Mysteries of Magic

Great Mysteries

Mysteries of Magic

by Stuart Holroyd
and Neil Powell

Bloomsbury Books
London

Editorial Consultants:

COLIN WILSON
DR. CHRISTOPHER EVANS

Series Coordinator:	John Mason
Design Director:	Günter Radtke
Picture Editor:	Peter Cook
Editor:	Sally Burningham
Copy Editor:	Mitzi Bales
Research:	Sarah Waters
General Consultant:	Beppie Harrison

This edition published 1991 by
Bloomsbury Books an imprint of
Godfrey Cave Associates Limited
42 Bloomsbury Street, London WC1B 3QJ
Printed in Hong Kong by Regent Publishing Services Ltd.
ISBN 1 85471 045 1

Introduction

Most of us would like to have power—power over our fates and power over other people. For centuries men and women have sought such power in the rituals and formulas of magic. This book tells how some have turned to the ancient wisdom of the Cabala; how others have looked for it in the hidden meaning of words and sounds; how yet others have thought they found the key in numbers. All have hoped that magic would help them understand and influence the world we live in. What have magicians discovered? Have they in fact succeeded in controlling certain forces? Did they, like the alchemists, have a deeper motivation than personal gain? The second part of this book reveals that many alchemists were notable scientific and philosophic figures of their day: Helvetius, Paracelsus, Dr. John Dee, Isaac Newton. They believed that the search for the secret of making gold was tied in with the search for spiritual perfection, and that success meant the achievement of immortality. There are traditions of alchemy in the East as in the West, today as in the past. Did anyone ever succeed in the alchemist's quest?

Contents

Chapter 1 Chance, Magic, and Synchronicity

Is it just accident when a person finds a lost book two years later? Is it more than accident when a man feels a pain in his skull at the moment that someone he knows is shot in the head? What is the theory of synchronicity developed by the great psychiatrist Carl Jung—and how does it tie in with magic? Like Jung's theory about coincidence, magic depends on the principle that all things in the Universe are bound by a fine network of relationships that continually interact. The old magical philosophy of "as above, so below" expresses these relationships. Can magicians use them to influence the course of events?

Some years ago George D. Bryson, an American businessman, was making a trip from St. Louis to New York. He decided to break his journey in Louisville, Kentucky, a town he had never visited before. At the station he inquired for somewhere to stay, and was directed to the Brown Hotel. He went there, found they had a room—number 307—and registered. Then, just for a joke and because he had nothing better to do, he idly wandered over to the mail desk and asked if there was any mail for him. To his astonishment and consternation the receptionist calmly handed him a letter addressed to Mr. George D. Bryson, Room 307. On investigation it turned out that the previous occupant of the room had been another George D. Bryson, who worked with a firm in Montreal.

We have all had similar strange experiences that we put down to coincidence, chance, or luck. Because these experiences are so common, scientists and philosophers have begun to wonder whether there is more to them than mere chance or coincidence. With this focusing of scientific and philosophical interest, more and more evidence has come to light that both the world we live in and the lives we lead are more mysterious than we usually suppose. In order to explain otherwise inexplicable events, many Westerners have taken a fresh look at magic and the psychic sciences.

Our normal way of looking at things in the West is from the standpoint of cause and effect. We have a built-in habit of mind

Opposite: this painting by German artist Gerfried Schellberger has strong overtones of death in it. Oddly, he was inspired to paint such a subject in such a way on the very day—but before—he learned about the accidental death of his brother.

Right: Schellberger at work. Just before his brother died unexpectedly, he was obsessed by images of a man with his hair swept forward into a point, by symbols of death, and by water lilies. He sensed uneasily that it all had some meaning.

Below: another of Schellberger's paintings of a man with pointed hair, this one with a beard. It was also done just before the artist's brother died.

that tries to make sense of events by seeing them as if they are linked in a chain, one leading to another. But, as the Scottish philosopher David Hume pointed out over two centuries ago, this is only a useful working method, not an absolute truth. When one billiard ball meets another and the second moves away, we cannot see cause and effect taking place. We can only assume that it does so. This kind of assumption is fairly safe as long as it is confined to practical observations, but unfortunately Western society has gone much further than that. It has raised the cause and effect link to the status of a general law, and in doing so has often tended to exclude other points of view. Events such as chance or coincidence, which cannot be explained by a logical cause and effect sequence, are all too easily dismissed by many people as incomprehensible.

Eastern philosophers did not fall into this pattern of thinking, and the growing attention being paid to Eastern philosophies in the West is both an indication of dissatisfaction with the mechanistic laws of cause and effect, and a realization that there are other ways of looking at life.

Chance and Coincidence

What we call coincidental or chance events are a challenge to our fundamental assumptions about reality. When many of them accumulate they build up a solid credibility barrier—like the sound barrier built up in front of an aircraft flying at supersonic speed. We then have to crash this barrier to break through. We have to acquire a new conception of a reality beyond the credibility barrier created by our expectations and assumptions, particularly the assumption of cause and effect. In 1973 a book called *The Challenge of Chance* was published in London. Written by Sir Alister Hardy, Robert Harvie, and Arthur Koestler, it contains many anecdotes illustrating apparent chance or coincidence. These examples may help us to look at things in a new way.

One is about a scholar who had been preparing some of his lectures for publication. He died suddenly, leaving a request for his son to see the work through. Checking the typescript and completing the footnotes took the son six months of devoted labor. Finally he was left with the last and most difficult query to solve. It was a reference from one of the 36 volumes of Sacred Books of the East. But which one? There was nothing to guide him. As a last resort he decided to take home three of the volumes that his father had once borrowed from the library. Sitting in his study late that evening, he uttered a sort of prayer to his father saying "Can't you be allowed to help me?" He picked up one of the volumes at random—and opened it at the very page he needed.

Another incident concerns a man who bought a house from two elderly ladies on the condition that a certain picture must never be removed from its position. It remained there until he sold the house several years later, when he sent the picture to a salesroom. The new owner of the house, who knew nothing about the picture, bought it and hung it back in the spot where it had always been.

The following story won a contest sponsored by an English newspaper to find the best example of chance. George Feifer, an American author living in London, lent a friend an advance copy of his new novel *The Girl From Petrovka*. It was covered with red marks because Feifer had been correcting it for the American edition. A week later the friend reported that he had lost the copy from his car. The author was understandably and exceedingly annoyed because he had to make the corrections all over again.

Two years later when Feifer was in Vienna for the filming of his novel, one of the actors told him about a strange incident. After the actor had heard that he would be in the film of *The Girl From Petrovka*, he tried one day to buy a copy of the book in order to familiarize himself with the character and plot.

Above: Norbert Schellberger, brother of the artist. He apparently died of a heart attack while gathering water lilies in a swamp. The fact of his death, the connection with water lilies, and the way his hair looked all conformed to Gerfried's disturbed feelings before the event.

Above: one of the men who found Norbert's body in the swamp pulls his hair into a point to show how the dead man's looked.

The Meaning of Synchronicity

He was unsuccessful. While waiting for his train in the London subway, however, he noticed a book lying on a bench. On picking it up he saw to his astonishment that it was *The Girl From Petrovka*, the very book he had searched for in vain all afternoon. He was puzzled by the many red marks in it and showed it to Feifer. The surprised author instantly recognized it as the copy that had been lost two years before.

To shrug off events like these as "just chance" may be to shut off a significant area of knowledge. The eminent psychologist C. G. Jung certainly thought they were worth serious investigation. Over the years he noticed that both he himself and his patients had had many experiences of what he called "meaningful coincidences." Many of these involved dreams or premonitions, and he devoted much time toward the end of his life in attempting to explain these experiences. Jung used the term *synchronicity* to describe incidents that seemed to be connected by time and meaning, but not by cause and effect. He felt that these coincidences, in some way, had their roots in very strong unconscious feelings that at certain times of stress or change came to the surface. He gives several examples of this happening in his own life.

One day, as he was returning home by train, he was overpowered by the image of someone drowning. He was so upset that he was unable to read, and could only wonder whether there had been some sort of accident. When he got home he was met by his grandchildren, and discovered from them that the

Below: a man reported a vivid dream that woke him "in a cold sweat," in which his car ran over a small boy who darted in front of him.

youngest had fallen in the lake and had almost been drowned. The little boy had been fished out just in time by his older brother. This nearly fatal accident had happened at exactly the time that the idea of someone drowning had occurred to Jung.

Many of us have had odd dreams and premonitions about our family or friends that have turned out to be true. As a psychoanalyst Jung also had a very close relationship with his patients. One night when Jung was sleeping alone in a hotel after a lecture, he awoke with a start. He was convinced that someone had opened the door and entered the room, but when he switched on the light, there was no one to be seen. He then tried to remember what had happened. He had been wakened by a feeling of dull pain as if something had struck his forehead and the back of his skull. The following day he received a telegram informing him that a former patient, whom he had lost touch with after helping through a severe crisis, had shot himself. The bullet had lodged at the back wall of the skull.

Synchronistic events of this kind frequently happened to Jung and his patients. He became convinced that they had a deep significance, and he applied his tremendous knowledge, experience, and diligence to the task of discovering their meaning. When he died he was working on the idea that physics and psychology would ultimately come together under a common concept that would be a unifying key to the forces at work in the physical and psychical worlds. Physicists had released the energy locked away in the atom. Might it not be possible, he wondered,

Below: weeks later, driving into Manchester, England, he saw a child dash out. He swerved violently, missing him by inches. He leaped out of the car—and was staggered to recognize the child of his dream.

The Subway That Stopped

It was November 1971 in London on a day like any other. In one of the city's subway stations, a train was approaching the platform. Suddenly a young man hurled himself directly into the path of the moving train. The horrified driver slammed on the brakes, certain that there was no way to stop the train before the man was crushed under the wheels. But miraculously the train did stop. The first carriage had to be jacked up to remove the badly injured man, but the wheels had not passed over him and he survived. The young man turned out to be a gifted architect who was recovering from a nervous breakdown. His amazing rescue from death was based on coincidence. For the investigation of the accident revealed that the train had not stopped because of the driver's hasty braking. Seconds before, acting on an impulse and completely unaware of the man about to throw himself on the tracks, a passenger had pulled down the emergency handle, which automatically applies the brakes of the train. The passenger had no particular reason for doing so. In fact, the Transport Authority considered prosecuting him on the grounds that he had had no reasonable cause for using the emergency system!

STER SQUAR

Above: Carl Gustav Jung, the world-famous Swiss psychiatrist who died in 1961. He worked for a time with Freud, but parted company with him and went on to develop his own theories of the unconscious and the importance it has in human life. For Jung, a most important problem was how the conscious mind communicated with the extended and enriched world of the unconscious so that it could play a full part in the life of the individual.

to likewise release the energy locked away in the human psyche? Throughout the ages magicians have aspired to just such a unity of the physical and psychical worlds, though they do not work in a scientific way.

One of the world's oldest books is the ancient Chinese book of wisdom and divination, the *I Ching* or Book of Change. The source of the *I Ching* is shrouded in myth, but it was systematized in its present form by King Wen in 1143 B.C., and later clarified by his son the Duke of Chou. This famous book has exerted enormous influence on the two main Chinese religions, Confucianism and Taoism. It is still widely revered and consulted in the Far East today. Since the first translation into English in 1882, the *I Ching* has gained many Western followers. One of these was Jung, who devoted a great deal of time and thought to its study.

The *I Ching* is based on a belief in the unity of man and the surrounding universe. The universe is thought to be made up of two equal and complementary forces, Yang and Yin. Yang is the active principle and stands for positive qualities. Yin, passive but equally important, stands for the negative. Yang stands for light and Yin for dark. Since everything is made up from Yang and Yin, differences between things are due to different proportions of Yang and Yin. According to ancient Chinese belief, every event results from an interaction between these two principles.

The *I Ching* contains 64 figurations, each a different combination of six broken and unbroken lines and therefore called a hexagram. The broken lines represent Yin, and the unbroken lines Yang. Each hexagram has a symbolic name signifying a different condition of life, and is accompanied by a short explanatory text attributed to King Wen. There is also a commentary on the text, possibly by Confucius, as well as explanations of the symbolism of the hexagram and the meaning of the separate lines in each hexagram. The *I Ching* does not regard the future as fixed. It does not aim to tell those who consult it what will happen, but tries to give guidance at the highest moral level so that an individual can determine what the correct course of action would be. Because this guidance depends to a large degree on perceptive interpretation, it is vital that the questioner approach the book in a serious frame of mind.

The *I Ching* is a system of wisdom containing advice, moral precepts, and insights that may guide the questioner. In order to find out which particular hexagram is relevant to his or her particular situation, the questioner tosses three coins six times. (Fifty yarrow stalks may also be used but coins are more common today.) Each toss will indicate a line in the hexagram, working up from the bottom line. For example, if the first throw of the coins shows two tails and one head, the bottom line would be an unbroken one. The hexagram formed in this way by the six tosses is the one to be consulted and interpreted.

The American psychologist Ira Progoff recalls an occasion when he consulted the *I Ching* with Jung's help. He had published a first book on Jung's work and had come to Europe from America to continue his research under the great man's guidance. One afternoon when they were sitting in the garden of Jung's

Consulting the I Ching

Left: Chinese priests in a temple tossing bamboo tallies to determine the success of their prayers. The picture is by an English artist, William Alexander, who accompanied Lord Macartney's embassy to China in 1792. Alexander kept a very detailed record of what he saw.

Below: a red lacquer panel with *pa kua*, the eight *I Ching* trigrams made up of broken and unbroken lines. Two trigrams together create a hexagram of the ancient book. The trigrams encircle the interlocking Yin and Yang symbols, seen as the opposing but complementary principles of the universe.

house beside Lake Zurich Jung asked him if he had ever used the *I Ching*. When Progoff said he had not, Jung suggested they do so there and then, and asked him what problem he would like to put to the *I Ching*. Progoff said he had no particular problem at that time, but he had general questions about his present situation and the meaning and eventual outcome of what he was doing. Jung produced three coins from an old worn leather purse. On tossing the coins six times, Progoff was directed to hexagram 59, named "dispersion." Hexagram 59 looks like this:

The Theory of Meaningful Chance

Below: a Taoist priest's robe embroidered with the *pa kua* trigrams. In the center are the all-important symbols of Yin and Yang. The origins of the *I Ching* are veiled in tradition and myth, but its elements are more than 4000 years old and so predate both Taoism and Confucianism.

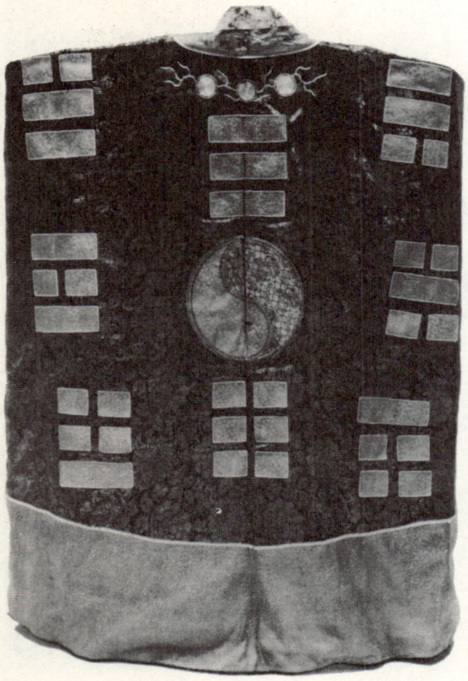

The text is as follows:

Dispersion. Success. The king approaches his temple. It furthers one to cross the great waters. Perseverence furthers.

This seemed relevant to Progoff's situation. He had just published a book that aimed to spread or disperse Jung's ideas, so he was encouraged by the indication that it would be a success. He had crossed "the great waters" of the Atlantic to come and work with Jung. He was enjoying a period of great good fortune in an idyllic situation (the "temple" in the second line symbolizes a place of safety). Finally, his chief worry was that in the circumstances he might be taking his life and work too easily, so the words "perseverence furthers" were particularly meaningful to him.

It was all relevant enough. But why, Progoff asked, should the act of throwing some coins in a garden in Switzerland in 1953 get a reading from an ancient Chinese text that had a specific personal meaning for him? It seemed impossible and absurd. Or was it just chance? Superficially it looked like chance, but a highly sophisticated civilization had made practical use of the book and of the principle underlying it over a period spanning many centuries. That was a fact that could not be lightly dismissed. A man like Jung had certainly not dismissed it.

In *Memories, Dreams and Reflections* Jung describes his long-standing fascination with the *I Ching*. He had begun experimenting with it in about 1920, and one summer he decided to launch an all-out attempt to solve the riddle of the book. Instead of the traditional yarrow stalks, he cut himself a bunch of reeds.

He wrote: "I would sit for hours beneath the 100-year-old pear tree, the *I Ching* beside me, practicing the technique . . . in an interplay of questions and answers. All sorts of undeniably remarkable results emerged—meaningful connections with my own thought processes which I could not explain to myself." Jung was preoccupied with the question of whether or not the *I Ching*'s answers were significant. If they were significant, how did this connection between the psychic and the physical come about? How could a problem in the mind of a questioner be answered by the interpretation of an ancient hexagram, seemingly selected at random?

Later he tried using the *I Ching* with his patients and found that a fairly high proportion of answers seemed to be appropriate. He describes one case involving a young man with a strong mother complex. He wanted to get married, and had found a girl who seemed suitable. However, he was uneasy, fearing that unconsciously he may have been attracted by another strong mother figure. He consulted the *I Ching*, and the text of his hexagram seemed appropriate to his predicament. It read "The maiden is all powerful. One should not marry such a maiden."

Jung's suggestion of how the *I Ching* works was the same as his theory on meaningful chance. This, as we have seen, was that events can be linked to each other by time and meaning, although they are in no way associated by cause and effect. In the idea of cause and effect, events evolve out of one another. In the idea of meaningful chance or synchronicity, objective events are in some way interdependent, as though bound together by a vast network of relationships. This network in turn is linked up with the psychic or subjective state of the person involved. In the case of the *I Ching* this person would be the questioner.

A belief in the interaction between man and the universe, or mind and matter, is fundamental to the theory and practice of magic the world over. Equally fundamental is the idea that there are favorable conditions for such interactions, conditions that involve the shapes, the patterns, and even the relationships in space between the elements in a given situation. These conditions do not appear to depend on any direct cause and effect relationship or, at any rate, any relationship that we at the moment can understand. For example, there seem to be favored positions for the siting of holy places. Propitious times for certain actions appear to depend on the positions of the planets. Certain shapes are said to afford protection, bring good fortune, or attract evil powers. Are all such beliefs merely superstitions? Anyone inclined to dismiss them as such without further thought might also consider that many strange facts have been demonstrated in recent years, for which there seem as yet to be no

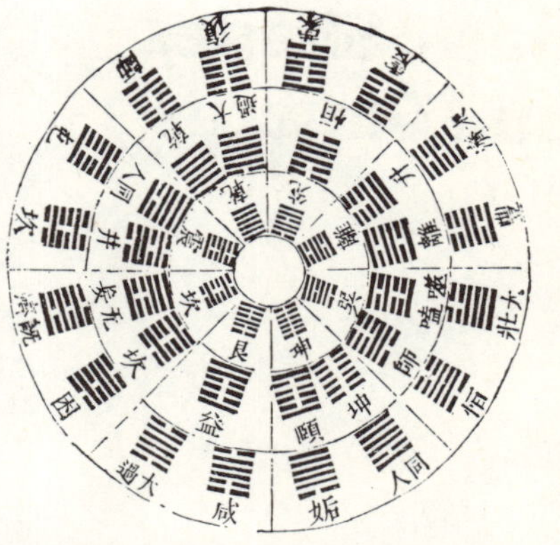

Above: the hexagrams of the *I Ching* taken from a 16th-century Chinese encyclopedia of wisdom.

Below: consulting the oracle. Steady concentration is required to calculate the lines properly. It is also necessary to keep the question clearly in the mind.

Basic Shapes and Patterns

One of the most fascinating of Nature's corresponding patterns is the spiral. It appears all around us. Our galaxy, like the galaxies around us, whirls into infinite space in the shape of a spiral; water spirals downward and to the right in a whirlpool; the hair on our heads grows in a spiral around the crown; and the head of a daisy is a double spiral as well. The foundation of life, the DNA molecule (far right) that carries the genetic message for each living cell, organized in a deceptively simple double spiral in which to lock its code.

known explanation. Blunt razor blades become sharp again if left inside a miniature model pyramid. Wounded mice heal more quickly if they are put in spherical cages. Shape, it appears, exerts some influence that we cannot explain.

Supposing we are prepared to recognize the limitations of looking at everything from the viewpoint of cause and effect, where does it get us? Perhaps not far, but it leaves us free to follow up clues and play with possibilities. Take, for example, the idea of shapes and patterns. We find that Nature, in fact, has only a small repertoire of basic shapes and patterns, and that the same ones tend to crop up in widely different contexts. A tungsten atom magnified two million times looks like a constellation of stars in the sky. When the 18th-century physicist Ernst F. Chladni found a way of making sound waves visible by mounting a metal plate covered with sand on a violin and drawing a bow across the strings, the sand arranged itself in patterns commonly found in living organisms. There is an intricate network of pattern and structure correspondences throughout the universe, and these patterns do not seem to have any causal connection.

Could events be thought of in the same way? Could a tiny change in the pattern of events existing at a given moment in time—a thing so small as a man throwing coins and formulating a question—affect the total existing situation and form a new pattern? Could this new pattern have the power to draw into relation to itself other events and situations remote in time and space? These were the kind of questions that Jung was asking.

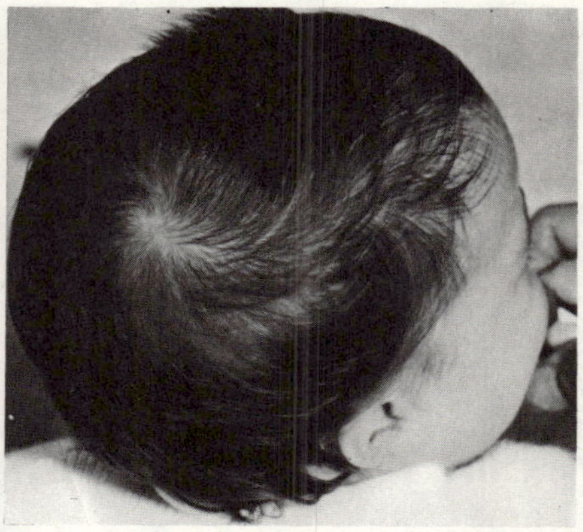

He even coined the term "magic causality" to describe such possibilities, which must have raised some eyebrows among his professional and academic colleagues. Here is an example of magic causality:

Henry, a patient undergoing analysis, had a dream in which his fate was decided by four Chinese who consulted an oracle "using little ivory sticks." His analyst drew his attention to the *I Ching*, and suggested that he should consult the book himself. Henry was 25 years old, highly intellectual, repressed, imaginative, and introverted. The hexagram he obtained when he consulted the book was the one called "youthful folly." Part of the commentary read: "For youthful folly, it is the most hopeless thing to entangle itself in empty imaginings. The more obstinately it clings to such unreal fantasies the more certainly will humiliation overtake it." Henry was shaken by the relevance of the reading. Till then he had denied the existence of anything except the purely rational. He had suppressed any feelings or thoughts that did not appear to be logical.

The *I Ching* had told Henry not to consult the book again. However, one night he had a vivid dream of a helmet with a sword floating in empty space. On an impulse he opened the *I Ching* at random. The first words he read were: "The clinging is fire, it means coats of mail, helmets, it means lances and weapons." He was amazed. He suddenly understood that the reason he had been forbidden to consult the book again was to give his unconscious an opportunity to express itself unhampered by his rational mind. After this experience, his analyst

The Collective Unconscious

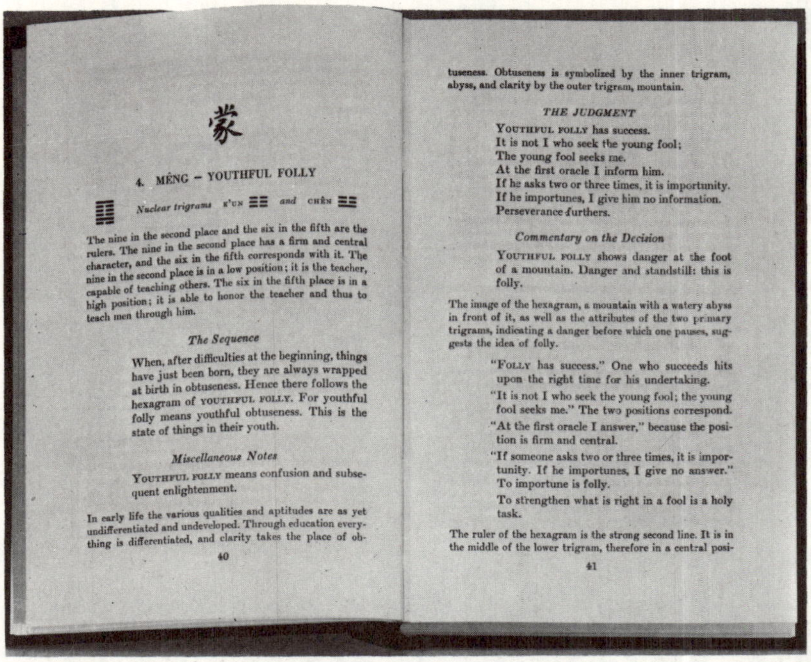

蒙

4. MÊNG – YOUTHFUL FOLLY

Nuclear trigrams K'UN ☷ *and* CHÊN ☳

The nine in the second place and the six in the fifth are the rulers. The nine in the second place has a firm and central character, and the six in the fifth corresponds with it. The nine in the second place is in a low position; it is the teacher, capable of teaching others. The six in the fifth place is in a high position; it is able to honor the teacher and thus to teach men through him.

The Sequence

When, after difficulties at the beginning, things have just been born, they are always wrapped at birth in obtuseness. Hence there follows the hexagram of YOUTHFUL FOLLY. For youthful folly means youthful obtuseness. This is the state of things in their youth.

Miscellaneous Notes

YOUTHFUL FOLLY means confusion and subsequent enlightenment.

In early life the various qualities and aptitudes are as yet undifferentiated and undeveloped. Through education everything is differentiated, and clarity takes the place of ob-

40

tuseness. Obtuseness is symbolized by the inner trigram, abyss, and clarity by the outer trigram, mountain.

THE JUDGMENT

YOUTHFUL FOLLY has success.
It is not I who seek the young fool;
The young fool seeks me.
At the first oracle I inform him.
If he asks two or three times, it is importunity.
If he importunes, I give him no information.
Perseverance furthers.

Commentary on the Decision

YOUTHFUL FOLLY shows danger at the foot of a mountain. Danger and standstill: this is folly.

The image of the hexagram, a mountain with a watery abyss in front of it, as well as the attributes of the two primary trigrams, indicating a danger before which one pauses, suggests the idea of folly.

"FOLLY has success." One who succeeds hits upon the right time for his undertaking.

"It is not I who seek the young fool; the young fool seeks me." The two positions correspond.

"At the first oracle I answer," because the position is firm and central.

"If someone asks two or three times, it is importunity. If he importunes, I give no answer." To importune is folly.

To strengthen what is right in a fool is a holy task.

The ruler of the hexagram is the strong second line. It is in the middle of the lower trigram, therefore in a central posi-

41

Right: Henry, a patient undergoing Jungian analysis, was referred to the *I Ching* by his therapist. This copy of the book is turned to the hexagram *Meng* or Youthful Folly, to which he was directed. He found it most relevant to his situation. However, in this hexagram he was warned against consulting the *I Ching* again—"If someone asks two or three times, it is importunity. If he importunes, I give no answer."

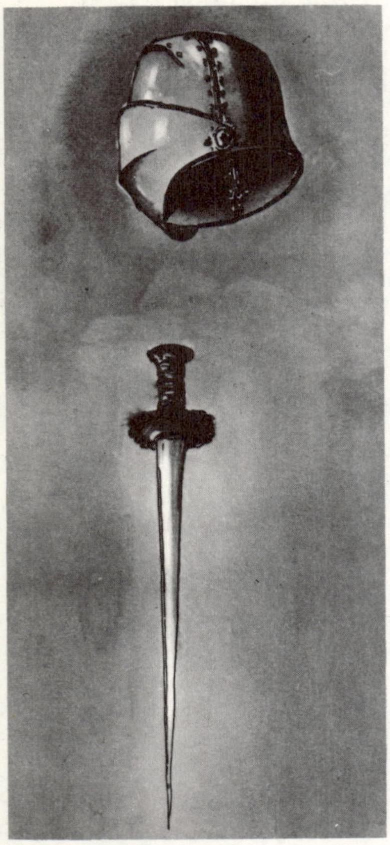

Below: Henry's drawing of the sword and helmet he saw in a dream. This dream led him to the *I Ching* again, and to a clearer appreciation of the part his unconscious played in his life.

reports, Henry "listened eagerly to the communications of his unconscious" and gradually became a changed man, "full of enterprising spirit."

Does magic involve the focusing of powers of the mind or the annexing of powers at work in the universe? This is a reasonable question. But it is wrongly phrased. The deeper we go into the matter the more clearly we realize that it is not a question of either/or but of both/and. Henry's case illustrates this. The images of a helmet and a weapon were *both* in his dream *and* in the external world as words printed in the book. A classic synchronistic event brought them together.

A fundamental principle of Jung's psychology is demonstrated in this. According to Jung the deepest structure of the human mind is the collective unconscious. This is made up from archetypes, which are not derived from personal experience but are in some way inherited. Archetypes in the Jungian use of the word are the distilled memories of the human species, and come from the common experience of mankind. They cannot be represented in verbal terms, but only by elusive symbols which, elusive as they are, we find are shared by all mythologies. They also provide patterns of behavior for all human beings in archetypal or stressful situations such as danger, conflict, death, or love. In such situations the archetypes, carrying strong emotions, invade the consciousness in the form of symbols.

According to Jung, it is by recognizing and coming to terms with the archetypal patterns in one's unconscious life that a person achieves wholeness, self-realization, and self-fulfillment. It was only when Henry listened to the communications of his unconscious that he was able to progress. It is at this unconscious level that humankind is in touch with the cosmic forces of Nature. It is by activating the archetypal symbol that a person acquires the extraordinary powers that are usually described as magical. Jung quotes the magician Albertus Magnus, who lived in the

13th century, as saying that everyone can influence everything magically if "he falls into a great excess." This corresponds with Jung's idea that by entering deeply into the unconscious we can activate the archetypes and achieve wholeness and power. It is like completing an electrical circuit. Until a contact is made nothing happens. But when it is made, power flows through the whole circuit. The contact on the psychic level is brought about when the individual's personal experience in depth corresponds with the universal archetype. This produces in the individual a sense of having an active and meaningful relationship to the whole, to life, and the world. This feeling is vital to psychological health.

Jung was interested in Albertus Magnus and in magic generally because he believed that the magician's power is of the same kind as that of the integrated individual, only greatly magnified. Magical power in his view is achieved by effecting a correspondence between the inner and outer, by completing a circuit that puts the individual into a dynamic relationship with the whole universe.

Bearing this in mind, let us take a closer look at the symbolic basis of the *I Ching*. As we have already seen, each of the 64 hexagrams consists of a different combination of unbroken and broken lines, the unbroken lines representing Yang, the active force in the universe, and the broken lines representing Yin, the equally important passive force. Each hexagram is made up of two trigrams, or groups of three lines. There are eight trigrams that are combined in 64 ways.

The trigrams are older than the *I Ching* itself. There is a tradition that they were first discovered by the Emperor Fu Hsi (2852–2738 B.C.), who saw them on the shell of a tortoise. In each trigram the lower line stands for earth, the middle line for man, and the top line for heaven. Thus man is seen as existing in a dynamic relationship of interaction between the heavens above and the earth below.

When three lines come together to form a trigram, there are eight possible combinations of broken and unbroken lines. Each trigram has an associated symbol, and these symbols form four groups of paired opposites: heaven and earth, mountain and lake, fire and water, thunder and wind. There are also associated pairs of qualities: the creative (heaven) and the receptive (earth), the violent (thunder) and the gentle (wind), the quiescent (mountain) and the joyous (lake), the clinging (fire) and the empty (water). When two trigrams come together to form a hexagram they will stand in varying degrees of accord or discord with each other. If they are in accord, the hexagram signifies something good, pleasant or fortunate. If they are in discord it signifies something bad, unpleasant, and unlucky. Take for example the following two hexagrams:

and

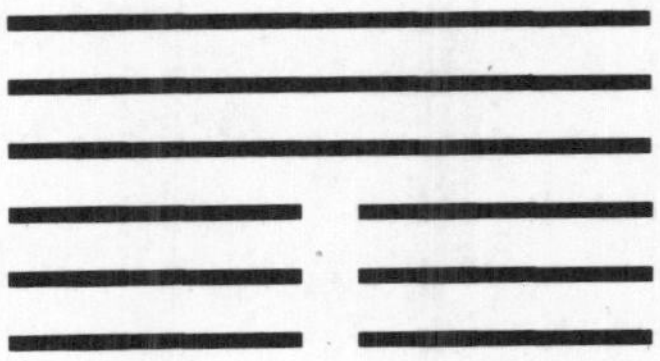

Above: during his analysis Henry recalled his earliest memory, which was of fetching a crescent roll from the baker's wife. His drawing of the roll is at the top. The middle photograph shows the crescent shape still in use on Swiss bakery shops. Interestingly for Henry's analysis, the shape has long been linked with the moon and the feminine principle, as exemplified here by a 3rd-century statue of the Babylonian goddess Ishtar wearing her crescent crown.

Above: the personification of the Self is not always wise and old. Here, in a painting of one of his dreams by the artist Peter Birkhäuser, the Self is a marvelous youth, riding on a mysterious beast.

The one on the left is Peace, and the one on the right is Stagnation. In each hexagram Yin and Yang are in equal proportion, but are not intermixed. The hexagram on the left stands for harmony and balance because the three Yang lines of the lower trigram provide the strongest possible support for the three Yin lines in the upper one. But to have a Yang trigram bearing down with all its weight on a passive, yielding Yin trigram, as in the hexagram on the right, is most unfavorable.

In 1962 there was a tense international situation when massive Chinese forces gathered on the India-Tibet frontiers. The world expected them to swoop down on the plains of India. John Blofield, an Englishman then in Bangkok, consulted the *I Ching* for a prediction of what would happen. The oracle not only correctly foretold the Chinese strategy, but also gave reasons for it. This prediction was confirmed in newspaper reports after the event. Blofield, who later published his own translation of the *I Ching*, could not help wondering whether the Chinese

"As Above, So Below"

generals had planned their campaign on the basis of the advice given by the venerable book. It was not improbable. In China's neighboring country of Japan, books of strategy based on the *I Ching* were required reading for military officers. Many Japanese believe that that fact accounted for the great victories they won in the early part of World War II, and one is reported to have said: "If the people at the very top had not been too 'modern' to consult the *Book of Change*, all those tremendous victories would not have been thrown away."

The significance of the hexagrams and their component trigrams is based on the assumption that all things in the universe, from solar systems to subatomic particles, are bound together in an intricate network of relationships, and are continually interacting with each other. Every part not only belongs to the whole, but also reflects the whole. The ancient Chinese considered the turtle sacred because its convex shell with its squares and lateral crossings corresponded exactly to the pattern of the heavens as they saw it. They would have agreed with the principle that is central to the magical system of the Hermetic philosophers. Their principle is expressed in the simple formula "As above, so below," which has significance in mysticism as well as magic.

The Hermetic writings are a group of works on many subjects including the occult. The authors are unknown and the tracts probably span several centuries, the earliest dating back to the 3rd century B.C. The writings have been grouped under the name of Hermes Trismegistus, or thrice-greatest, the Greek name for the Egyptian god Thoth. Thoth was believed to be the scribe of

Above: in Jung's ideas, his concept of archetypes—unconscious memories of the experiences of our ancestors which come into our consciousness as symbols during stress—plays a central role. Among the archetypes that appear in our dreams is that of the Self personified as a wise old man. This painting by Jung is a personification that appeared in one of his own dreams—a winged old man who carried keys. Jung said that this was a symbol representing superior insight.

Left: another archetype is that of the fallen angel Lucifer, shown here as the resplendent bringer of light, but carrying the dual aspect of Satan. The idea of the basic duality of the universe runs through many of the philosophies that humans have evolved to explain the cosmos and their own place in it.

The Symbolism of the Alchemists

Opposite: a 16th-century manuscript illustration, rich in alchemical symbolism, which was of much interest to Jung and which he studied. It shows the rebirth of the soul in terms of medieval alchemy, which compares it to base metal that is transmuted into gold. The blackened soul emerging from the mire represents the first stage of transformation. The substance used to revive and whiten it is personified as the refined and all-powerful queen.

Below: this illustration from the 1650 edition of Albertus Magnus' *Philosophia Naturalis* shows man as the *anima mundi*, or world spirit, containing in his body the four elements of earth, water, fire, and air, and characterized by the number 10. This number represents perfection because it is the sum of 1 plus 2 plus 3 plus 4. These concepts play an important part in the alchemical tradition.

the gods and the inventor of writing and all the arts dependent on it, including medicine, astronomy, and magic. The Greeks identified him with their own god, Hermes, the messenger of the gods, whose staff of entwined serpents symbolized wisdom. Hermes Trismegistus still remains an important figure in the occult tradition of the West.

One of the underlying hermetic beliefs was that the universe, or Cosmos, was a unity, and all its parts were interdependent. The relationship of all the parts was governed by the laws of sympathy and antipathy, but these could only be understood by divine revelation. The hermetic writings on alchemy included the system of occult sympathies, or correspondences, which underlies much magical tradition. This system aims to reveal secret links between various and apparently unconnected parts of the universe. Hermetic philosophy was of special interest to Jung, although he discovered it late in life—but not too late to devote ten years and two of his major works, *Psychology and Alchemy* and *Mysterium Coniunctionis*, to the study of it. This was a brave action at a time when alchemy was regarded as a discredited pseudoscience, and its devotees as absurdly misguided dabblers in chemistry or grasping charlatans. The professed aim of the alchemists—to change base metals into gold—seemed to personify human greed and credulity until Jung pointed out that the process was symbolical of man's attempt to change his own personality to attain a higher level of perfection. Jung discovered in the neglected hermetic literature a rich store of "archetypal motifs that . . . appear in the dreams of modern individuals." An archetype, remember, is an image or experience at a profound level, that enables the individual to come into contact with the universal and acquire extraordinary powers. Could the alchemists have found the secret of releasing the energy locked away in the human psyche, as the physicists later released the energy in the atom? Could they have succeeded in bringing together in dynamic interaction the physical and psychical worlds? Could they have been not misguided charlatans but profound philosophers and genuine magicians with powers over the material world?

The theory of synchronicity, Jung said, was an offshoot of his studies of the alchemists. It was a descriptive theory only, a statement that noncausal events are not mere accidents or chance but a significant part of reality that may provide the clue to some of the ultimate mysteries of life and the world. He stated that synchronistic events happened and were important, but he considered it beyond his mission as a scientist to say *how* they happened or whether they could be *made* to happen. Down the ages, however, there have been men less cautious about these questions—the magicians themselves.

XXVII
XXXV
XXX
XXXIII
XXV
XXIIII
XXVIII
XXVI
XXXI

Chapter 2
The Magical Correspondences

Magicians, like astronomers, have a strong belief in the cosmic influence on human lives and events. Magicians try to harness the power of the planets in a different way, however. They often use the ancient system of *correspondences*—that is, affinities of certain metals, colors, animals, and substances with certain planets—in ritual magic in order to arouse and control cosmic forces. That is why talismans are so important in ritual magic, and why they must be prepared according to their correspondences. Can it be that hypnotism, Kirlian photography, and color healing are modern manifestations of the magical correspondences?

In 1934 the notorious gangster John Dillinger was gunned down by the FBI in Chicago. People rushed to the spot and mopped up the blood with handkerchiefs and coats. It is said that afterward there was a brisk trade in the area in fake Dillinger blood—and some enterprising hustlers made another kind of "killing."

Long ago when a gladiator was killed in a Roman arena, epileptics rushed out to drink the fresh blood spurting from the wounds. In 1610 the dead bodies of over 50 peasant girls were found in the cellars of the Hungarian countess Elizabeth Bathory after she had been arrested. She had been in the habit of bathing in their blood in the hope that it would preserve her youthful looks.

Witches drank bats' blood believing that this would enable them to fly by night. Legends of vampires that suck human blood in order to sustain their vitality are worldwide, and so are black magic ceremonies involving bloody sacrifices. Belief in the magic properties of blood can be traced back to the fundamental principle of all magic: that the part reflects and contains the whole.

Aleister Crowley, a modern magician, took great care not to let his fingernail clippings or hair fall into anyone's hand in case a rival magician got hold of them and used them against him. What he had to fear is illustrated in the story of the Scottish schoolmaster who dabbled a bit in magic. He developed a passion for the elder sister of one of his pupils, and bribed

Opposite: a 15th-century pack of Tarot cards, traditionally used for reading fortunes. The 12 signs of the zodiac illustrating this pack were believed to have a kind of magical correspondence, not only with human characteristics and destinies, but also with parts and functions of the human body—for example, Pisces with the feet and Aries with the head. By means of such magical correspondences, people thought they had found the key to understanding celestial influences.

Correspondences and Their Meaning

Top: celestial influences could of course be unfavorable, and the prudent man created talismans to protect himself. This one was designed to give invisibility.

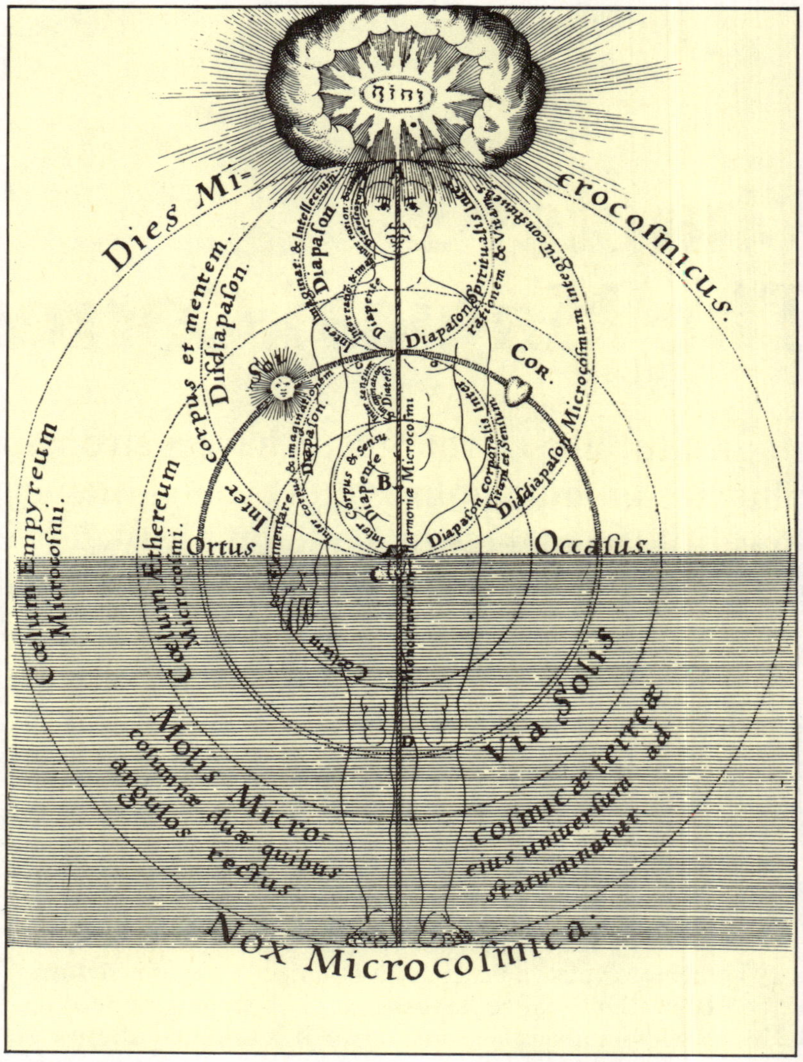

Right: Robert Fludd's concept of the correspondences between the universe—macrocosm—and man—microcosm. Like many other philosophers, Fludd envisioned the universe as a human organism on a gigantic scale. Fludd was an English physician active in the early 17th century. He became one of the leading members of the school of medical mystics who believed that their work was the key to universal science.

the boy to bring him three of the girl's pubic hairs. While the boy was engaged in the delicate operation of obtaining the hairs from his sleeping sister, their mother caught him and made him tell her what he was doing. She sent the boy back to the schoolmaster with three hairs plucked from the udder of a heifer, and when the amateur magician worked his spell, he had an amorous heifer prancing around him and following him everywhere.

The crudest superstitions have in common with the subtlest arts of magic the belief that there exists a link between the part and the whole, and vice versa. This is a belief that is endorsed by great traditions of religious, philosophical, and scientific thought.

From earliest times magicians have been concerned with the influence of the sun, the moon, and the planets—all referred to as the planets for convenience—on human lives and events. They believed that there was a natural affinity between certain planets and certain colors, metals, animals, and plants. Magicians called these affinities *correspondences*. They were convinced that by understanding and using these correspondences correctly, they would be able to draw on the power of the

Left: pages from a 1548 German edition of *Naturalia* by Albertus Magnus. In it he links the magical and medicinal properties of herbs with planetary and zodiacal influences—the Martagon lily (left) with Saturn, and chicory (right) with the Sun, for example.

planets. This system of correspondences is the basis of all ritual magic. Some of the main correspondences are shown in the table below.

Planet	**Color**	**Metal**	**Stone**	**Creature**
Saturn	black	lead	onyx	crocodile
Jupiter	blue	tin	sapphire	eagle
Mars	red	iron	ruby	horse
Sun	yellow	gold	topaz	lion
Venus	green	copper	emerald	dove
Mercury	gray	mercury	agate	swallow
Moon	white	silver	crystal	dog

Some of the correspondences seem fairly obvious, such as the association of the sun with the color yellow and the metal gold, and the moon with white and silver. Mercury, the fastest moving planet, is linked with the most mobile of metals of the same name, and with the fast-flying swallow. Saturn, the dimmest and slowest moving planet, is associated with the color black and the heavy metal lead. Venus is the ruling power of nature as well as of love, and its association with nature's predominant color green follows logically. Since copper turns to green, it is the metal associated with Venus.

A magician who seeks to arouse and control the force of Venus, for example, would surround his working area with green draperies, and would wear a green robe possibly with a dove motif embroidered on it, a ring of emerald set in copper, and a Venus talisman. He would use a copper wand, or a wooden one capped with copper, and would burn the appropriate incense in a copper burner. He might also—though this is not essential—make a ritual sacrifice of a dove. He would then be well disposed to draw down the cosmic influence of Venus, which may be employed to foster love or friendship, to secure pleasure, or to acquire beauty.

Below: the 15th-century Italian philosopher-doctor Marsilio Ficino based his belief in talismans on the idea that a charm made up of images and materials associated with a particular planet would hold within it the *spiritus* or essential substance of that planet. Magical correspondences would make it effective against unfavorable planetary aspects.

The Influence of the Planets

In 1489 Marsilio Ficino, a Florentine philosopher and physician, published a textbook of magical medicine, the *Libri de Vita* or Book of Life. It was based on a belief in sympathetic or natural magic, which used the system of correspondences. Powerful influences from the planets were said to be constantly pouring down on the earth. Colors or objects or plants especially associated with a particular planet would react to the planet and focus its influence.

Ficino suggests how men might use planetary influences to their best advantage. Young students are advised to avoid plants, herbs, stones, animals, and people that come under the influence of Saturn, because Saturn is the planet of melancholy

Right: Jupiter with its zodiac signs Pisces and Sagittarius, from a 15th-century Italian manuscript. Occupations thought in medieval times to be under Jupiter are shown at the bottom: an apothecary weighing out his materials, an alchemist sieving bags of sand to find precious metals, and a mathematician being consulted by a client. Each of the five then-known planets were given two zodiac signs, but the sun and moon had one each.

influence and saps the forces of life and youth. Students should expose themselves to the more cheerful and life-giving influences of things associated with Jupiter, Venus, or the Sun. An illness is seen as often being the result of bad stellar influences, and a cure can be affected by drawing down from the heavens a stream of beneficial influences from the appropriate planet. To do this one must know which plants, stones, or metals belong to that planet, how to make the appropriate images, and at what astrological moment to do so. A substantial part of Ficino's book was devoted to instructions on making planetary images or talismans for medical use.

A talisman is an object that is worn or carried as a charm. It serves the purpose of either attracting or repelling various influences. To be effective, a planetary talisman should be made at a time when the relevant planet is pouring out its influences at maximum intensity, and should consist of an image engraved on the stone or metal associated with the planet. It should be made by the person who is going to wear it, who should cast his own horoscope to determine the hours most favorable for the work. The talisman should then be consecrated by being exposed to fumes produced by a prescribed mixture of herbs burned in an earthenware vessel over a fire made of certain types of wood. When this complex process has been completed the talisman should be worn on the breast in a silk pouch of a particular color.

Here is a brief description of the seven planetary talismans, their manufacture and use, and the powers traditionally ascribed to them:

1. The talisman of **Saturn** is engraved on a plaque of pure lead. On one side is an image of a bull's head enclosed in a six-pointed star, and on the other a scythe in a pentagram or five-pointed star. It must be made on a Saturday (Saturn's day), and consecrated over flames of alum, scammony, and sulfur burned on a fire of cypress and ash. It is worn in a blue silk pouch. It protects the wearer against death by apoplexy, cancer, consumption, or paralysis, against being buried alive while in a coma, and against assassination, poison, and ambush. It protects women in childbirth and is also useful in war because the enemy will not be able to cross any place that it is hidden.

2. The talisman of **Jupiter** is engraved on a plaque of pure tin. It has on one side an image of an eagle's head in a six-pointed star, and on the other a crown in a pentagram. It must be made on a Thursday, and consecrated over fumes of frankincense, ambergris, balsam, cardomom, and saffron on a fire of oak, poplar, and fig. It is worn in a sky blue silk pouch. It protects the wearer against death by diseases of the liver or lungs or by unforeseen accidents, and it draws good-will and sympathy.

3. The talisman of **Mars** is engraved on a plaque of pure iron. On one side it has a lion's head in a six-pointed star and on the other two crossed swords in a pentagram. It must be made on a Tuesday, and consecrated over fumes of absinth and rue. It is worn in a red silk pouch. It protects the wearer against death by malignant ulcers or epidemic, and affords powerful protection against enemies. If concealed in a besieged citadel, it insures that no attack from outside will succeed.

Above: a talisman of Jupiter. According to one authority, it must be made of tin with the image of an eagle's head in a six-pointed star on one side and a crown in a pentagram on the other. It can only be done on a Thursday. If all directions are carried out exactly, the talisman will protect the wearer against accident and certain diseases, as well as help to gain good-will and sympathy.

The Consecration of a Talisman

In ritual magic the consecration of a talisman, or object worn as a charm, must be done in accordance with the law of correspondences which says that each planet is associated with a certain metal, color, animal, and plant. This illustration shows the consecration of a talisman for a person whose planet is Jupiter. It was one of the special and important ceremonies of the Order of the Golden Dawn. The talisman had to be prepared in Jupiter's metal, which is tin, or color, which is violet, and was engraved with the symbols and numbers associated with Jupiter. Then, after performing banishing rituals to remove all outside influences, the members who had reached the grade that qualified them for performing the ceremony would chant invocations associated with Jupiter, and burn the particular incense of Jupiter. Next, with the most intense concentration and imagination, they used their psychic energies to summon down the energy from the sphere of Jupiter, drawing it down into the talisman. Finally, in a last banishing ritual, they would request "all spirits bound by this ceremony . . . to depart in peace unto their places." Only after all this, done exactly right, was the talisman ready.

4. The talisman of the **Sun** is engraved on a plaque of pure gold and has a human head enclosed in a six-pointed star on one side, and a circle in a pentagram on the other. It must be made on a Sunday, and consecrated over fumes of cinnamon, saffron, and red sandalwood on a fire of laurel and dried heliotrope stalks. It is worn in a pouch of yellow silk. It protects the wearer against death by heart disease, epidemic, or conflagration, and draws the favor and good-will of people in high places.
5. The talisman of **Venus** is engraved on pure copper. On one side there is a dove in a six-pointed star, and on the other is the letter G in a pentagram. It must be made on a Friday, and consecrated over fumes of violets and roses on a fire of olive wood. It is worn in a green silk pouch. It protects the wearer against death by poisoning and, women in particular, against cancer. It preserves harmony in marriage, and if dipped in an enemy's drink, it will turn him into a friend for life.
6. The talisman of **Mercury** is engraved on a plaque made of an alloy of silver, tin, and mercury. It has a dog's head in a six-pointed star on one side, and a caduceus in a pentagram on the other. It must be made on a Wednesday, and consecrated over

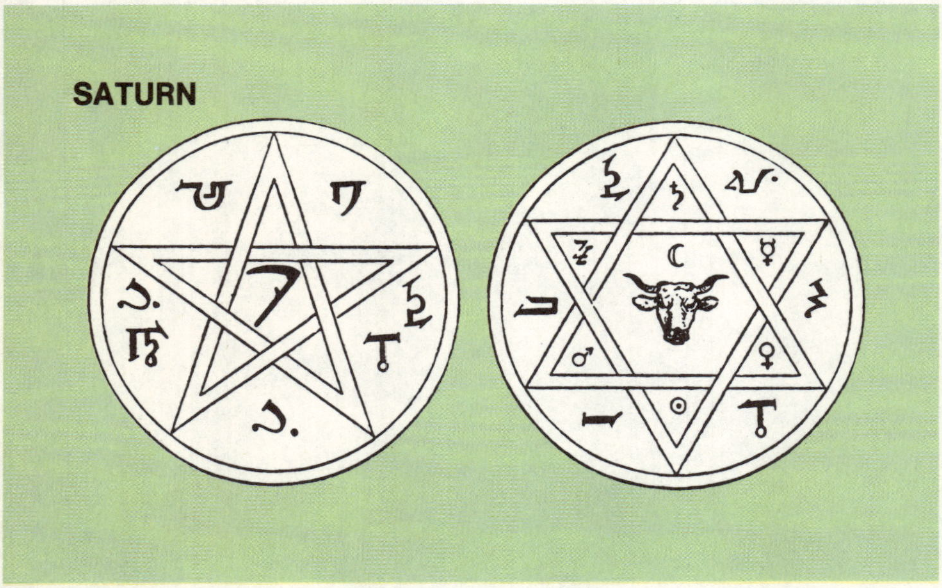

At about the same time that Ficino was working out his instructions for making talismans, the Swiss magician-physician Paracelsus was also studying the ancient works on talismans. Both he and Ficino were using authorities who took the doctrine from the secret traditions of Jewish mysticism, which were themselves believed to be derived from the occult sciences of Chaldea and Egypt. The talismans illustrated here are based on both Ficino's and Paracelsus' descriptions of effective planetary talismans.

The Planetary Talismans

fumes of benzoin, mace, and storax on a fire of dried stalks of lilies, narcissus, and marjoram. It protects the wearer against attacks of epilepsy or madness, and against death by murder or poison. It is worn in a pouch of purple silk. If buried under a shop or place of business it insures prosperity, and if placed under the head during sleep, it brings prophetic dreams.

7. The talisman of the **Moon** is engraved on a plaque of pure silver and has on one side a goblet in a six-pointed star, and on the other a crescent in a pentagram. It must be made on a Monday, and consecrated over fumes of white sandalwood, camphor, aloes, amber, and cucumber seeds on a fire of dried stalks of artemisia, selenotrope, and ranunculus. It is worn in a white silk pouch. It protects the wearer against death by dropsy, apoplexy, madness, or shipwreck, and also protects people traveling in foreign lands.

The making of a personal planetary talisman involves detailed astrological calculations, and requires enormous patience and dedication. It might work to a certain extent purely because of the faith invested in it. If it didn't work, the believer could always attribute the failure to some miscalculation, omission, or error

SONNE

MOND

Above: the making of a talisman from a Persian manuscript, dating from the early 16th century. The talisman in this case was believed to keep evil away from children. The painting shows pupils at a Koran school. They have a writing board with the word *nushreh*, which means talisman in Arabic, written on it. The text explains that this talisman is given to boys after they succeed in reading one of the 30 sections of the Koran.

in the complex process of making and consecrating it. However, we are not mainly concerned with the question of the effectiveness of talismans, but with the philosophy that lies behind them—the philosophy of a system of correspondences linking together nature, man, and the cosmos.

There is a story in Idries Shah's book *Oriental Magic* which shows that knowledge of a system of correspondences and belief in its power is worldwide. The story was related to the author by a Scotswoman who was married to an Afghan. She had an opportunity to witness and participate in the work of an Afghani alchemist, and she was convinced that he could actually make gold.

The process took days. On the first day the alchemist, Aquil Khan, led the woman and a friend miles into the jungle to find some plants like tall dandelions, from which they had to collect a thick white sap by breaking and squeezing the stalks. Throughout the long ritual Aquil Khan maintained complete silence and only communicated by signs. It was hours before he indicated that they had collected enough and could go home. On the second day at dawn they started out on another three-hour walk into the jungle, this time to collect some creamy yellow mud from beside a stream. Out of this Aquil Khan made two deep bowls when they got back to his cave. On the third day they went out to collect special types of wood, and on the fourth to collect stones of a specific color, shape, and size. The fifth day they built a fire, starting it off with pieces of paper on which some squares were drawn, then putting layers of the special wood and charcoal, and on top a mixture of nutmeg, cinnamon, incense, and the dried and powdered blood of a white goat.

They had to wait for the first night of a new moon to light the fire, and while they were waiting Aquil Khan cast the horoscopes of his two assistants to make sure that there were no bad planetary influences that might spoil the work. The fire had to be kept burning for four days and nights before it was used. The alchemist put a stone and a small lump of silver in one of the bowls he had made, and covered them with the dandelion sap. He then put the other bowl on top of the first and bound the two together with long strips of cotton dipped in clay. At every stage of the operation he kept looking at the stars, like a man consulting a watch. The bowl remained in the center of the fire for seven days and nights. When it was removed, cooled and the two halves prised apart, there was a nugget of yellow metal. A jeweler later confirmed that it was pure gold and offered to buy it. At the conclusion of the process Aquil told the woman: "It took me 30 years to learn this; 30 years of water and nuts, berries and starvation, contemplation and experiment. I had to learn to read the heavens, tame animals, read signs."

Many Years of Dedicated Work

The Afghan's account of his art is similar to accounts by European alchemists. There is the same emphasis on purification, contemplation, and years of dedication to work. There is the hint that powers drawn down from the heavens bring about the magical transmutation. There is the statement that knowledge of signs is an essential part of the work.

The 16th-century German alchemist Oswald Crollius published a volume under the title *The Book of Signatures, or True and Vital Anatomy of the Greater and Lesser Worlds* in which he demonstrated that everything in the natural world carries the signature of the cosmic force with which it is linked. He maintained that the initiate who knows how to read signs can see at a glance the sympathies and antipathies between things, and learn their secret properties. It was precisely such knowledge that the Afghan alchemist claimed to have.

The literature of alchemy contains many stories of successful transmutations of metals, not all of them easy to dismiss. We know that transmutation of the elements can and does take place through making changes in their atomic structure, and that such changes can only take place at extremely high temperatures. We also know that the art of the alchemist culminated in the act of drawing the forces of the heavens into the material world.

There is a good deal of evidence in the world that ancient man knew of technologies that baffle even the scientists of our highly technological age. For example, in 1960 archaeologists found in China the grave of a general who had lived in the 3rd

Alchemy and the Spirit of the World

century A.D. In it were objects made of alloys that could not be made today, and that would require a very high temperature for their production. There were also aluminum objects. Until then it had been thought that man had only known how to make aluminum for about a century. Another instance of early technological knowledge is in Delhi, India. An ancient column of iron there, probably made between 376–414 A.D., does not corrode. These are but two of numerous inexplicable phenomena that make it difficult to dismiss the claims of alchemists, and suggest that magic may be a forgotten science or technology.

Ficino's sympathetic or natural magic was based on the belief that throughout the universe there exists a very fine and subtle substance which conducts the stellar and cosmic influences down to earth. He called this substance the *spiritus mundi*, or spirit of the world.

In Ficino's day only two states of matter were known, liquids and solids. It was the 17th-century alchemist Johann Baptist van Helmont who discovered that matter can exist in a state thinner than fluidity, namely as a gas. Since his day many scientists have wondered whether there might not be yet another state of matter. Then, about 30 years ago, plasma was discovered. In technical language plasma is a gas that has had the electrons stripped off the nuclei of its atoms, and has become ionized. But its properties are greatly different from those of gas. It is a superconductor of electricity. It can reach temperatures of millions of degrees. It is luminous. Its energy can be contained and directed by a magnetic field. Most of the matter outside the earth's surface is plasma. In the light of these recent discoveries, Ficino's idea of a subtle substance that conducts stellar influences, the *spiritus mundi*, looks prophetic.

In the 1780s the fashionable people of Paris were flocking to a clinic where there were some queer goings-on. They sat in a tub filled with a mixture of water and iron filings. From the tub protruded iron rods which, from time to time, those under treatment applied to the parts of their anatomy that were giving them trouble. Their therapist, dressed in a lilac gown, wielded a long magnet that he would point at his patients or touch them with. They might then form a chain—men and women alternating—and press their thighs against each other. Some remarkable cures were reported—which is perhaps not surprising in the light of what we now know about psychosomatic illnesses and the therapeutic value of getting rid of inhibitions. But it is the theory behind the therapy that is particularly interesting, the theory formulated by Franz Anton Mesmer, the gentleman in the lilac gown.

Mesmer's theory was that there is an invisible fluid that passes through everything in the universe, including the human body, and through which the influence of the planets is transmitted. He called this invisible fluid "animal magnetism." It was also known as "etheric fluid" or "psychic fluid." The human, he believed, is like a magnet with opposite poles on the left and right sides of the body. Disease is caused either by an imbalance of the animal magnetism, or obstructions to its circulation. Illness could therefore be cured by applying magnetic forces to move the fluid in the body so as to restore a correct

Opposite: by the middle of the 19th century when the British artist Sir William Fettes Douglas painted this picture entitled *The Alchemist*, alchemy itself had fallen into almost total disrepute. But the figure of the alchemist himself was still that of a fabulous and wise old man, who was acquainted with secrets of supernatural power.

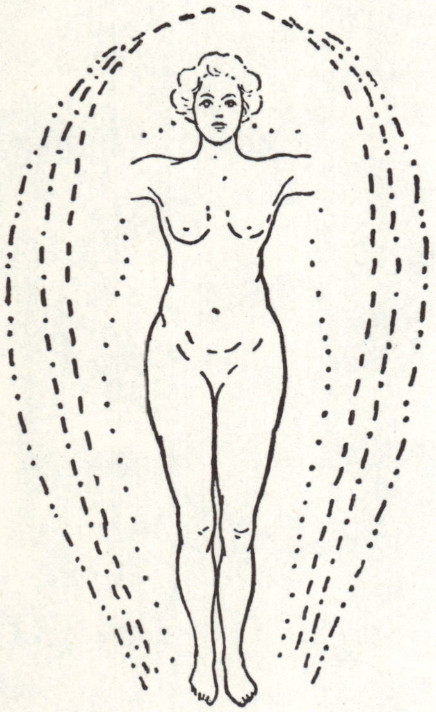

• • • • • • • Inner aura.

— — — — Outer aura, when not well.

—•—•—• Outer aura, when in good health.

—••—••— Outer aura, after electrifying positively.

Above: the aura as defined by Dr. Walter Kilner. He observed the aura through special colored glass. Although it was the Spiritualists who gave his work the warmest welcome, Kilner was emphatic that his ideas were not metaphysical, and not founded on occult principles or clairvoyance of any kind. He had been educated as a conventional medical doctor, and to his death firmly insisted that his work was purely scientific.

balance between the poles. At first Mesmer used actual magnets in his experiments. Later he claimed that he could transmit animal magnetism from himself to his patient simply by stroking the patient and bringing on some sort of bodily convulsion. He was, in fact, not the first healer to use magnetic therapy. Paracelsus had claimed to cure epilepsy by checking the flow of fluid to the brain. He did this by placing the negative pole of a magnet on a patient's head, and the positive pole on the stomach. He had also used magnets in treating other ailments, apparently with success. Mesmer's successes, too, were spectacular, though how much they owed to the power of suggestion is difficult to assess.

Cranky and comical though his methods were, Mesmer's theories for a time exerted a great influence, and all over Europe people went around magnetizing each other, animals, and plants. It seemed to be an amiable and pleasant occupation, and in some cases, also a beneficial one. A Dr. Picard accelerated the growth and flowering of a rose bush by magnetizing it daily for five minutes morning and evening, and made one branch of a peach tree produce fruit more abundantly and

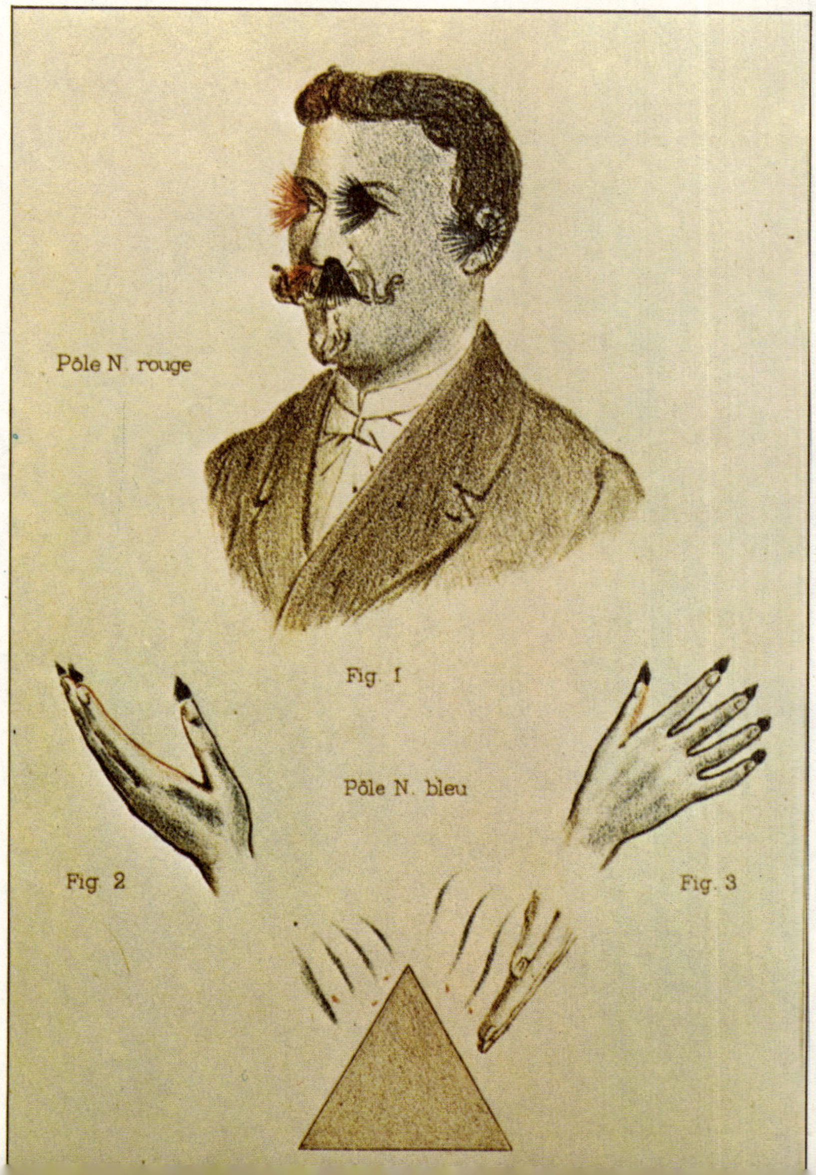

Right: during the 1890s in Paris, Albert de Rochas hypnotized subjects who were then able to distinguish colored rays emitted from the human body, as shown in this illustration from his book. Using Mesmer's theory that the body has two poles, they reported that generally the north pole appeared to produce blue rays, and the south pole red ones—although this was not invariable.

earlier than others on the tree. The stories of the experiments of the magnetizers make fascinating reading, but what concerns us here is Mesmer's theory behind the experiments. He believed that animal magnetism or psychic fluid is the invisible link between man and the cosmos through which man emits a kind of energy that can affect other organisms, and even the world of matter.

The 19th-century French writer on magic Eliphas Lévi declared boldly that "Mesmer rediscovered the secret science of Nature." He identified Mesmer's animal magnetism or psychic fluid with the "astral light," which is "either latent or active in all created substances." He quoted in support of his idea the 4th-century poet Synesius who said: "A single source, a single root of light, jets out and spreads itself into three branches of splendor. A breath blows around the earth, and vivifies in innumerable forms all parts of animated substance." Allowing for the poeticism, this seems to be much like a definition of recently discovered plasma. So, too, is Lévi's definition of the astral light as both a force and a substance, for plasma, though intangible and invisible, has the metallic properties of responding

Animal Magnetism or "Astral Light"?

Below left: Kirlian photography, which by use of long radio waves reveals that living things—plants and animals—have a pattern of flares surrounding them. The process was invented by Semyon and Valentina Kirlian working in South Russia. This picture of the fingertip of a healthy human being shows the luminous gas around it. Curiously, when illness strikes, the "aura" shows the earliest signs of change and irregularity.

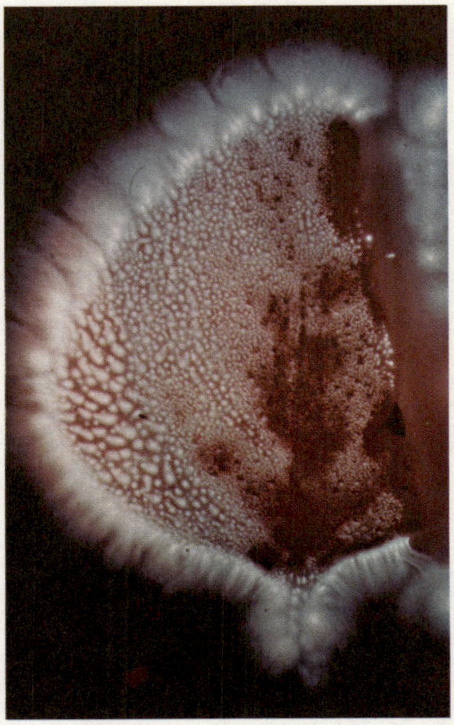

Above: a rose leaf with a portion cut away is seen to go on emitting its entire aura. This "phantom" aura lasts for about 15 minutes.

Below: an ordinary photograph of a healthy leaf from a geranium.

Bottom: a Kirlian photograph of the leaf showing its surrounding aura. At this stage the aura is of bluish flares that glow strongly and evenly in a flashing pattern around the tips of the entire leaf.

to magnetism and conducting electricity.

Since Mesmer's day, numerous researchers have sought to demonstrate the existence of the etheric or psychic fluid. Between 1845 and 1868 the German chemist Karl Reichenbach published several books demonstrating the existence in all matter and all organisms of a natural energy that he called *od*. His evidence was the testimony of a number of sensitives (people with sharper sense perceptions than usual) who, if kept in the dark for an hour or more, could see gleams of light like flames emitted from the poles of magnets, from crystals, and in some cases from the fingers of a human hand. They also felt sensations of heat and cold in connection with these lights.

In 1891 a Colonel de Rochas and a Dr. Luys began a series of experiments in Paris developing Reichenbach's work. They used hypnotized subjects. In 1912 an Englishman, Dr. Walter Kilner, published the results of a long series of experiments. By looking through colored glass screens he found that he could see a radiant fringe or aura about six inches wide around most bodies. He claimed that this visible aura was in three distinct layers, and varied with the age, sex, mental abilities, and health of the subject. He also believed that it could be used as an aid to medical diagnosis. In 1921 a French researcher, Du Bourg de

Living Auras and "Fluidic Forces"

Bozas, produced photographic evidence that certain psychic subjects could emit from their hands a "tube of fluidic force" that would penetrate a sheet of lead five centimeters thick. Another Frenchman, Boirac, discovered that he could anesthetize an area of a person's body simply by pointing his hand at it. A blindfolded subject would be able to describe sensations of touch on all parts of his body except the area that the experimenter was pointing at. Two doctors in Bordeaux conducted many experiments with a woman who could halt natural processes such as the fermentation of wine and the decay of animal organs by holding her hands over them. She apparently emitted some energy that was lethal for bacteria, and was able permanently to mummify the corpses of birds and small animals by means of that unusual energy.

In recent years research into human energy fields has become more sophisticated and more scientifically controlled. The process known as Kirlian photography has demonstrated that all living things emit vivid patterns of light and color, which are not visible under normal conditions. For example, a leaf or hand placed in the middle of two plates, between which a high-frequency electrical field is passed, are seen to have an aura of light with vivid flares streaming from the pores. Healing by

Below left: the same geranium leaf after it has been deprived of light for 72 hours. The shape of the aura has become rounded, and a reddish color has spread over the center.

Below: the dead leaf. The outer flashes have been extinguished and the leaf is almost completely red.

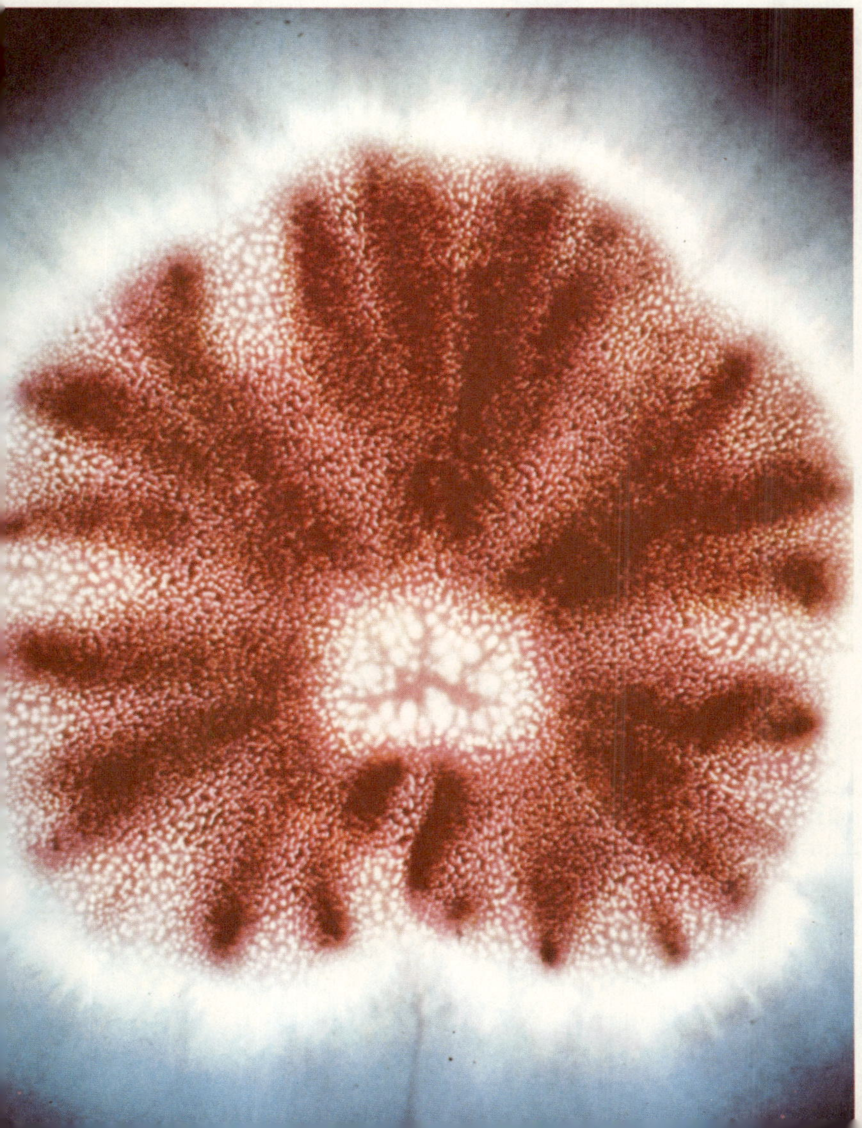

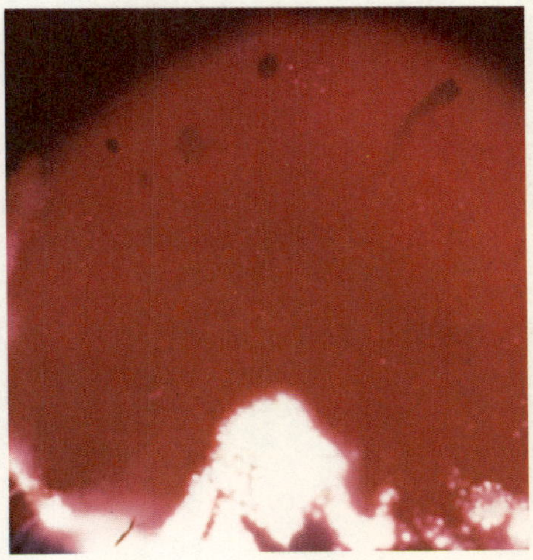

Leadbeater and the Human Aura

For C. W. Leadbeater, the world was a wonderfully complex place, containing much more than was ordinarily visible. This English clergyman became a leading figure in the Theosophical Society, which believed in and explored the invisible spirit world unknown to most of us. By using clairvoyance, he believed that a greater reality was available to all of mankind.

In no way was this greater reality more obvious to Leadbeater than in the aura which he saw surrounding each person. According to him, this aura was an emanation of the astral body, and gave a key to peoples' state of spiritual development and individual temperament. It was clearly visible to the trained clairvoyant, Leadbeater said. The savage or an uncivilized man will have a weak and pale-colored aura, but the developed man or woman—described as "a seeker after the higher truth"—will have a finely colored aura. This expresses capacity to serve as a channel for the higher force. Such people are possessed of a crown of brilliant sparks that rise from the upper part of the body, adding greatly to their dignity. This sparkling aura surrounds them whatever they might be doing with their physical body.

touch, or the laying on of hands, has long been practiced all over the world, and now Kirlian photography has shown that the emissions from the fingers of a healer are of exceptional intensity and length.

Until quite recently acupuncture—the ancient Chinese practice of sticking needles into the body to prevent and cure diseases—was regarded by many in the West as strange and unscientific. Now, through Kirlian photography, an exact correspondence has been discovered between the points where the body gives off its most intense emissions of light and color, and the points where the acupuncturists stick their needles. In 1973 an American book reported the proceedings of a conference on "the human aura in acupuncture and Kirlian photography." It said that "the function of the acupuncture stimulation was primarily to take energy out of one limb of the circuit and put it into another—to shift these energies around so that one obtained a balanced system." This is remarkably similar to Mesmer's idea that disease can be cured by shifting the etheric fluid in the body, and restoring a balance between the magnetic poles. The title of this American book, *Galaxies of Life*, serves to remind us that all these developments in the sciences come back to the central theme of the hermetic philosophy and of magical traditions: as above, so below. Kirlian photographs of the energy fields of living organisms have a striking and weird resemblance to pictures of astronomical formations and constellations, such as the milky way, the spiral and crab nebulae of distant galaxies, and solar flares.

Color healing is not new. In Heliopolis in ancient Egypt there were temples of light and color that were used for purposes of therapy. Present-day enthusiasts claim that perfect health can be insured, and even the severest diseases can be cured, by applying knowledge of the principles and functions of light and color. Techniques for breathing certain colors, for bathing in them, or for absorbing them through specified food and drinks are prescribed by Dr. Roland Hunt in his book *The Seven Keys to Color Healing*, published in 1971. Dr. Hunt, like Dr. Kilner 60 years ago, claims that illness can be diagnosed by observing the condition of and the colors in the etheric aura that surrounds the human body. His treatments involve the use of metals as well as breathing, diet, and exposure to light. He declares that red radiations can be absorbed from iron, yellow from gold, green from copper, and blue from tin. A glance at the table on page 31 will show that these are the same correspondences handed down in magical lore.

Orthodox scientists and doctors may scoff at the idea of the human aura or energy body, but magicians and psychic healers down the centuries and throughout the world have produced a body of remarkably consistent testimony for its existence. Magicians claim that their powers come from the etheric or astral plane, and that their art consists in knowing how to channel a stream of astral light into and through the body. The recognition of the magical patterns of correspondences between man, nature, and the cosmos is an important introduction to how practical magic is actually done.

Emotions and the Astral Body

These illustrations, showing the effect that various emotions have on the aura as seen clairvoyantly, are from the book *Man Visible and Invisible* published in 1907. It was by C. W. Leadbeater, who wrote widely on occult subjects. In his view the true shape of the mental and astral material around the physical body is roughly ovoid.

Top left: the astral body when convulsed with fear. Terror will "in an instant suffuse the entire body with a curious livid gray mist," according to Leadbeater.

Top right: the calm scientific man. The large quantity of golden yellow at the top shows a well-developed intelligence, and the orange cone rising through the yellow shows there is justifiable pride and ambition in connection with the knowledge indicated. The scientific and orderly habit of mind has an obvious effect upon the astral colors, which fall into neat and regular bands.

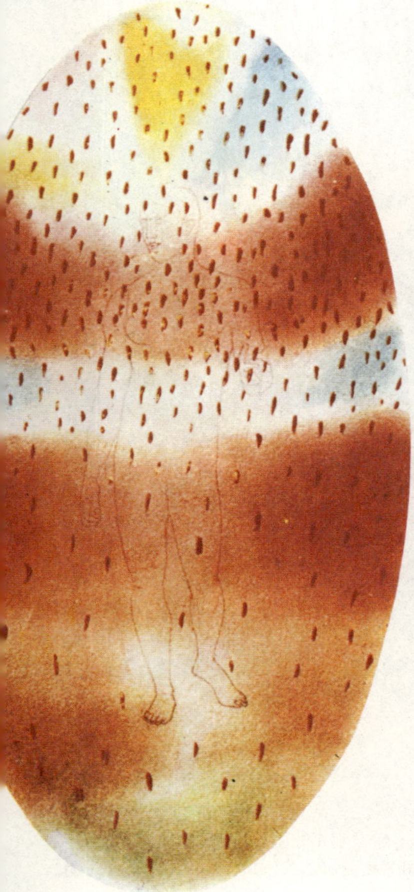

Bottom left: the irritable man. His astral body is filled with small floating scarlet specks showing outbursts of temper over the vexations of ordinary life. Some flecks are cast out in the direction of the person assumed to be responsible for whatever has gone wrong, but many remain floating around in his astral body. Although they gradually fade away, there is likely to be a continuous source of new ones as the irritable man finds new subjects for his annoyance.

Bottom right: the angry man. The faint outline of the man is almost hidden by the heavy, thunderous masses of sooty blackness as the man gives way to a fit of passion. Fiery arrows of rage shoot through the black, and the terrible flashes penetrate other astral bodies like swords. Therefore, though he may be able to restrain himself from giving way to physical violence, he is nonetheless injuring others on the astral plane.

BINAH
CHOKMAH
DIN
GEBURAH
TIPHARETH
CHESED
NETSHAH
HOD HOD
YESOD
YESOD
MAIKUTH
MAIKUTH

Chapter 3
Mysteries of the Cabala

Were the ancient cabalists magicians? Did they ever intend their mystical writings to be adapted by magicians? What are the likenesses between the Cabala, which is a collection of occult speculations by Hebraic mystics over many centuries, and magic? Many magicians have found in the Cabala a method of possible access to powers beyond the self. Like the cabalists, they study means of projecting their body into other levels of existence, getting ever closer to the ultimate source of life. Can such magic rituals open up new paths of awareness?

There is a legend that God whispered the secret wisdom of the Cabala to Moses on Mount Sinai, that Moses communicated it to the 70 elders, and that they in turn passed it on to their immediate successors. It remained a secret, oral tradition known to very few until centuries later, when various anonymous authors began to write down their different versions. There are those who maintain that even today the most profound truths of the Cabala are known to only a handful of initiates. They are passed on either by word of mouth or through closely guarded, ancient, unpublished manuscripts to those who have proved themselves especially worthy of carrying on this mystical tradition.

Cabala is a Hebrew word that means knowledge or tradition. It is used to refer to a large body of mystical speculation that includes writings by many authors, and that spans many centuries. Among the vast amount of literature two books stand out as the most important. One is the *Sefer Yetzirah* or Book of Creation, which was probably written in Palestine or Babylon between the 3rd and 6th centuries A.D. The other is known as the *Zohar* or Book of Splendor, and was probably written in Spain in the late 13th century by Moses de Léon.

The ideas of the Cabala have much in common with those of gnosticism, which also flourished in the countries of the Eastern Mediterranean around the time of Christ. *Gnosis* means knowledge of spiritual things obtained by divine inspiration. Unlike

Opposite: a modern artist, Godfrey Dawson, produced this image of the cabalistic Tree of Life. He drew freely on all the elements which have come to enrich the cabalist tradition.

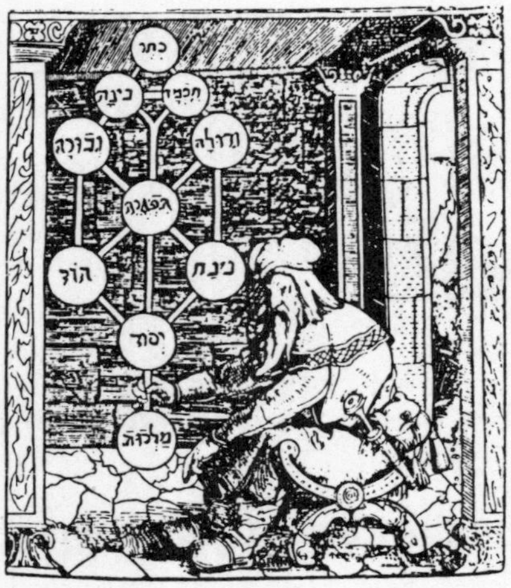

Above: a 16th-century woodcut of a Jewish cabalist holding the Tree of Life. The Tree is visualized as growing downward with its roots above. The circles give the Hebrew name for each of the sefira. Together the sefiroth—or 10 aspects of the Divine—are seen as making up God's name.

the Christians, who believed that the road to salvation was through faith, love, and good deeds, cabalists and gnostics held that it was only possible to reach God through knowledge. They believed that the chosen were those who had obtained this knowledge, and that we are cut off from God not by sin in the Christian sense, but by ignorance.

The tradition of the Cabala is predominantly Jewish, but since the Renaissance humanists, philosophers, psychologists, and occultists have seized on it with enthusiasm. Each have extracted from its great diversity and richness those features that best fit in with their particular scheme of thought. The Cabala is in some ways the *I Ching* of the West, worthy of a lifetime's study and contemplation. It is complex and inexhaustible, but at the same time accessible in its basic conceptions.

Magicians and occultists have, of course, been attracted by the mystery and secrecy surrounding the Cabala. But they have also found themselves in sympathy with many of its underlying beliefs. Common both to the Cabala and to occultists is the idea that all things in the Universe are part of an organized whole, governed by secret laws, and with hidden connections or correspondences between many things that do not overtly appear to be linked. Shared, too, is the notion that all phenomena contain something of the divine, and that man is, in some way and on a minute scale, a reflection of both God and the Universe. The idea of a path that we can climb in stages to reach God is fundamental both to the Cabala and to theories of magic throughout the centuries.

Behind the cabalist system of thought is the basic doctrine that God is completely unknowable. He cannot even be directly addressed in prayer. He is everything and nothing. He cannot be ascribed qualities of good and evil. He is known as *En Sof*, Infinite Radiance. He did not create the Universe, and therefore cannot be responsible for it. The Universe emanated or flowed out from Him. According to the *Zohar*, a single ray of light burst out from the closed confines of En Sof, and from this light came nine further lights. This process of emanation was the way in which the unknowable God revealed certain aspects of Himself. Each of the ten lights can be seen both as facets of God and as stages in His revelation of Himself. They are known as the *sefiroth* (one light is a *sefira*), and are seen as constituting God's name because they are the identity that he has revealed.

The 10 sefiroth are regarded as underlying the construction of the Universe and of man, both of which are in the image of God. They are also the forces behind man and the Universe. There are 22 paths connecting the 10 sefiroth to each other. As we shall see later, the 10 sefiroth, each of which has its own name, are linked to the numbers 1 to 10, and the 22 paths are linked to the 22 letters of the Hebrew alphabet. The sefiroth and paths are usually depicted by circles and lines in the Tree of Life, and this Tree embraces and classifies everything in the Universe. This is shown at the top on page 53.

The Tree of Life also shows how God descended in a flash from *Kether*, the first emanation or Crown, through the sefiroth to *Malkhuth*, the Earth or the Earthly Kingdom. To reach God the soul has to make the journey in reverse through the sefiroth, a long and arduous climb beset with many pitfalls. This route is shown at the bottom of page 53.

The idea of the Tree of Life has much in common with the widely held belief in the construction of the Universe that existed from classical times right up to the 16th century. This stated that the Universe was made up of nine concentric spheres. God was accorded the outer sphere, the stars made up the second sphere, and each of the planets then known were allotted one of the next seven spheres. Of these, the moon was the innermost sphere. It contained the earth, which was not considered a separate sphere. Cabalists were influenced by Pythagorean theories based on the numbers 1 to 10. In order to make the planetary spheres correspond with the 10 sefiroth and the first 10 numbers, they increased the spheres in this scheme to 10, making the earth a sphere on its own to correspond with Malkhuth or Earth on the Tree of Life. The seven sefiroth above Malkhuth correspond with the seven planets; *Hokmah* or Divine Wisdom with the sphere of the stars or zodiac; and Kether, the Crown, with God.

In the early centuries after Christ, the idea of the soul's descent

The Tree of Life

Above: a miniature of Moses from a medieval Bible. In spite of the tradition that Moses received the secrets of the Cabala while on Mount Sinai, it seems clear that what we now call the Cabala grew out of the Merkabah or "Throne" mysticism of Judaism. This flourished from the 4th to 10th centuries in the Middle East.

Left: one unorthodox form of Christianity which had much in common with Cabalism was the heresy Gnosticism. In the 12th century, a Gnostic sect known as the Cathars arose in Europe and was savagely repressed. Here St. Dominic is shown burning Cathar books. One "pure" book rises, untouched, from the flames consuming the rest.

Ego sum rerum naturaliū doctor

and ascent through the spheres took shape in the countries of the Eastern Mediterranean. This idea was absorbed by the cabalists and adapted to the Tree of Life. It was believed that the human soul originated in God and descended through the spheres, picking up the characteristic of each like a new skin as it passed through. For example, from Venus it took love and from Mercury it took intelligence. Finally it reached the earth and added the last layer or skin, the physical body. It was now a miniature image of the Universe, each layer corresponding to a sphere, or sefira in cabalistic terminology. This idea is the clearest illustration of the cabalist belief that man is a reflection of both the Universe and God.

Once in the body, the soul longed to return to its origin, to go back up through the spheres and be reunited with God. It could begin its ascent at the moment of death. But the way was difficult and hazardous because each sefira was guarded by angels that would try to prevent the soul from continuing. The lower spheres were also full of evil spirits that would try to ensnare unwary souls. The soul's progress would depend on the knowledge it had gained in life of the secrets of each sphere, and of how to overcome its guardian angels. It can be seen clearly that knowledge, rather than a pious life, was all-important for the progress of the soul, although there have doubtless been many pious and religious cabalists. Cabalists also believed that the soul might begin its ascent before death through the mastery of certain techniques and knowledge. It is probably mostly this belief that attracted magicians as well as religious and other mystics to the Cabala.

The correspondence between the sefiroth on the Tree of Life and the planetary spheres is shown even more clearly when the sefiroth are represented, as they sometimes are, by 10 concentric spheres. In the diagram on page 54 the planetary correspondence for each sefira has been given in order to make the link clearer. When the Cabala is used as a basis for magical operations, it is essential to know the planetary association of each sefira in order to make use of the appropriate symbols and system of correspondences.

Illustrating the sefiroth as concentric spheres clearly shows that, because the spheres decrease in power and dignity as they reduce in size, it takes an immense expansion of consciousness for each stage of the journey by the soul from the inner circle to the outer. Outside of showing this, the Tree is a much more suggestive and versatile representation. It can be contemplated in different ways, various patterns within it can be focused and, with the exercise of a little imagination, everything in the Universe can be fitted into it and assigned to one or another of the sefira. It is, as Aleister Crowley said, like a great card-index file.

Our understanding of the sefiroth and the relationship between them may be increased by looking at them in different groupings. They are sometimes thought of by cabalists as forming three pillars, as in the diagram on page 56. Those on the right side of the tree bring together the male, positive, light principles of the Universe (like the Yang of Chinese philosophy). Hokmah is the father of the Universe, the force behind everything active, creative, and changing. *Hesed* or Love, is the force that civilizes and governs, the merciful loving father, the guide and protector.

Different Groupings

Opposite: an illustration from the 15th-century work *Opera Chemica* by Ramón Lull, showing the Hermetic philosophy of Nature. At the center of the picture is the Serpent of Wisdom, twined around the Tree of Life.

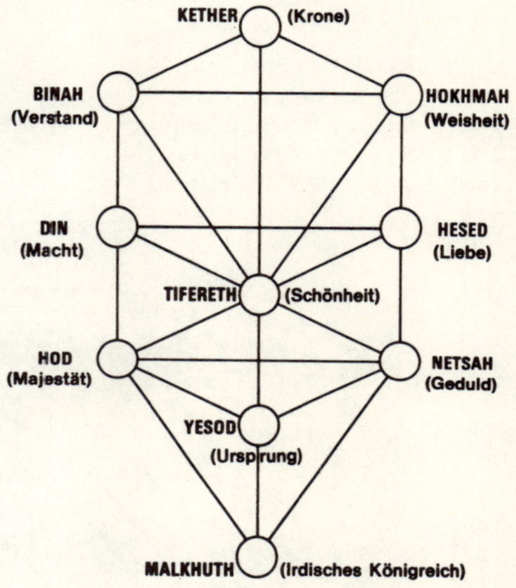

Above: the 10 sefiroth with the 22 pathways connecting them. The sefiroth shown here are the emanations of En Sof, the totally unknowable, uncomprehensible God.

Below: the lightning flash by which God descended from Kether to Malkhuth to create Adam Kadmon, the metaphysical counterpart of the biblical first man, Adam.

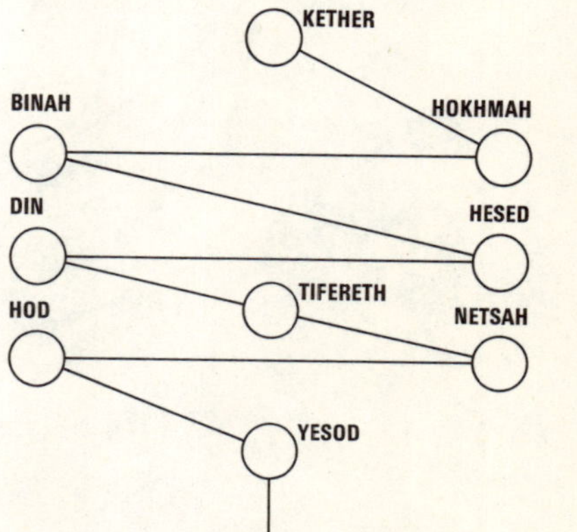

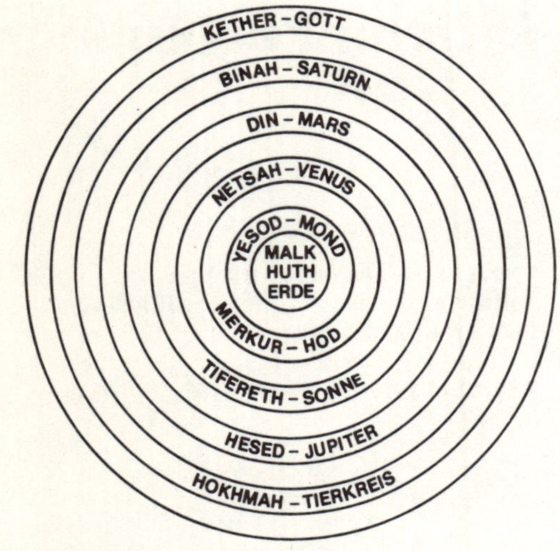

The Ptolemaic concept of the Universe (below) was the only one accepted from ancient Greek times to the 16th century. Yet it is based on the same thinking as the concept of the cabalists (above).

Netsah or Victory and Endurance, at the base of the male pillar, represents the force of Nature, of human instincts, impulses, and emotions. These three male sefiroth together make up the Pillar of Mercy.

On the left side of the tree are the three sefiroth that represent the female, passive, dark principles (like the Yin). At the top is *Binah* or Understanding, the mother of the Universe, passive and receptive until fertilized, and then prolific. Binah represents slumbering potentiality and all-embracing understanding. It is the stable counterpart to the dynamic Hokmah at the head of the male pillar. The counterpart to the loving merciful Hesed is *Din* or Power (also known as *Geburah*), standing for severity and discipline. Din is the force that destroys, whereas Hesed builds. But it also stands for energy and realism. At the bottom of the female pillar is *Hod* or Majesty, the counterpart of the male Netsah. Where Netsah stands for animal instincts and emotions, Hod represents the higher powers of the mind such as intuition and inspiration. These three female sefiroth form the Pillar of Severity.

Reconciling the male and female pillars is the Pillar of

Equilibrium. It is also known as the Pillar of the Soul or of Consciousness. The *Zohar* calls it the perfect pillar, mediating between the forces of light and darkness, but not dependent on them for existence. At the top of the pillar is Kether, the first emanation of the unknowable Godhead or Divinity. Then comes *Tifereth* or Beauty, and *Yesod* or Foundation. Yesod is connected with mystery and magical power. Finally, at the base is Malkhuth, the Earth.

Another way of looking at the sefiroth is in terms of three triangles with Malkhuth, the 10th sefira, at the bottom. Each triangle will contain two opposing forces from the male and female pillars, and one reconciling force from the central pillar. The top triangle of Kether, Hokmah, and Binah or Divinity, Wisdom, and Understanding, represents the ideal intellectual world. The next triangle of Tifereth, Hesed, and Din or Beauty, Mercy, and Power, represents the actual moral world, and the third triangle of Yesod, Netsah, and Hod, or Foundation, Victory, and Majesty, represents the astral or magical world.

The parts of the Tree of Life are upside down in comparison to a real tree. Kether, at the top, represents the roots of the Tree. The branches containing the other sefiroth spread and grow downward. Another common way to portray the sefiroth is in the form of a man, this time the right way up, with Kether representing the head. The first three sefiroth are the three cavities of the brain, the fourth and fifth are the arms, the sixth the torso, and the seventh and eighth the legs. The ninth represents the sexual organs, and the tenth either the total image of man or, in a different interpretation, woman.

The correspondences and attributes of the sefiroth are sometimes unexpected. Many of the qualities that we normally think of as being masculine appear in the female sefiroth, and vice versa. Planetary associations too are not immediately obvious. But the Cabala has its own fascinating logic. For example, Binah, the female force behind everything stable and potential, is linked to the planet Saturn, the planet of stability, old age, and fate. Netsah, the male force behind nature, animal drives, and passions, is linked to Venus, the goddess of sensuality and nature. All the sefiroth are rich in imagery and association, which is especially important when the Cabala is used for magical purposes.

Kether, the Crown, is the first emanation and corresponds with the number 1. The soul that reaches this sefira achieves union with God. It is guarded by the creatures described in the first chapter of *Ezekiel*: "and everyone had four faces, and everyone had four wings." Its symbols are the point, which stands for 1, and the crown. When meditating on Kether the cabalist must concentrate on the image of an old bearded man seen in profile.

Hokmah, Wisdom, is the father of the Universe. It is the next emanation from Kether and therefore its number is 2. Because it is the force behind activity, its guardian angels are the Wheels in *Ezekiel*, which moved around and had the spirit of life in them. Hokmah's symbols are the phallus, the tower, and the straight line, and the image to be used in contemplation is a bearded man.

Binah, Understanding, is the mother of the Universe. Being the third emanation, it is associated with the number 3. Its

Spheres, Pillars, or Branching Tree

Below: in the Hermetic version of the soul's progress toward God, the soul spiraled its way through the spheres which—as in cabalistic thought—reversed the original process of creation. This illustration comes from an anonymous 12th-century Hermetic manuscript; but the Hermetic tradition itself dates from around the time of Christ, a period of profound civil uproar and ideological chaos—the period in which Gnosticism and Cabalism were also taking shape. Mysteries and magic fascinated philosophers.

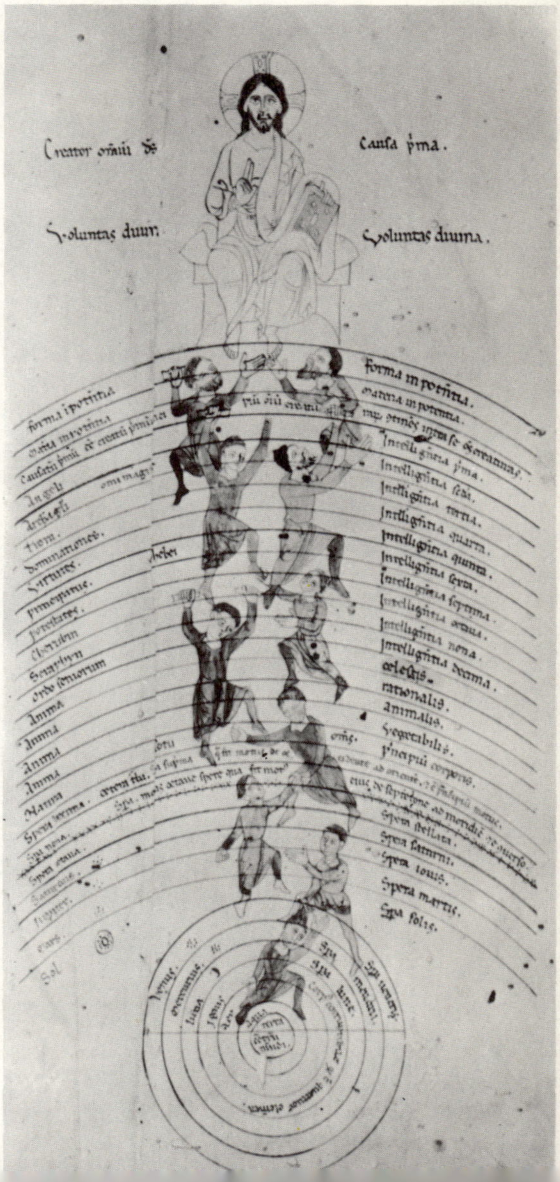

Interpreting the Secret Symbols

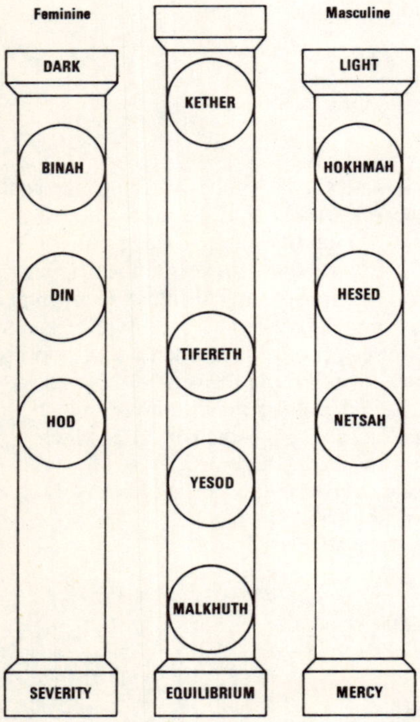

Above: another way of looking at the sefiroth is to consider them as three pillars, which creates a whole new set of relationships. In this way the theme of opposites is emphasized, with the masculine sefiroth on the right-hand pillar, and the feminine on the left-hand. The middle pillar acts as a balance between them. This pillar in addition provides a direct line from the divine (Kether) to the material (Malkhuth), which are the supreme cabalistic opposites.

symbols are the female genitals, the cup, the circle, the diamond, and the oval. As with the other female sefiroth, Binah has conflicting attributes—of life and death, of goodness and evil. It is associated both with the mother goddesses and with Hecate, goddess of witchcraft and sorcery. Its image for contemplation is a mature woman.

Hesed, Love, is accorded number 4, and is the male force that organizes and builds things up. Its symbols are the king's scepter, the magician's wand, the bishop's crook, as well as the Greek cross (+) and the pyramid. It is linked to the unicorn, which stands for virility and power, and its image for contemplation is a powerful king on a throne.

Din, Power, is number 5 and the female counterpart of Hesed. It lies behind all destruction, hatred, and war. Its planet is Mars and its symbols are the sword, spear, scourge, chain, and the pentagon, which is linked with the number five. Many cabalists see Din as the source of evil. There is even a theory that its destructive energy overflowed and created its own Tree of evil emanations. Din is associated with the mythical basilisk, a fierce deadly creature. Its image for contemplation is a warrior in a chariot.

Tifereth, Beauty, is number 6, and linked to the sphere of the sun. It is vital energy, and it balances the destructive and constructive forces of Din and Hesed. Christian cabalists associate Tifereth with Christ, both because of its direct descent from Kether, which stands for God, and because the sun had an early symbolic association with Christ. Tifereth can be represented by a lion, the beast of the sun, or by a phoenix or child, the symbols of immortality and mortality. Its images for contemplation are a majestic king and a sacrificed child.

Netsah, Victory, is number 7, the male force behind nature. It stands for the senses and passions. It is the sefira of the arts and of rhythm, movement, and color. Its sphere is Venus, and the bird associated with it, the wryneck, is used in love charms. Its image, again associated with Venus, is a beautiful naked woman.

Hod, Majesty, is number 8. It is the female force standing for the higher qualities of the mind, such as intuition and insight. But it also stands for qualities of reason and logic, distrusted by the Cabala. Like the other feminine sefiroth, there is a conflict between good and evil. It stands for wisdom as well as trickery and cunning. Its planet is Mercury, the god of intelligence and magic, and the twin serpents from Mercury's wand are often associated with Hod. Likewise, its image for contemplation is a hermaphrodite, which is also a symbol for the metal mercury in alchemy.

Yesod, Foundation, is the ninth sefira and the basis of all active forces in God. It stands for creativity, both sexual and mental. When the sefiroth are depicted as a man, Yesod is shown as the genitals. Its number is 9, and 9 is the number of initiation into magic and the occult. Its sphere is the moon, and the moon is the planet of magic. Its reconciliation of the animal drives of Netsah and the intellectual faculties of Hod give it great potential magical power. It is associated with the elephant, the animal that combines strength and intelligence, and its image for contemplation is a beautiful naked man.

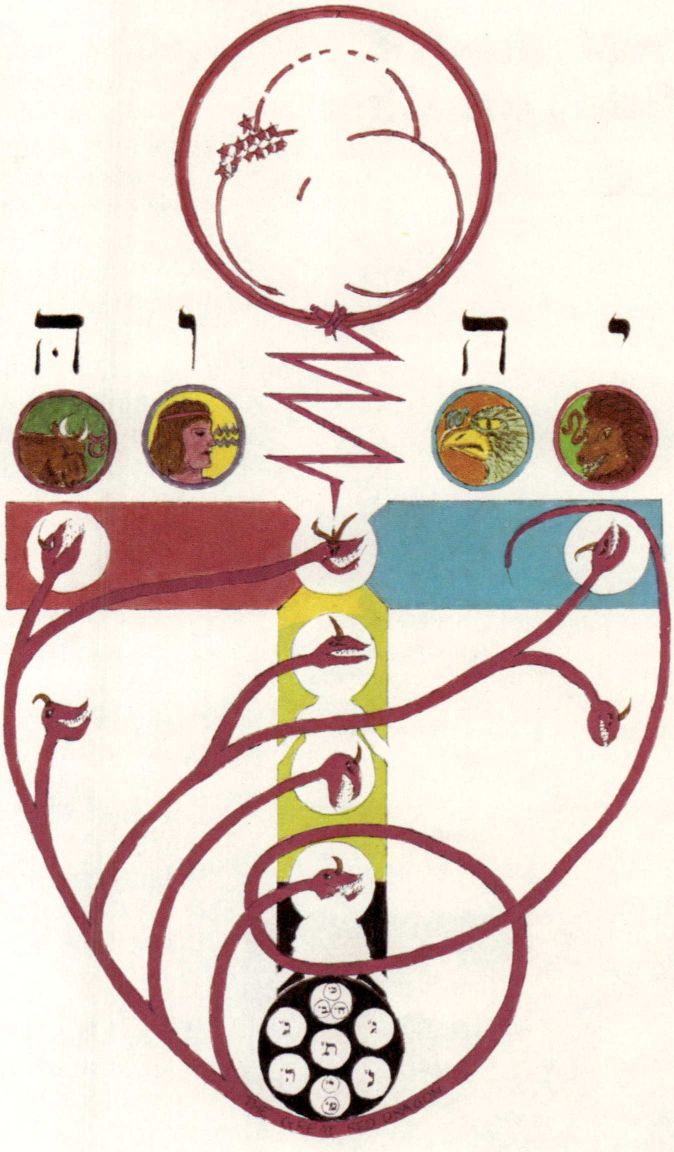

Above: two modern drawings, *The Garden of Eden Before* (left) and *After the Fall*, show how the story from Genesis, like other religious and mythic episodes, is enriched by cabalistic symbolism. Before, Adam and Eve are free and vigorous, Adam in Tifereth with his arms stretched out, and Eve in Malkhuth, supporting the two great pillars. Below them the Serpent of Wisdom encircles the seven palaces, giving the key to paths on the Tree of Life. After the fall, the serpent has become the Red Dragon, the apocalyptic monster with eight heads and 11 horns and both Adam and Eve are caught hopelessly in the tangles.

Malkhuth, the Earthly Kingdom, is the tenth sefira. The number 10 means "all things," and Malkhuth unites all the sefiroth in one somewhat like man is seen as uniting all the features of the planetary spheres. It is associated with the sphinx, which stands for the unity of heaven and earth. This sefira is also known as *Shekinah*, the bride of God. The purpose of the Cabala is to unite God, the first emanation, with His lost bride Shekinah, the tenth emanation or, put differently, to ascend from the tenth sefira to the first. The image for contemplation is a young woman, crowned and seated on a throne.

Ambiguities abound in the Cabala, particularly when we come to the lower sefiroth, for each sefira receives influences from others connected with it on horizontal, vertical, and diagonal planes. But ambiguities also abound in life, and cabalists believe that contemplation based on the Tree and its patterns may reveal more about life and the universe than any explicit and unambiguous philosophical statement could. The attributes of the sexes and the relations between them, for example, are

"A Method of Using the Mind"

Opposite: a modern painting of Aleister Crowley, most notorious magician of the 20th century. Crowley encountered the Cabala early in life and was deeply influenced by its concepts from then on.

Below: Crowley as a young man. His ideas still attract new followers today.

certainly more ambiguous than commonly accepted patterns of thinking and living allow for. The contemplation of the structure and symbolism of the Cabala, therefore, could probably revitalize many an ailing marriage. Dion Fortune, who was the leading modern English cabalist, writes, "The Tree is a method of using the mind, not a system of knowledge." The fascination of the Cabala is that it leads the mind beyond ambiguities to profound truths and insights.

Magic too is a method of using the mind, or rather the powers of the mind. Aleister Crowley, the modern magician, defined magic as "the science and art of causing changes to occur in conformity with will." The cabalist who wished to make the journey through the sefiroth during his lifetime had to learn to detach himself from the physical world by mastering the powers of concentration and imagination. He learned to achieve a trancelike state in which he could visualize a clear image of his own body in front of him, like a double. He then had to transfer his consciousness to the second body so that he was functioning through it, and he was ready to begin the long hard ascent.

Modern magicians and occultists employ many of the same techniques as the cabalists, but they think of the journey through the sefiroth as a journey in the astral plane, another dimension of the world, and of the body on that plane as the astral body. The astral plane includes the ordinary world, but it extends beyond it to the realm where the products of thought and imagination have reality. The astral body is the spiritual replica of the physical body, and is able to travel through space and solid objects. In the Tree of Life, the gateway to the astral world is Yesod, which corresponds to the sphere of the Moon. It is the link between Earth and the rest of the Universe.

The Cabala has had a great influence on modern occultists and magicians. Eliphas Lévi, whose books are still widely read today, spent much time working on a theory of correspondences. He studied both the Cabala and the Tarot, that curious pack of fortune-telling cards of uncertain origin. Lévi related the 22 symbolic cards of the Tarot to the 22 letters of the Hebrew alphabet. These letters, as we have seen, are related to the 22 paths of the Tree of Life. Thus the Tarot cards were linked to the Cabala.

Lévi's theories on correspondences were greatly expanded by the Order of the Golden Dawn, the magical society that flourished in England in the 1890s. With amazing thoroughness, members of the Golden Dawn elaborated one of the most complex and all-embracing systems of ritual magic. Mythologies and religions were combed and out of them Greek, Roman, and Egyptian gods, and Christian and Jewish spirits, were apportioned among the sefiroth and the 22 paths. Colors, animals, stones, and scents were among the other objects and attributes that were classified. The magician who wished to find the appropriate ritual for each sefira could thereafter look it up in a Table of Correspondences.

The 22 connecting lines between the 10 sefiroth are called the Paths of Wisdom. According to Dion Fortune "the sefiroth are natural forces, the Paths states of consciousness." Each path represents an equilibrium between the forces of the two sefiroth it connects. Each is associated with a planet or zodiac sign, a

Tree of Life
עץ חיים
אין סוף אור Boundless Light
אין סוף Eternity
אין Void
כתר
PRIMUM MOBILE
IPSISSIMUS
The Crown.
11. The Fool (O)
12. The Magician (I)
13.
The High Priestess (II)
בינה
MAGISTER TEMPLI
Understanding
חכמה
ZODIAC
MAGUS
Wisdom
14. The Empress (III)
THE VEIL OF
THE ABYSS
דעת
Knowledge
BASE OF THE ABYSS
18. The Chariot (VII)
17 The Lovers
15 The Emperor
16. The Heirophant (V)
גבורה
ADEPTUS MAJOR
Severity
חסד
ADEPTUS EXEMPTUS
Mercy
19. Strength (VIII)
22. Justice (XI)
20. The Hermit (IX)
23. Hanged Man (XII)
21. Wheel of Fortune. (X)
THE VEIL OF
THE TEMPLE
תיפארת
ADEPTUS MINOR
Beauty
24. Death (XIII)
25. Temperance (XIV)
26. The Devil (XV)
27. The Lightening-Struck Tower (XVI)
הוד
PRACTICUS
Splendour
נצח
PHILOSOPHUS
Victory
28. The Star (XVII)
יסוד
THEORICUS
Foundation
31. The Last Judgement (XX)
29. The Moon (XVIII)
32. Universe (XXI)
מלכות
ZELATOR
The Kingdom
The Four Worlds
1.Archetypal World
2.World of Creation
3.World of Formation.
4.World of Action
Coloured in the Minutum Mundum, with the Grades attributed to the Sefiroth, and Tarot attributions to the Paths.
The Serpent of Wisdom touches all the Paths in numerical order, and the Lightening Sword shows the descent of power.
The Three Triangles.
1 Supernal Triangle.
2.Ethical Triangle.
3.Astral Triangle.
SEVERITY
BALANCE
MERCY

Using the Cabala

color, certain plants, a symbolic Tarot card, and various animals and birds, among other things. It is by "working" the paths that the Tree is employed in meditation or magic. Working a path means visualizing intensely a trip along it while seeing all the things associated with it, such as scents, colors, plants, and creatures. Each sefira also has a negative aspect or *qlifah*, and there is a point in every magical operation when this negative force has to be dealt with and conquered.

The following description gives a good idea of how a modern magician might use the Cabala. A room will be suitably curtained and supplied with an altar, candles, a gong or gavel, and enough space for the magician to make some sweeping flourishes with his ritual sword. He begins by drawing the magic circle in which he is going to operate. This may be done with chalk or, in a carpeted room, with string or cotton. The circle keeps out evil forces, and in drawing it the magician leaves a gap to enter through when he has completed his preliminary preparations.

To the east of the circle the magician draws a triangle, the purpose of which is to confine any demonic or angelic being that is conjured up. These preparations completed, he puts out all lights except his altar candle, steps inside his circle, closes it, and drives all undesirable influences from the area by making the cabalistic cross. Standing in the middle of the circle, he visualizes a great cloud of light above his head. This is the light of Kether. Raising his right hand, he draws some of the light down to his forehead, then touches in turn his solar plexus, his right shoulder, and his left shoulder, saying "Malkhuth," "Din," and "Hesed" as he does so, and all the time visualizing the stream of ketheric light trailing from his finger. He is projecting his body onto the Tree of Life, and he imagines both the Tree and his body growing to a tremendous size so that he is standing above the Universe with the stars at his feet. Returning to his normal size, he next traces pentagrams in the air in front of him with his ritual sword, one for each of the four points of the compass. These pentagrams represent extra barriers against inimical forces, and are also his points of contact with the astral world. There is an archangel associated with each of them, and he greets these archangels—Raphael, Gabriel, Michael, and Uriel—with great compliments chanted in Latin. At the same time he visualizes them in all their splendor. Above his head he imagines a six-pointed star comprised of two interlaced triangles. These represent the fusion of his temporal physical self with the eternal cosmic forces.

Now the magician is ready to travel from Malkhuth, the earth, to Yesod, the gateway to the astral world and to the other sefiroth. He travels along path 22, the Path of Saturn. On the way he may well meet the Tarot symbol corresponding with this path, which is a naked young woman garlanded with flowers, carrying two wands, and dancing. This stands for joy, release from earthly concerns, and entry into the higher magical world. On the other hand he may meet a crocodile, the symbolic creature of Saturn. Arriving at the threshold of Yesod, he gains entry in the name of Gabriel and humbly confesses to the guardian angels his ignorance of the mysteries that surround him. He informs them which sefira he wishes to work with, and then proceeds from Yesod along the appropriate paths toward his

Opposite: the Tree of Life as it was interpreted by the Golden Dawn, well-known magic society of the period around the turn of the century. The Tree played an extremely important part in the organization of the Golden Dawn. In fact the progression of the initiate through the degrees of the Order was based on the progression of the soul up the pathways of the Tree to Kether.

The Magic Power of Cabalistic Rites

Above: Arthur Edward Waite, historian of magic, was fascinated by the Cabala. A member of the Golden Dawn, he translated Lévi's book on magical dogma and ritual. He also wrote a good many other massive and dense volumes on various aspects of the "secret tradition" which he claimed existed as a common element in Christianity, alchemy, the Cabala, Freemasonry, and the legend of the Holy Grail.

destination. As he travels he visualizes around him all the creatures, plants, colors, and other attributes that he would expect to find on each particular path. Of this stage of the operation Dion Fortune writes: "To project the astral body along the paths it is necessary . . . to hold the degrees of initiation to which they correspond; [for] unless one has received the grade, one will be unknown to the guardians of the paths, and they will be inimical rather than helpful, and do all in their power to turn the wanderer back."

Assuming that he has the necessary degree of initiation and can satisfy the guardians, the magician now conjures up in the triangle outside his circle the required sefirothic form. He will probably make it materialize in the shape of the traditional image associated with the particular sefira. If he is working with the powers of Hesed, for example, the form will be a crowned king on a throne, and if with Netsah, it will be a beautiful naked woman. It is at this stage that the magician has to be prepared to contend with and banish the evil negative qlifahs. The sefirothic form cannot enter the circle, but the force it represents can through one of the archangels and the pentagrammatic gates. The force may even be visible as a swirling cloud of vapor. In order to build up the force even more, the magician also has to conjure up in the triangle the planetary form associated with his chosen sefira. When sufficient force has built up, he has to gather himself up for the climax of the operation.

The object is to draw into himself the elemental force that he requires to accomplish his purpose. To do this he must, in the words of Albertus Magnus, "fall into a great excess." He has to lose his reason and whip himself into a frenzy. It is at this stage that sex, drugs, alcohol, or bloody sacrifice may enter into the ritual, though they are not necessary. The frenzy may be by self-hypnosis, induced by chanting a word over and over again. Behind him, within the circle, the magician visualizes a god- or goddess-form materializing, growing, towering immensely above him. He must not turn and look at it for fear that it may be so hideous or so ravishing that the sight could prove fatal to him. Then comes the moment when the god- or goddess-form takes control of him, taking over and convulsing his body. At this same moment the magician visualizes the thing he wants to accomplish. He expels the accumulated force and bids it go to fulfill its mission. If his magic involves another person, an article of that person's clothing, a lock of hair, or some nail clippings may be used in order to put the magical force on target.

Having summoned up the magical forces, the magician now makes the return journey to Malkhuth. He goes back the same way as he came, politely thanking the guardians of the paths and sefiroth for their help and hospitality as he passes them. The archangels too have to be thanked. Finally the magician forms the cabalistic cross again to banish unwanted hangers-on—for minor psychic forces hover around a magical operation like moths around a candle, and he does not want his normal life disrupted by poltergeists, ghosts, or suchlike.

In 1963 the *Journal of Parapsychology* carried an article by the Czechoslovakian doctor Milan Ryzl entitled "The Focusing of ESP on Particular Targets." Dr. Ryzl reported on some telepathic experiments he had made in which a person tried to transmit intense sensations to another person miles away. When the sender concentrated on a sensation of suffocation and anxiety, the receiver suffered a choking fit. When he took a depressant drug and concentrated on feelings of despair and gloom, the receiver suffered from a prolonged headache and a feeling of nausea. The effects were clearly not produced by suggestion, for the receiver had no way of knowing what kind of sensations were being beamed at him. Dr. Ryzl's experiments caused some of his readers to adopt a more open-minded attitude than they had previously held on the effectiveness of magical rituals. If such strong effects could be produced under experimental laboratory conditions, how much greater might be the effect of the discharge of the intense emotions built up in the cabalistic ritual?

Below: Waite was absorbed with the relationship of the Tarot cards to the Cabala in which each card symbolized one of the 22 paths between the sefiroth. He designed a set, of which six are shown. It became one of the best-known versions of the Tarot.

THE SORCERER
H.M. BROCK
D'OYLY CARTE OPERA CO.

Chapter 4
Magic Words and Spells

Magicians claim the knowledge of secret words and names by which they can call forth special powers. What are these words and where do they come from? Does a person's name contain that individual's character and destiny, and can they be interpreted through numerology? Magic words are related to magic spells. Can a magician fly or cause two friends to have a fight by writing certain letters in a certain way to form a square? Will vile potions of usually inedible animal parts make someone who consumes them faithful or submissive? Do magic words and spells work?

The Elizabethan astrologer John Dee had a most curious way of communicating with the spirit world. Before him on a writing table he would place a chart of over 100 squares, each with a letter in it. His assistant Edward Kelley would sit nearby at what they called the Holy Table, on which a similar chart of numbered squares lay before him. Kelley gazed into a crystal and concentrated until the figure of an angel appeared in it. Using a wand the angel pointed to a succession of squares on Kelley's chart. Kelley called these numbers out to Dee, who wrote down the corresponding letters. When the angel had finished, words of the message were rewritten backward.

The words were in a language that Dee called Enochian, and which he said had been dictated to him by the angels. The curious thing about Enochian is that it has grammar and syntax like established languages do, and it can be translated into other languages. Whether Enochian was the invention of the scholarly Dee or his inspired but scoundrelly medium Kelley, or whether it was really the language of the angels, its effectiveness in magical work has been attested by many practicing magicians. The language consists of apparently genuine words of Powers, and was used by Aleister Crowley in this invocation:

Eca, zodocare, Iad, goho,
Torzodu odo kikale qaa!
Zodocare od zodameranu!

Opposite: the mysterious powers ascribed to magicians most often make them figures of fearsome drama, but in Gilbert and Sullivan's *The Sorcerer*, first performed in 1877, the magician was John Wellington Wells ("I'm a dealer in magic and spells"). He dispensed a love potion in a teapot, which put a spell on the whole town with most unexpected—and disconcerting—results. At the end, the spell is broken by the magician agreeing reluctantly to give up his life.

To Know the Name is to Tap its Power

Zodorje, lape zodiredo Ol
Noco Mada, das Iadapiel!
Ilas! Hoatahe Iaida!

The idea that words, names, and sounds have special powers is common to all magic. In numerology, the character and destiny of a person or thing is contained in the name. The same principle applies to the gods, angels, and demons. To know the name, and how to pronounce and use it, is to be able to tap its power.

The ancient belief in a secret name that had power over everything in the Universe was fairly widespread. For the Jews this secret name was the true name of God. In the Old Testament, God is referred to by various names such as Adonai or Elohim, and these are used in magic. But the personal name of God was considered so sacred that it was rarely pronounced aloud. It was known as the Tetragrammation, or word of four letters. The four letters are Y H V H, which in Hebrew are yod, he, vau, he. The correct pronunciation is uncertain partly because there are no printed vowels in Hebrew, and partly because the word was spoken so rarely that there is no traditional pronunciation to follow. Scholars on the whole prefer to write and say it as Yahweh, although the English Bible renders it as Jehovah. Correct pronunciation is essential in magic, which may be why some magicians claim to be among the very few who know the secret.

More powerful even than the Tetragrammation was the Shemhamforash. It was the name of 72 syllables that Moses is said to have used to divide the waters of the Red Sea to

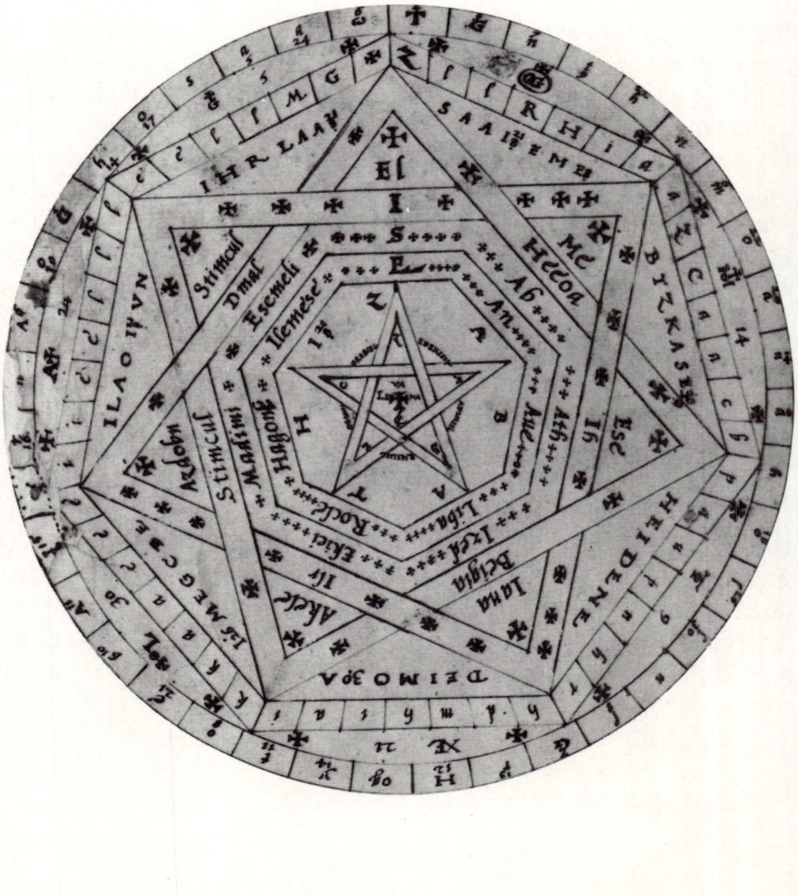

Right: design for a Great Seal by John Dee, Elizabethan investigator into magic. This drawing is from one of the notebooks in which he made a careful record of his magical experiences. The writing on the Seal is partly in Latin, and partly in Enochian, Dee's so-called language of the Angels.

Left: beginning of a manuscript that gives the magic ritual for invoking Venus. It is known to have been in Dee's possession and indicates that he had some involvement with conventional ritual magic. The following pages tell how to make the horn and circle, and summon the spirits. Throughout the ritual the color green—the color sacred to Venus—plays a very important role.

יהוה

Above: the Tetragrammation, the name of God, in its four Hebrew letters. Even in early times, it was pronounced only once a year. Tradition says that the sages were allowed to pass it on verbally to their disciples every seven years. That ancient pronunciation has been lost, and it is now, in normal Jewish religious reading, vocalized as Adonai, the Lord.

enable the Israelities to escape the pursuing Egyptians. The true pronunciation of this name is unknown, and it is too cumbersome to be widely used in magic. But the number 72 has a mystic significance, and the Renaissance cabalist John Reuchlin ingeniously managed to link the Shemhamforash to the Tetragrammation by means of gematria, the cabalist method of assigning numerical values to letters. The numerical equivalents of Y H V H are: Y = 10, H = 5, V = 6, H = 5, totaling 26.

However, if the name is built up progressively and then totaled, it is found to equal 72, the same number as the syllables of the Shemhamforash.

Y	= 10
YH	= 15
YHV	= 21
YHVH	= 26
	72

This was the kind of exercise that delighted the cabalist, for the cabalistic mind avidly sought order in the mystery and multiplicity of the world. When cabalists found order they believed that they had also found arcane knowledge. And in

Below: preparing a magic circle. Outside the circle is the first symbol of the Tetragrammation.

Right: a device invented by Dr. Hans Jenny to show sound visually revealed that the vowel O formed a perfect sphere shape.

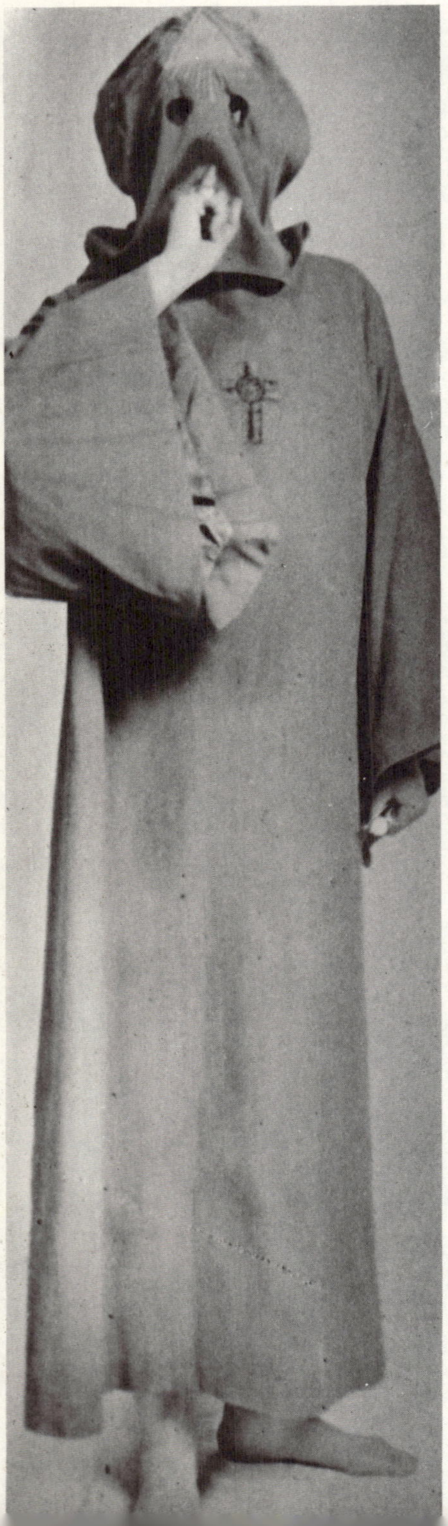

Below: Aleister Crowley, robed in one of the Golden Dawn ritual costumes, "vibrates" a magical name as part of a ritual for invoking a specific spirit. This kind of exercise demanded tremendous powers of concentration, and required a great deal of practice for success.

cabalistic thought knowledge was power. Knowledge of the names of the sefirothic guardians overcomes their resistance, and knowledge of the names of demons summoned up in ritual magic gives the magician power over them.

That it is not enough to know the words of power without knowing how to use them correctly is illustrated by a story told by the modern cabalist Israel Regardie. A young English student of the occult arts proposed to summon up an *undine*, a spirit associated with water. To make the invocation easier, he decided to perform his ritual beside the sea. He packed all his paraphernalia—robes, sword, gong, incense, candles, collapsible altar—and took a train to a respectable seaside resort. There, late one night at low tide, he went down to the sea's edge, set up his altar and lit the candles on it, drew out his magic circle and triangle in the sand, and began his conjurations, bellowing out the words of power in the still night. No undine responded. What the apprentice magician did succeed in conjuring up was "a wrathful creature clothed in blue—a policeman."

Israel Regardie explains how the names of power ought to be used. When the time comes for pronouncing the divine name in the ritual, the magician should inhale deeply, slowly, and forcefully, imagining that the God-name is being inhaled with the air. He should picture the name in the air in letters of fire and flame and, breathing deeply, he should draw it down into his lungs, then further down through his abdomen, thighs, and legs into his feet. His entire body should be filled with the fire of the divine name. Then, adopting one of the poses of the god

Horus, as shown in the Egyptian Book of the Dead, the magician should exhale the breath that is now charged with the power of the name, imagine it surging up from his feet through his body, and pronouncing the name with "a mighty shout of triumph." If at this moment the magician feels his body full of force and energy, and if the name thunders through his entire being, he will succeed in magically vibrating the name. The effect of this vibration, Regardie matter-of-factly explains, "is to set up a strain in the upper astral light, in response to which the intelligence evoked hastens."

The Power of Sound

We know that at certain frequencies sound is destructive, that it can shatter glass and even kill a person. Magicians believe that the reverse is also true, that sound can be constructive and creative. Up to a point, science agrees. In an issue of the *Science Journal* in 1968 a Swiss physicist, Hans Jenny, wrote an article entitled *Visualizing Sound*. Jenny coined the term "cymatics" for the study of the effects of sound waves on matter. His work was a development of that of the 18th-century physicist Ernst Chladni, who discovered that sand scattered on a metal plate will arrange itself in beautiful patterns at certain sounds from a violin. Jenny extended his research to the human voice. He invented a machine that he called the "tonoscope," which converts sound to three-dimensional forms. He discovered that the sound of the letter O produces a perfect sphere—exactly the shape that we use for the sound in our

Below: one of the central premises of magic operations—that sounds (magic words and spells) can have a physical effect—is verified by science. Here, in another of Dr. Jenny's experiments, a highly viscous liquid is vibrated at an ultrasonic frequency, producing a fascinating physical turbulence.

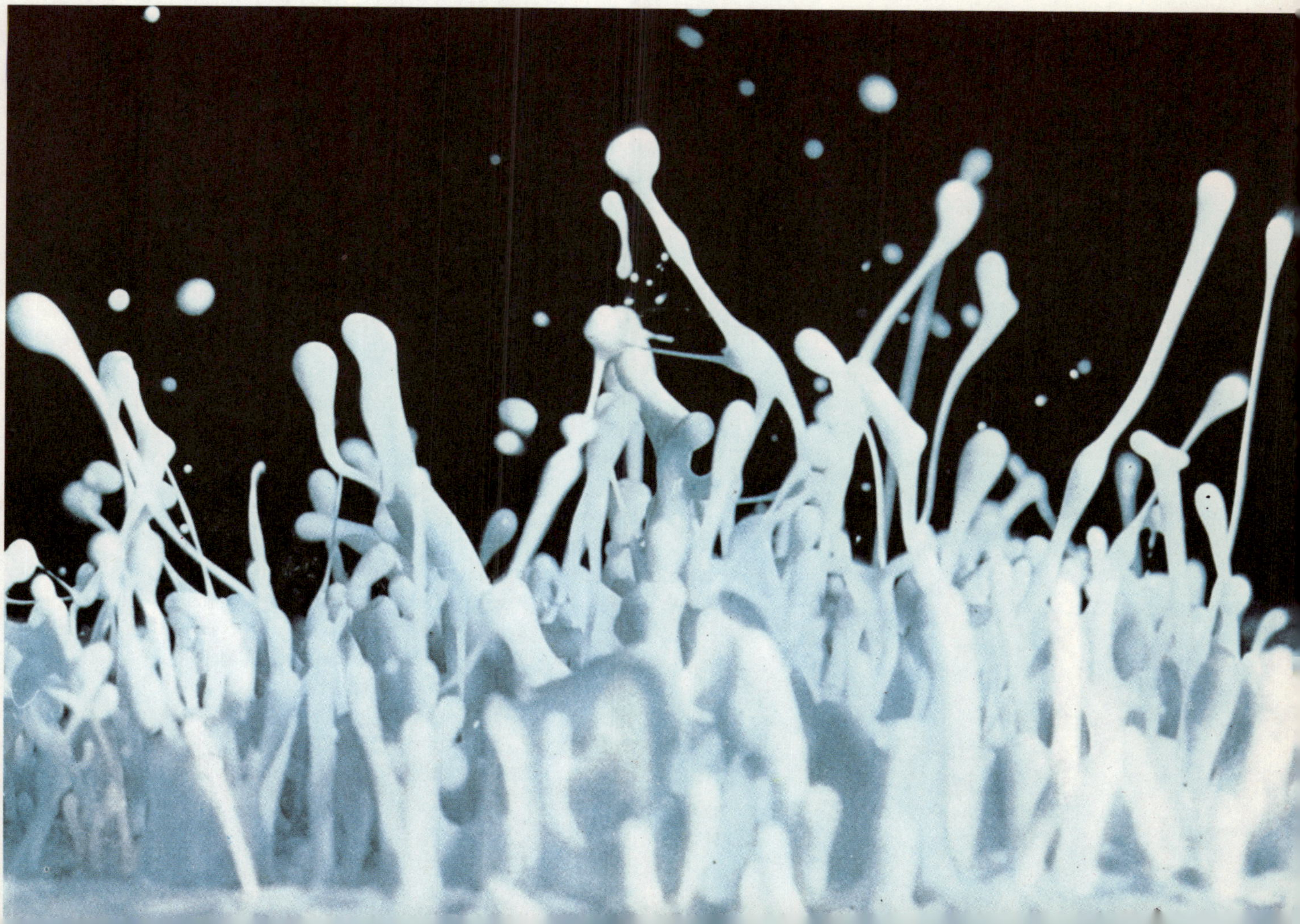

In the story of creation in the Bible, God created the heavens and earth by the Word. "Darkness was upon the face of the deep" till God said, *Fiat lux*—"Let there be light." And there was light.

Above: in one of Michelangelo's frescos for the Sistine Chapel in the Vatican, the Creation is expressed by gesture—which is more common to most than the concept of Creation by sound.

Below: the cabalistic seal of Cornelius Agrippa. It is made up of abbreviations formed by having each letter represent the first letter of another word, thus compressing and presumably heightening the power of the entire phrase. In this seal, the word is "Araita," which uses the initial letters of each of the Hebrew names of God.

script. Jenny's research has shown that sounds—and therefore also words and names—have properties and powers of their own. This is something that occultists and magicians have never doubted.

The ancient belief in the constructive power of sound is illustrated by the account of creation given in *Genesis*. The Universe was created by the *Word* of God. The divine intention or will was not enough in itself. It has to be expressed in the Word. The cabalistic belief in words of power ultimately derives from the *Genesis* creation myth. The power that God employed to create the Universe, the power of the Word, was believed to be a power that man too could acquire and use.

Among certain Buddhists and Hindus there arose a belief, similar to that of the cabalists, that there were words or sounds of power which, if repeated over and over again, could give man control over the spirit world. These were known as *mantras*. They consist of short verses with fairly clear meanings, cryptic words that needed deciphering to be comprehensible, or even single syllables. Some mantras were composed, some were the result of meditation or inspiration, and others represented the reduction of a large body of writing to a short formula. For example, thousands of verses of a holy book might be summarized in a single chapter. This would be further reduced to a few sentences, then to a single line and, finally, even to one syllable. This syllable would be extremely powerful since it would contain the essence of the whole writing. It was believed that the mastery of the mantra of this syllable would give an intuitive understanding of the complete holy book.

Mantras might be addressed to certain parts of the body where they would set up certain vibrations. This was considered particularly important in healing. It was thought that sound vibrations underlay the whole universe, and that by chanting an appropriate mantra, all problems could be solved.

The mantra could be used in all kinds of ways as a magical spell. Strings of dried seeds were often used to keep count of the number of times a mantra had been repeated. Sometimes, when the purpose of the mantra was evil, small bones of dead animals or humans were strung together and used in the same way. Extraordinary powers were associated with the repetition of certain mantras. It was said that if a special mantra were repeated 100,000 times, the chanter would get complete obedience from other humans. If it were repeated 200,000 times, the chanter would gain power over all natural phenomena, and if it were increased to a million and a half times, the chanter would be able to travel through the Universe.

Some of the most famous mantras are those using seed sounds, single syllables that usually end with an n or an m and therefore have an echoing, humming note. The best known of these is *Om*, which symbolizes all the sounds in the Universe. Its echoes are thought to encompass Heaven, Hell, and Earth, and it is supposed to be the key to the Universe.

In describing word magic thus far we have been concerned with the highest aspiration of the magician to contact and use divine or elemental forces. Magic at this level is the secret and cherished art of the few, the initiates, the priesthood. It is an expression of man's aspiration to be like a god. But in all countries, cultures, and ages, verbal magic has been practiced on a lower level—for personal gain or satisfaction, to insure success in love or war, to repel evil influences, to cure ailments, or to procure the fulfillment of any conceivable human wish or whim. Magic with such aims is appropriately called "low" magic. This generally combines some action, which may be simple or elaborate but is never as emotionally demanding as the action of ritual magic, with a verbal formula or spell.

Many ancient Greeks and Romans believed that the power of a spell was without limit. When in Homer's *Odyssey* Ulysses is wounded in the thigh, the bleeding is stopped by a magic spell.

Mantra Magic

Below: in an illustration for a book about the cosmos written by a 17th-century Englishman, the word of God takes an oddly serpentine form as it coils in an explosion of light, incorporating the dove which symbolizes the spirit of God.

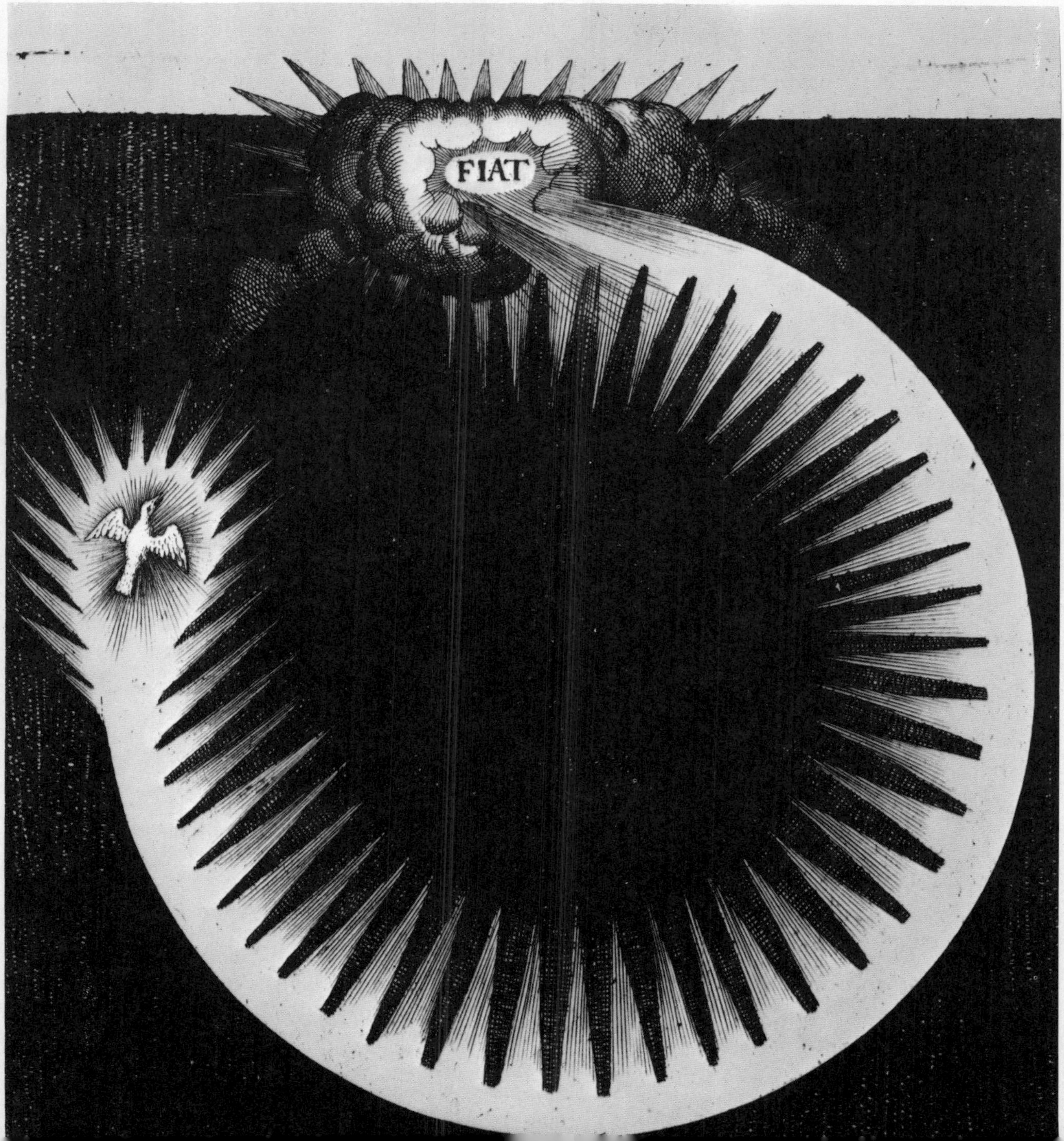

Magical Spells and Incantations

"The wound of Ulysses the blameless, the godlike, they bound up skillfully, and by incantations staunched the dark blood." Circe, the enchantress, could change men into beasts with her incantations. According to the Roman writer Pliny the belief that the women of Thessaly could enchant the moon out of the sky was so strong that during an eclipse the people set up an incessant din with brass trumpets to prevent the moon from hearing the spells. Fire could be controlled, rivers made to change their course or flow backward, crops could be blighted or enticed from one field to another, men rendered impotent or women submissive—all by the power of incantation or the magic spell.

Spells are often associated with plants or herbs. It was believed that the reason the Thessalian witches wished to bring the moon down to earth was to concentrate its influence on the plants they used for magical purposes.

The most famous magical plant is the mandrake. The true mandrake, the *mandragora*, grows only in Mediterranean countries, but there are plants with similar characteristics and properties throughout the world. In the East it is the ginseng, in northern Europe white bryony, in America the may apple. All

Right: the beautiful Circe, using her magical spells to change Ulysses and his men into snorting swine. The idea that such powerful spells could exist was common in Ancient Greece.

these plants have a root that seems to resemble a human figure. Throughout recorded history and all over the world, the mandrake has been prized for its medicinal or aphrodisiac properties, or as a talisman, and a mass of legend and superstition has gathered around it.

The most potent mandrakes were supposed to grow under gallows, and were believed to be produced from the semen involuntarily ejaculated by a hanged man. They were thought to be living creatures, and to unearth them was a hazardous business. The recommended way was to attach one end of a

rope to the plant and the other end to the neck of a strong dog. Then pieces of meat were to be thrown just out of reach so that in struggling to get them, the dog would drag the mandrake out of the earth. When uprooted the mandrake would let out a terrible cry that would kill any hearers. This meant that the dog was usually lost. The mandrake-seeker had to take the precaution of blocking his ears.

This is one of the more grisly and far-fetched of the mandrake legends. A pleasanter one is the Celtic spell known as Lover's Mandrake, a fairly elaborate procedure to win love.

Above: magic practically forms the plot in Shakespeare's *Midsummer Night's Dream*, with many spells accidentally misfiring. However, the spell on the Fairy Queen to make her love the rustic with the ass' head was intentional mischief.

The Magic of the Mandrake Root

Below: a 15th-century drawing from a medical treatise showing a mandrake plant being pulled up by a dog. In fact, the mandrake plant is not particularly unusual in having a forked root—even the humble parsnip often has that—but the root does contain an alkaloid that can be used as a narcotic drug. In ancient times it was used as a painkiller and sleeping drug. It early developed a reputation as an aphrodisiac.

When the lover has found his mandrake he must dig it up with great care before dawn at a time when the moon is waxing. As he digs he recites the words, "Blessed be this earth, this root, this night." He must take the mandrake root home, and trim and shape it with a knife until he gets as near as possible to a female figure. Then, holding it in his left hand and forming a pentagram or five-pointed figure over it with his right he must say, "I name you____." Of course he gives the name of the unsuspecting object of his passion. He next should bury it in his garden, and pour over it a mixture of water, milk, and a little of his own blood while chanting: "Blood and milk upon the grave/will make____evermore my slave." The plant remains buried until the night of the next new moon, when, an hour before sunrise, the lover must dig it up while reciting: "Moon above so palely shining/Bestow this night thy sacred blessing/On my prayer and ritual plea/To fill____'s heart with love for me."

The mandrake now has to be dried out, a process that can take weeks. In the course of the drying out it should be frequently passed through a certain kind of incense that attracts the influence of Venus. The drying process is also accompanied by a verbal spell saying: "This fruit is scorched by that same heat/Which warms my heart with every beat." When the little mandrake-figure is thoroughly dried out, the magician-lover takes a silver pin and thrusts it through its heart, concentrating his thought on the loved one as he does so. Finally, he leaves the mandrake on a window sill where it will be exposed to the moon at night.

The obvious drawback of this Celtic love spell is that it takes time, which some might feel would be more profitably spent wooing the lady with a more direct form of verbal sorcery. However, not all lovers are gifted with eloquence and some become tongue-tied with unrequited passion. For quicker results with less trouble the impatient lover may prefer to try an Indian love spell. One such is given by Idries Shah in his *Oriental Magic*, with the instruction that it should be recited over and over again while the moon is waxing.

"With the all-powerful arrow of Love do I pierce thy heart, O woman! Love, love that causes unease, that will overcome thee, love for me!

"That arrow, flying true and straight, will cause in thee burning desire. It has the point of my love, its shaft is my determination to possess thee!

"Yea, thy heart is pierced. The arrow has struck home. I have overcome by these arts thy reluctance, thou art changed! Come to me, submissive, without pride, as I have no pride, but only longing! Thy mother will be powerless to prevent thy coming, neither shall thy father be able to prevent thee! Thou art completely in my power.

"O Mitra, O Varuna, strip her of willpower! I, I alone, wield power over the heart and mind of my beloved!"

All that the lover-magician has to do in addition to reciting this spell repeatedly is to make an arrow, which represents the arrow of love, and wave it about as he speaks.

Other methods to gain a woman's love by means of a magic

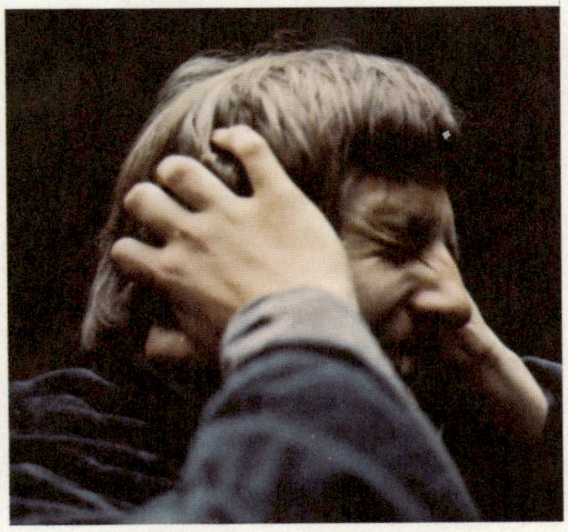

Even in Roman times the mandrake could only be collected with special ceremony. Unless this was followed precisely, the plant would run away. Later, the root came to be considered one of the Devil's plants, bestowing infernal powers. The superstition that the root shrieked when dug up was probably linked with this idea. The mandrake's cry was fatal to anyone who heard it. One treatise warns all to beware of a changing wind carrying the deadly sound. Extraction of the mandrake root is started by gently loosening the surrounding soil around the growing plant. Then a dog is fastened to the root and, enticed by a piece of meat, is induced to pull the mandrake from the ground. The mandrake's scream is fatal to the dog, but the protected collector can safely pick up the root, then fill in the hole with bread and coins to placate the earth. The root should be wrapped in the finest white silk cloth.

Love Crystals For Sale!

Dieudonne Langston, mother of three and a housewife, lives in the English countryside. She is an antique dealer. On one of her trips to a stately home where an auction was being held, she found and purchased a book of herbal medicines, published in 1790. About that time she was asked to run a stall at the local church fair, and she decided to make up some pink love crystals from an old recipe she had found in her book. Following the directions meticulously, she made up 50 portions the size of an egg cup. She sold them cheaply, and the whole lot was bought up enthusiastically. That, thought Mrs. Langston, was that.

However, strangers began to appear at her door asking for the pink crystals, and customers from the fair came back for more. They claimed that their marriage beds were happier places because of them.

Now Dieudonne Langston sells her crystals by mail all over the world. To get the right atmosphere for concentration, she does her brewing alone in her kitchen in the middle of the night, stirring her secret ingredients into a mysterious pink brew as she chants the proper incantation. Once, she says somebody walked in on her—and everything went wrong.

spell are given in the medieval black magic books known as *grimoires*. One is very simple, though it could possibly arouse the woman's laughter rather than her passion. While conversing with her alone, the would-be lover makes her look straight into his eyes and says in a compelling voice, "Kaphe, kasita, non Kapheta et publica filii omnibus suis." The book offers this advice and assurance: "Do not be suprised at or ashamed of these enigmatical words whose occult meaning you do not know; for if you pronounce them with sufficient faith you will very soon possess her love."

Love and lust are not always easily distinguishable, even by those concerned, but there are spells in the black books that seek to fulfill only erotic fantasies. According to the *Grimorium Verum*, it is a simple matter to make a girl dance in the nude against her will. All the man needs to do is to write the word *Frutimiere* on virgin parchment with the blood of a bat. The parchment is laid on a stone over which a Mass has been said, and then put under the threshold of a door the unsuspecting girl is sure to pass. It will compel her to enter that house or room, take off all her clothes, and dance wildly until the spell is removed. The book warns, however, that her "grimaces and contortions will cause more pity than desire," so this spell will appeal more to sadists than to lechers.

According to another grimoire, anyone can be made to dance wildly—thought not in the nude—by putting under a threshold a parchment with the words SATOR AREPO TENET OPERA ROTAS written on it in bat's blood. Even your good old solemn minister will not be able to resist the power of this spell, the book says, and anyone who tries the trick will be assured of a good laugh.

Absurd though these spells are, they show that men's idea of entertainment has not changed much over the centuries—except that today they go to the cinema for erotic fantasies and slapstick comedy. It is another area in which the skills of the technologist have usurped those of the magician.

Love by Magic

Opposite: a maiden consulting a witch, who is dropping herbs onto the fire to produce an image of the girl's beloved knight. Love spells are one form of magic which appear to have an endless popularity.

Left: in *Love's Enchantment*, a 17th-century Flemish painting, a young witch anoints herself with herbs such as henbane, belladonna, and hemlock to prepare herself for a magical experience of love.

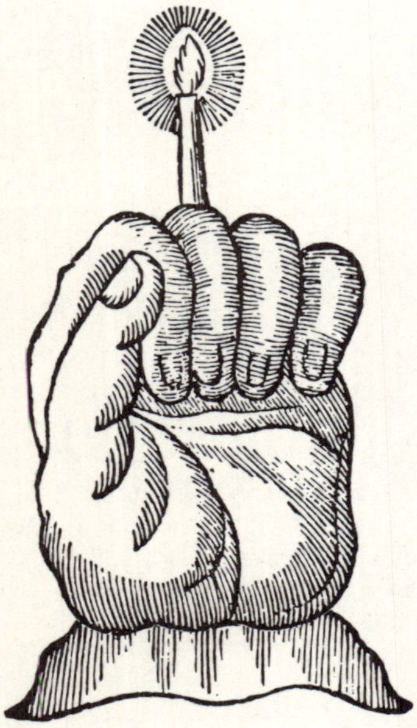

The written spell in this last example is of particular interest because it forms what is known as a magic square. *Palindromes* (words or phrases that read the same backward or forward) are believed by magicians to have extraordinary power, and when they can be arranged in a square their power is all the greater. The Sator square is the most perfect because the words remain the same whichever way they are read:

S	A	T	O	R
A	R	E	P	O
T	E	N	E	T
O	P	E	R	A
R	O	T	A	S

In addition to making people dance against their will, this formula was believed to be useful for discovering witches because they could not stay in a room where it had been placed. It also gave protection against various ailments. This square was believed to have sinister power:

C	A	S	E	D
A	Z	O	T	E
B	O	R	O	S
E	T	O	Z	A
D	E	B	A	C

The Hand of Glory, a charm made from a human hand cut from a hanged man, then dried and pickled. It was reputed to prevent sleepers from wakening, or to stupefy anyone who was awake.

Above: a 19th-century Hand of Glory used as a candle holder.

Below: a dried Hand of Glory. The fingertips themselves are used as candles when set alight.

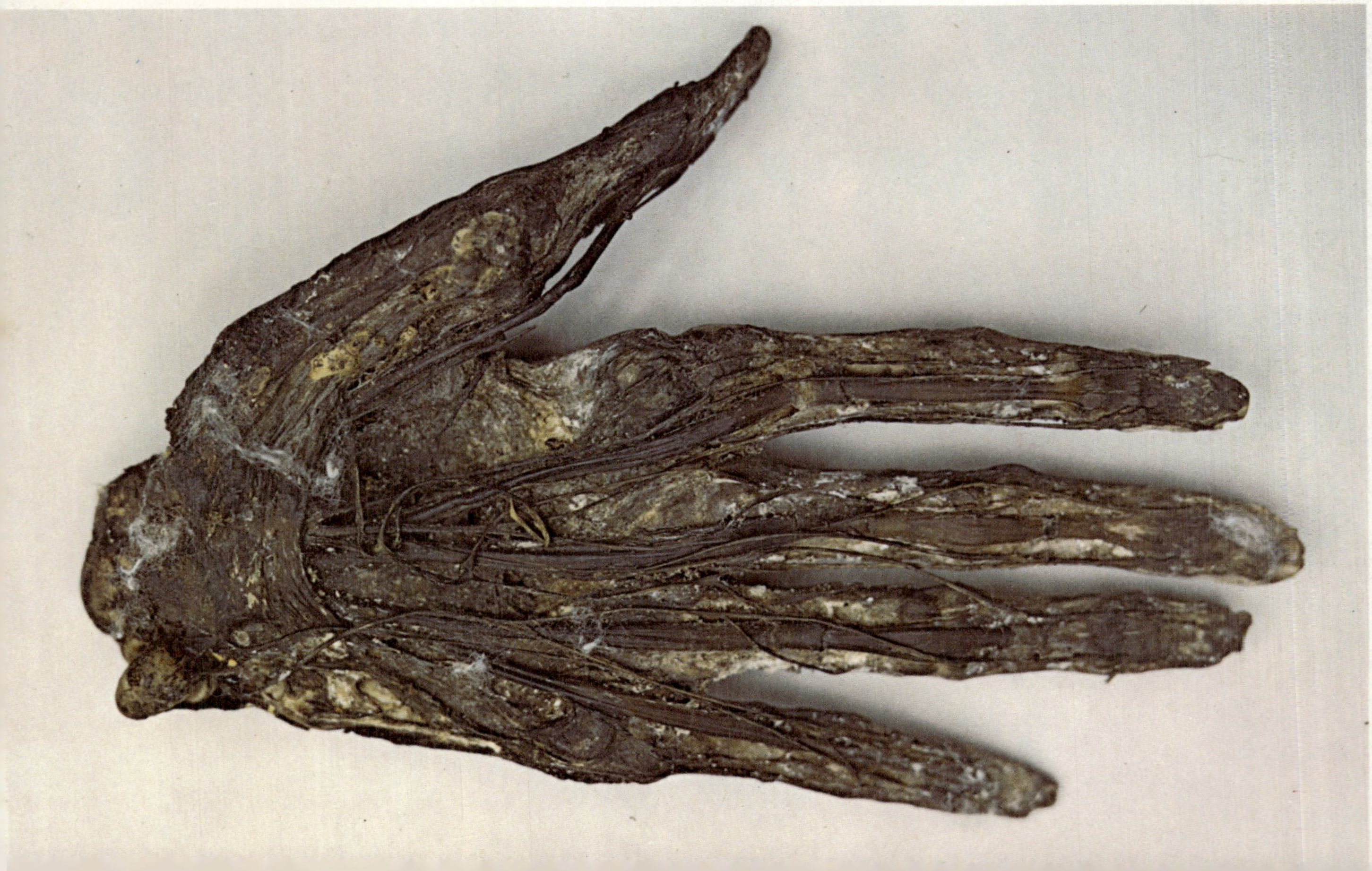

This one conferred the dubious privilege of being able to fly through the air in the form of a crow:

R O L O R
O B U F O
L U A U L
O F U B O
R O L O R

It is not essential for a magic square to have the characteristics of a palindrome. According to the *Kabbalistic Secrets of the Master Aptolcater, Mage of Adrianople, Handed Down from the Greatest Antiquity*, a book published in England in 1724, the following square can be used to cause discord:

H D H D H
I D I D I
D H D H D
D I D I D

Master Aptolcater's instructions for using this square state that it should be scratched with an iron point on a piece of lead, and worn in a leather pouch around the neck. When you start two people quarreling or fighting, you shout seven times to each quarter of the globe the words *Roudmo* and *Pharrua*, say their names and, under your breath, urge: "Fight, fight, Roudmo." The fight will be savage and unremitting, but the magician can stop it simply by saying the word *Omdor*. "In this way were many wars stopped in former times," Master Aptolcater assures us.

There are numerous spells that do not involve words or written symbols, but rather apply the basic magical principle of the system of correspondences.

Sage is a herb that receives the influences of Jupiter and Venus, and in magical tradition it has properties that the housewife who uses it in cooking would never suspect. The magician is advised to pick a quantity of sage at a time when the sun is passing through the sign of the Lion, grind it into a powder, and bury this powder in a pot in a dung heap for 30 days. At the end of this time it will have turned into worms. These worms should be burnt between two red-hot bricks, and made into a powder. This powder is very versatile. By sprinkling some of it on your feet you will insure that any favor you may ask of princes or powerful men will be granted. Put some under your tongue and everyone you kiss will love you. Mix a little with the oil of a lamp and everyone sitting in its light will imagine that the room is full of serpents.

Everyone would like to know how to double his money without much trouble, and the *Grimorium Verum* has a formula for this. Pluck a hair from near the vulva of a mare in heat saying "Drigne, Dragne, Dragne" as you do so. Buy an

To Command an Unclean Spirit

In any invocation of spirits, particularly evil ones, it is crucial that the magician be of pure and devoted heart. Otherwise the spirit will gain command over the magician who invokes it. According to an old grimoire, or book of spells, this is how to invoke unclean spirits:

Find a virgin black hen and seize it in its sleep so that it does not cackle. Go to the main road, find a crossroads, and on the stroke of midnight, make a circle with a cypress rod. Stand directly in the middle and tear the fowl in two, repeating "Euphas, Metahim, frugativi et appelavi." Turn to the East, kneel down, recite a prayer, finish with the name of God, and the unclean spirit will appear to you—dog-headed, ass-eared, and with the legs of a calf, dressed in a scarlet surcoat, a yellow vest, and green breeches. He will ask for your orders, which you will give as you please, and since he must obey you, you may become rich and happy on the spot.

As with all grimoires, the spell has been altered to fool the uninitiated. A magician will recognize the alteration. Someone else who tries it as it is will have "only his pains for his trouble."

A Medieval Spell

A modern reconstruction of a complex medieval spell to preserve the chastity of a noble maiden while her betrothed is away at the wars. The magician begins by making a magic circle.

Above: he then waves his censer, exactly as the ritual commands, over the circle he has prepared.

Above right: the maiden enters, clothed only in a white veil. She carries in her left hand a rose, which symbolizes human love, and in her right hand a lily, which symbolizes human mortality.

earthenware pot with a lid, fill it with water from a spring, put the hair in it, and hide it away for nine days. When you remove the lid, you will find a little snake that will rear up. When it does so, say, "I accept the pact." Put the snake in a box made of new pine and feed it daily with wheat husks. When you want gold or silver, put some coins in the box, and lie down for three or four hours. At the end of this time you will find that your money has been doubled. You should not try to obtain more than a hundred coins in this way at any one time, the book cautions. However, if the snake has a human face, as sometimes happens, you may get up to a thousand.

The black books of the sorcerers contain a number of unpleasant love spells (or perhaps, more appropriately, lechery spells). For example, to gain a woman's submission, take a dove's heart, a sparrow's liver, a swallow's womb, and a hare's kidney, dry them, and reduce them to a fine powder. Add an equal quantity of your own blood, leave the mixture to dry, and—difficult as it may seem—make the woman you desire eat it. She will then find you irresistible. The book does not say how she will rate your culinary skills.

If you want to make sure that your woman will not desire another man, take the genitals of a wolf and some hairs from his cheeks, eyebrows, and beard, burn and pulverize them,

and give the potion to the woman in a drink.

To discover a woman's most intimate secrets, tear out the tongue of a live toad and place it on her heart while she is asleep. She will then talk in her sleep and answer all your questions truthfully.

The spell that is designed to subject one person's will to another's is the most ignoble of the magician's arts. It is far removed from the aspiration of the great magicians of the Renaissance and the ancient world to work in harmony with cosmic forces. Magic originates in our desire for power. This desire is not in itself ignoble, and it is often the origin of achievements in the arts and sciences. The fascination of the story of magic is that it sounds and charts the deeper waters of the human spirit, the dreams, hopes, and longings with which we aspire to transcend ordinariness, limitation, and death. We should not therefore be surprised to find in the story as it unfolds a mingling of the baser and the nobler aspects of human nature.

Top: directed by the magician, the girl lays her flowers in front of the skull within the circle as homage to the magical power that the ceremony is about to invoke for her protection.
Right: she places rosemary and verbena herbs next to her heart.

7
20
0
1
21
31
17
10
34
4
11
19
9
25
24
12
0 32 15 19 4 21 2 25 17 34 6 27 13 36 11 30 8 23 10 5 24 16 33 1 20 14 31 9 22 18 29 7 28 12 35 3 26

Chapter 5
Number Magic

Why is the number seven so closely associated with magical powers? Could Joshua have won the battle of Jericho by using number magic? Cabalists and magicians have worked out systems of assigning number values to letters in order to analyze people's character and predict their future. This analysis can be extended to foretelling what kind of a day will be experienced. Is a person with a name number of 9 really destined for great achievements? Should a soldier avoid fighting when his day number indicates harmony? Would Napoleon have won at Waterloo on a 1-day instead of a 6-day?

In the 1880s Matthew Arnold, the famous English poet, attended a dinner party given in his honor by Sir John Millais, the equally well-known artist. There were 13 people seated around the table. One of the guests drew attention to this fact, and to the old superstition that the first person to leave a table at which 13 are seated would be dead within a year. Arnold laughed and suggested that, "to cheat the fates for once," he and two of the younger members of the party should rise and leave the table together. They did so. Within the year Arnold had died of a heart attack, one of the young men had committed suicide, and the other had been drowned. The superstitious prediction of death had come to pass.

Of course, this could be chance. There must have been thousands of occasions on which 13 had been at table and the first to rise had survived the year. The idea that 13 is an unlucky number is sometimes thought to stem from the fact that there were 13 at the Last Supper. But in pre-Christian civilizations, as far apart as India and Italy, it had already been said to be a bad omen for 13 to sit down at the same table. Belief in the occult significance of numbers is deep rooted and widespread.

In the ancient world science and magic went hand in hand, but where science investigated nature, magic sought to control it. Science of necessity evolved concepts of number and measure, and in doing so, came across certain odd patterns and correspondences. Magic was quick to seize upon these patterns and

Opposite: numbers and gambling have always gone together—on this early 20th-century post-card from Monte Carlo, Lady Luck poses.

The Significance of Certain Numbers

correspondences and to use them for its own ends.

The recurrence of the number seven must have been one of the first discoveries of investigations. The week of seven days, for example. Of the heavenly bodies, the moon has the most obvious influence on the rhythms of life on earth. Its cycle, which we call a lunar month, consists of four phases of seven days each. This is our week. Seven was considered to be the number governing the rhythms of life, and also the number of completeness. There were seven colors in the spectrum, and seven notes in the musical scale. In antiquity there were thought to be seven planets governing events on earth, and these could be linked not only to the days of the week, the colors, and the musical notes, but also among many other correspondences to seven metals, seven vowels in the Greek alphabet, and seven features of the human head. Seven occurs frequently in the Bible, and it is the number most associated with mysterious magical powers.

It is alleged that Joshua used number magic to bring down the walls of Jericho. He marched his army around the city walls for seven days, accompanied by seven priests carrying seven trumpets. On the seventh day they circled Jericho seven times, shouted, and the walls fell down. Various explanations for this feat have been put forward. It could be held that Joshua actually succeeded in invoking the aid of cosmic forces. Another theory is

Below: Titian's *Last Supper*. It has been suggested that the idea that it is unlucky to have 13 at table comes from the last meal of Christ and his 12 apostles, one of whom betrayed him.

that the final great shout of the Israelites produced sound waves of a frequency to set up vibrations in solid objects, rather like a soprano's high note can shatter glass. The belief favored by skeptics is that all the marching and ritual activity was merely a diversionary tactic designed to distract attention from some of the Israelites who were busy undermining the wall's supports.

Sound is energy. The training of former Japanese Samurai, or warriors, included instruction in producing the "kiai," a fighting cry. The sound of the kiai causes a sudden lowering of the blood pressure, and is said to produce partial paralysis in the hearer. Our language recognizes this kind of phenomenon in the description of a cry as "blood-chilling." Science has discovered that low frequency sound of 3 to 5 cycles per second can rapidly kill human beings. The discovery of the relationship between sound and numbers is generally credited to Pythagoras, the Greek philosopher and mystic of the 6th century B.C. There is a legend that Pythagoras once happened to pass a blacksmith's shop and noticed that four anvils of different sizes produced four distinct notes when they were struck. Investigating the phenomenon, he discovered that the weights of the anvils were in the proportion 6, 8, 9, and 12. He suspended four weights of the same proportions from a ceiling on strings, and found that he could produce the same four notes as those the anvils had made

Above: among the Tarot cards, too, the number 13 is unlucky—card 13 is the card of Death.

when he plucked the taut strings.

A plucked string sounds a certain note. If the length of the string is doubled, the new note will be the octave of the first. It may have been Pythagoras who discovered that the octave could be expressed numerically as a ratio of 2 to 1, and the other known musical intervals as ratios of 3 to 2 and 4 to 3. The fact that only the first four numbers were needed to express these ratios probably inspired the belief that the first four numbers were the basis of all numbers. This was given added weight by the fact that the first four numbers totalled 10 when added together and only the numbers 1 to 10 were considered to have great significance. Other numbers were thought merely to repeat 1 to 10 in different combinations. It was also found that the first four numbers were essential in the construction of solid objects. One stood for a point, 2 a line, which is the distance between two points, 3 a triangle, which added breadth to length, and 4 a pyramid, which is the simplest of solid objects. These observations led Pythagoras and his followers to conclude that number was the key to understanding the Universe. They evolved a complete philosophy that demonstrated order and pattern where there had been chaos.

A man who works in a power station will soon become unaware of the constant hum of the generators. Similarly, according to Pythagorean philosophy, human beings are unaware of the "music of the spheres." Pythagoras anticipated the Copernican theory of two thousand years later in conceiving the earth and the planets as globes revolving around a central

The Power of Seven

Above: in the Bible, particularly in the Revelation of St. John, or the Apocalypse, the number seven occurs again and again. In this case one of the seven beasts gives the seven angels the vials of the Wrath of God.

Left: the plan of the seven walls of Jericho as illustrated in a 14th-century Bible. Joshua's feat of demolishing the walls with trumpet blasts has fascinated scholars for hundreds of years. Archeological evidence seems to show that something of the sort did occur, but offers few new suggestions to explain how.

Opposite: in this early 15th-century German altarpiece of the Apocalypse are illustrated the seven epistles addressed to the seven original Christian churches.

Sound and Number

Opposite: Joshua and his army, and seven priests with seven trumpets, circled Jericho seven times, then shouted and blew, and the walls came tumbling down. This 15th-century miniature shows the dramatic collapse of the city walls.

Below: a Japanese Samurai, or warrior. In his arsenal of weapons was his voice, trained to produce a horrendous shout—the kiai—which had the physical effect of suddenly lowering the blood pressure in an opponent.

luminary. On the principle that strings of different lengths sound different notes, the Pythagoreans believed that each of the planets sounds a different note depending on its distance from the center, and that the combination of the sounds forms a harmonious cosmic octave.

All magic is based on the idea that everything in the Universe is bound together in a great design. Number magic stems from the assumption that this design is numerical, and that it involves assigning different properties to the various numbers.

The Pythagoreans believed that the odd and even numbers formed pairs of opposites in the Universe. The odd numbers were assigned the male, active, creative characteristics, and the even numbers the female, passive, receptive qualities. This idea has remained the basis of numerology down to the present day. It is not quite the arbitrary division it seems. It is based on the way the ancients represented numbers by certain arrangements of dots. Shown in this way the odd numbers look like this:

The even ones look like this:

The Pythagoreans saw phallic significance in the odd numbers because they have "a generative middle part," and they saw female sexual characteristics in the even numbers because they have "a certain receptive opening and a space within."

Furthermore, when an even number is divided in two, there is nothing left over, but an odd number divided in two had a part remaining. The odd number is therefore regarded as stronger, or male. Another reason for regarding the odd numbers as dominant is that the addition of an odd and even number together always results in an odd number.

The Renaissance magician Cornelius Agrippa in his *Occult Philosophy* lists the characteristics of the numbers from 1 to 9 as they would appear in a Pythagorean scheme. This is as follows:

1 stands for purpose, action, ambition, aggression, leadership
2 stands for balance, passivity, receptivity
3 stands for versatility, gaiety, brilliance
4 stands for steadiness, endurance, dullness
5 stands for adventure, instability, sexuality
6 stands for dependability, harmony, domesticity
7 stands for mystery, knowledge, solitariness
8 stands for material success and worldly involvement
9 stands for great achievement, inspiration, spirituality

It will be seen immediately that the odd numbers have all the higher and more interesting characteristics. No doubt there was a certain amount of what is today called male chauvinism behind the allocation of characteristics to the numbers—both Pythagoras and Cornelius Agrippa lived in male-dominated societies—but

to regard the system as a crude and primitive example of male wishful thinking would be to miss the point made earlier: that the characteristics of the numbers are derived from their *mathematical* properties. For example, 6 stands for harmony because it is a "perfect" number—that is, it equals the sum of its divisors (1+2+3 = 6), and it is divisible both by an odd number and an even number (2 and 3), so harmoniously combining elements of each. Eight is the number of success and involvement because when halved its parts are equal (4 and 4), and when halved again they are still equal (2 and 2, 2 and 2). The other numbers, likewise, have mathematical properties corresponding to moral and psychological characteristics.

Cagliostro, the 18th-century adventurer and miracle healer

Above: Pythagoras, who believed that numbers were the key to the universe. A Greek philosopher active around 530 B.C., he is traditionally believed to have traveled widely, and certainly was familiar with ideas that originated in Asia Minor.

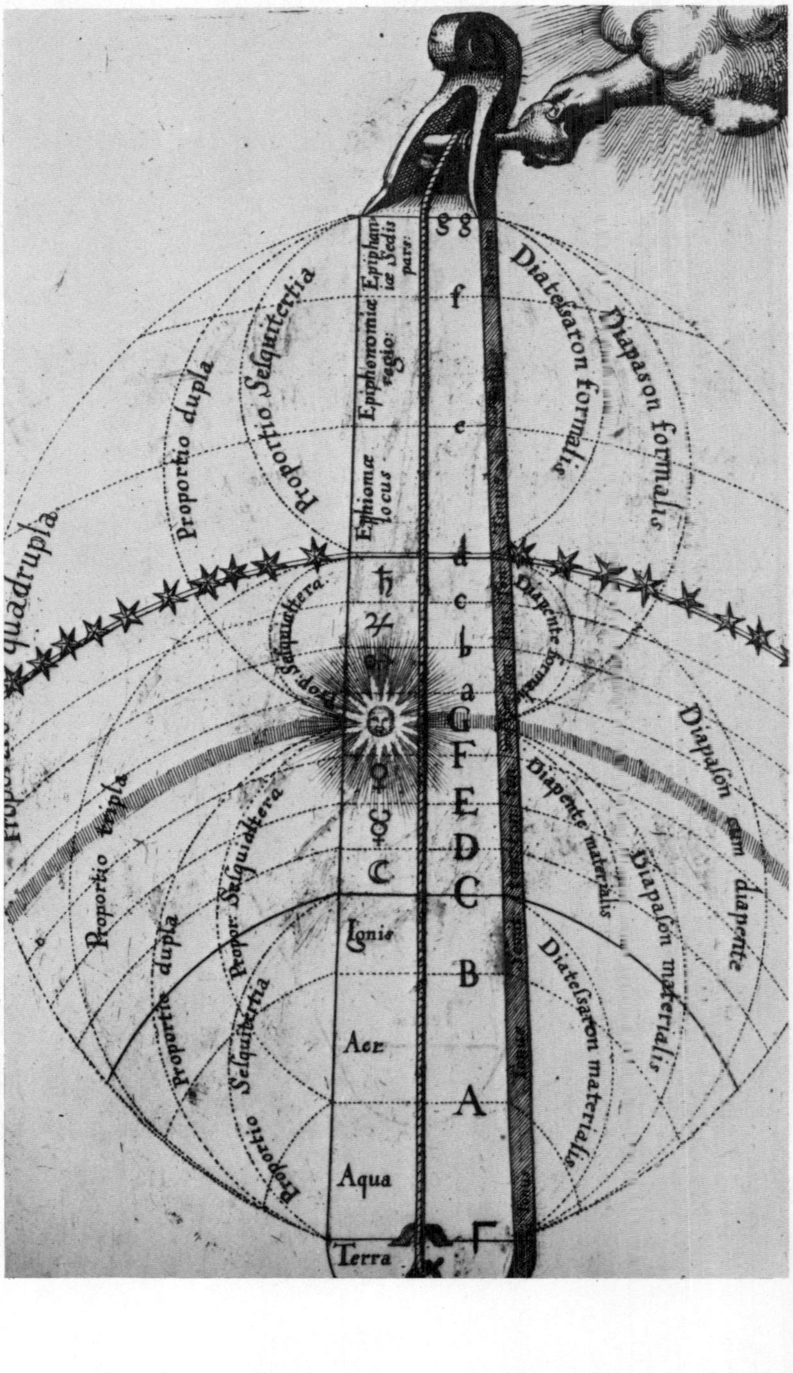

Right: the Music of the World, from Robert Fludd's book printed in 1617 and based on Pythagorean ideas. The universe is presented in terms of musical intervals along a great monochord that stretches from heaven to earth. Fludd was an English physician who was greatly influenced by John Dee and followed him in speculation and investigation of various metaphysical concepts.

Numbers the Key to the Universe

Left: four illustrations taken from a book published in Italy in 1492. They show Jubal, the biblical father of music, with Pythagoras and a student aide, experimenting with the tones of different musical instruments.

who has been called "the last of the magicians," had all Paris at his feet in 1785 because of the wonders he worked. He came to Paris from Strasbourg where he was said to have carried out 15,000 cures in three years. He seemed able to win as much money as he liked at the Paris gaming tables. He also forecast the winning numbers in the lotteries three times for a certain Baroness, refusing to do so a fourth time on the grounds that he had already given her enough information to make three fortunes. Healing and gaming were not his only occult accomplishments. At a gathering in the home of a friend one day he demonstrated his skill as a numerologist. Analyzing the names of King Louis XVI and Queen Marie Antoinette, he made predictions about their fate. The king, he said, was "condemned to lose his head before his 39th year for being guilty of war." Marie Antoinette would be "unfortunate, unhappy in France, a queen without a throne or money, wrinkled prematurely through grief, kept on a meager diet, imprisoned, beheaded." These were to prove two of the most remarkably accurate predictions ever recorded.

Cagliostro employed a system of numerology passed down from Cornelius Agrippa and, in turn, based on the Hebrew

Below: the frontispiece to *Raphael's Witch* or *Oracle of The Future* published in England in 1831. It shows the Wheel of Pythagoras, a device used in one method of numerical fortune-telling. Among the decorative figures are a witch (in the center) and an astrologer, who is contemplating the heavens in the bottom left corner. By that time, the name of Pythagoras had become associated with almost any form of magical numerology.

alphabet. Although the cabalists developed numerology as a method of prediction, character reading, and divination, numbers were most important as the basis of cabalistic philosophy. The gematria was the part of the Cabala that dealt with the conversion of words into numerical values. It was believed that God had created the world by pronouncing the names of things, and that each of the 22 letters of the Hebrew alphabet were divine instruments of creation. Each letter was allocated to one of the 22 paths of the Tree of Life, and each letter had

Numerology and Magic

its own numerical equivalent.

The cabalists believed that a name mystically encodes the essential character of a person or thing as well as information about its destiny. The gematria was a method of reading a code by reducing names to number values, and discovering information about them through words of the same number value.

In the Book of Daniel, which was written in the second century B.C., the name Nebuchadnezzar was used to hide the identity of King Antiochus Epiphanes. It was carefully chosen so that the numbers of the letters in it added up to 423, just as did Antiochus Epiphanes. Cabalists believed that God, like the author of Daniel, used numbers in mysterious ways. For example, they believed that the three men who stood by Abraham on the plains of Mamre were the three senior archangels because the words in *Genesis*, "and lo three men stood by him," add up to the number 701, and this same number is obtained by adding together the number equivalents of the letters in the words, "these are Michael, Gabriel, and Raphael."

Cabalists throughout the centuries have devoted years of their lives to proving the hidden meanings of the scriptures by the methods of gematria. No records exist of those who became mentally deranged in the process, but the most notorious caballistic magician of modern times, Aleister Crowley, had a gematria mania. He identified himself with the Great Beast that comes out of the sea in the Book of Revelation and signed his letters To Mega Therion because the letters of these words add up to 666, the number of the Beast. The historian Macaulay would have disagreed with him, however. He thought the House of Commons was the Great Beast because the number of its members and permanent officials was 666 at that time.

The gematria provided a means of decoding material by converting letters to numbers. The Pythagoreans furnished a method of interpreting the numbers by the qualities they assigned to them. Judaism and Christianity contributed additional interpretations—and thus numerology was born.

The method of conversion that Cagliostro used gives numerical values to the letters of the alphabet as follows:

1	2	3	4	5	6	7	8
A	B	C	D	E	U	O	F
I	K	G	M	H	V	Z	P
Q	R	L	T	N	W		
J		S			X		
Y							

This system is based on correspondences between the Hebrew alphabet and ours, and there are no letters for the numerical value 9 because the Hebrew letters that stood for it have no equivalents in our alphabet.

An alternative method assigns the values by putting the alphabet in its normal order:

1	2	3	4	5	6	7	8	9
A	B	C	D	E	F	G	H	I
J	K	L	M	N	O	P	Q	R
S	T	U	V	W	X	Y	Z	

Above: ladies consulting the magician Cagliostro about the royal lottery of France. His brilliance in selecting winning numbers helped make him the darling of Paris society for a time, until he became entangled in the Affair of the Diamond Necklace of Marie Antoinette. Although innocent of the swindle, he was thoroughly disgraced. Cagliostro was one of the leading magicians of his day, but came to a miserable and unhappy end.

"Name Numbers"

Different numerologists favor one system or the other, though on the whole the Hebrew system is preferred because of its antiquity. To determine the meaning of a name, and therefore the essential character of its owner, the name must first be reduced to one of the numbers below 10. To do this, the numerical values for each letter are added up, and then the individual numbers of that total are added together. If the new total is still more than 10, the individual numbers are again added. Eventually the total will be under 10. Here is an example using my own name.

S T U A R T H O L R O Y D
3 4 6 1 2 4 5 7 3 2 7 1 4 = 49;
(4+9) = 13; (1+3) = 4

My "name number" comes out to be 4. Two further significant numbers may be obtained by adding the vowels and the consonants separately. Because vowels are not written in Hebrew, they are taken to signify the hidden self in numerology, whereas the consonants represent the outer personality. In my name it will be seen that the vowels total 21, which reduces to the number 3. The consonants total 28, which yields the "personality number" 1 (2+8 = 10; and 1+0 = 1). My numerological character reading suggests that my essential character and destiny is a 4, my secret life is a 3, and my outward personality is a 1.

In the following key to the interpretation of the numbers, it will be seen that the basic characteristics ascribed by the Pythagoreans remain, but have been expanded and modified by Judaic-Christian thought and attitudes.

1: the number of God, the One, the Father, the Jehovah of the Old Testament. It signifies dominance, drive, leadership, singleness of mind and purpose, self-mastery, independence. People with the number one are powerful individuals, capable of great achievement, but also capable of obstinately following a path that leads to disaster. They set little store by friendship or cooperation, and are inclined to put themselves first.

2: the number of the eternal female. It signifies passivity, subordination, even temper, conciliatoriness, and desire for peace and balance. People with this number can be characterized by sound balanced judgment, generosity, and friendship. On the other hand, two also carries associations with the Devil, and a person of this number can be cruel, deceitful, and malicious. Two is a neutral number that can become good or evil by a combination of factors and its possessor is likely to be indecisive and susceptible to influence.

3: the number of creation and procreation representing both spiritual and sexual creative power. It is a powerful number, signifying the reconciliation of the opposites apparent in two. People with this number are talented, imaginative, gay, versatile, energetic, and often lucky. Its association with the Christian concept of the Holy Trinity endowed this number with a more profound, mystic, and spiritual significance than it had for the Pythagoreans.

4: endurance, firmness of purpose, accomplishment, will. It

Above and opposite: *Melancholia*, an engraving by the medieval artist Albrecht Dürer, with an enlargement of the magic square shown in the picture. In a magic number square, each number from one to the highest present must appear only once, and the verticals, horizontals, and two long diagonals must all add up to the same total. Engraving the magic square on the appropriate metal at the appropriate time creates a powerful talisman. This particular square is the square of Jupiter, and each row adds up to 34. Thought to have healing properties, it was used to treat various diseases.

MELENCOLIA I
16 3 2 13
5 10 11 8
9 6 7 12
4 15 14 1

Right: one favorite numerological exercise is to analyze the names of the famous to see if their known characteristics match up with the traits one would guess from their name numbers. For numerologists, Mark Twain is a particularly knotty problem. Born Samuel Langhorne Clemens, he was known at various times in his life as Samuel L. Clemens, Sam Clemens, and finally and most famously as Mark Twain. An analysis of his name involves tracing the development of his name number each time it was changed. He began life as a 4, with a plodding nature. When he went on the Mississippi as a river pilot, he shortened his name first to Samuel L. Clemens (name number 1) and then to plain Sam Clemens (name number 5). The number 5 would indicate his uncertainty and indecision at this period. But with the change to Mark Twain, his name number became 2, proving to be the perfect and stable balance.

Above right: George Washington's birth number was 1, and his name number was 7. This would indicate such attributes as his dominance and leadership, and his idealism and intuition. The frequency number 5, which occurs five times in Washington's name, indicates an adventurous vibration, offsetting uncertainty.

was a sacred number for the Pythagoreans representing completion, solidity, equilibrium, the earth. However, it is not a very inspiring number, and its possessor is likely to be rather down-to-earth, stolid, practical, and industrious. In its negative aspects it implies joylessness, dullness, and a tendency to gloom and melancholy.

5: sexuality pure and simple. It brings together the first feminine number of 2 and the first masculine number of 3. (One is considered the number of God and therefore not the first masculine number.) People with this number are likely to be adventurous, restless, quick-tempered, nervous, unstable. Number 5 is the natural man, the sensualist; but on a more profound level he is also the magician, the adept, the controller of the powers of nature.

6: the number of love, harmony, domesticity, union, fidelity, dependability, honesty. Having the power of 3 doubled, those with the number 6 can be very creative though on the whole they tend to lack the energy and flair of 3s. The negative aspects are conventionality, complacency, triviality, and fussiness over detail.

7: mysticism, solitariness, introversion, contemplativeness, aloofness, signifying the triumph of spirit over matter. There is a tradition that the seventh son of a seventh son will have magical powers. Seven is the characteristic number of poets, philosophers, scholars, highly intuitive and imaginative people. But 7s can be given to impractical dreaming, depression, and moodiness. They need success and recognition to fulfill themselves, or else they become frustrated and out of touch.

8: worldly involvement and success, drive, efficiency, capacity for concentrated effort. It is the number of struggle, tenacity, and materialism. Ruthlessness and obstinacy are the negative aspects of this number, and failures can be as spectacular as successes for those with it.

9: the pinnacle of mental and spiritual attainment. Passion, impulsiveness, broad sympathy, and inventiveness are characteristics of people with this number. It is another powerful number, tripling the creative power of 3, and standing for completeness. It has the peculiar mathematical characteristic that when it is multiplied by any other number, the sum of the digits making up the final number is always 9. For example, $2 \times 9 = 18$ and $1+8 = 9$; $3 \times 9 = 27$ and $2+7 = 9$. This signifies a tendency toward egotism.

Another point to be considered by those wanting to try their hand at numerology is that the name used to arrive at their number should be the one by which they are most commonly known, even if it is a stage name or pen name. Any change of name in life is believed to be significant. Certain sects of medieval Jews nurtured on the Cabala believed that it was possible to overcome persistent ill health or bad fortune by a change of name. Few numerologists would go so far, but most would claim that the name a person is given at birth signifies his basic character and potentialities, and that any name later acquired or adopted yields what is known as his "number of development."

In addition to the separate vowel and consonant counts, numerologists pay attention to any "frequency" number—that is, a number which recurs several times in a name. It is also significant if a name lacks one or more numbers. In such a case the person is likely to lack the corresponding qualities of the missing numbers, and could therefore be unbalanced.

One English expert on numerology, Richard Cavendish, has analyzed a famous stage name as follows:

M A R I L Y N M O N R O E
4 1 2 1 3 1 5 4 7 5 2 7 5

Name number: 2—the number of the eternal female (total count 47; $4+7 = 11$; $1+1 = 2$).

Vowel number (inner character): 3—signifying talent, gaiety, luck, versatility.

Consonant number (outer character): 8—signifying worldly success, power, wealth.

Frequency numbers: 1—drive, ambition, and 5—restlessness, instability, sexuality.

Missing numbers: 6—signifying domesticity, harmony, love.

The analysis would appear to be fairly consistent with what is known of the life and character of Marilyn Monroe.

Numerologists also take account of numbers in relation to time for purposes of character analysis, prophesy, and determination of auspicious and inauspicious days. A person's birth number—which is obtained by adding the day, month, and year of birth, and reducing the resulting number to a number below 10, as in name analysis—is believed to indicate the influences existing at the time of birth. Most numerologists stress that these influences get weaker as a person develops, and are modified by the characteristics inherent in the name.

The birth number is frequently used for the purpose of finding out a person's good or bad days. Everyone finds that some days

Name Numbers Interpreted

Below: Henry Ford in his first car, the "Quadricycle," made in 1896. He was 33 at the time. His birth number was 1, and his name number 5. He overcame the uncertainty associated with number 5, and with the purposefulness of number 1, made a fortune and built a worldwide car business.

Prediction by Numbers

Right: the Battle of Waterloo, which ended Napoleon's career.

Above: Napoleon. Had the great French leader consulted a numerologist about his chances at the Battle of Waterloo, he might well have been told that June 18, 1815 was not his day for winning. For him it was a 6-day—which is one for harmony rather than conflict.

are better than others, and that there are days when everything seems to go wrong, and other days when everything goes right. Some numerologists believe that it is possible to predict such days by adding together the person's birth number, name number, and the number of the day itself, reducing the total to one of the numbers below 10. For example, my date of birth was 10/8/1933, (total 25 = 7) so my birth number is 7. The date today is 31/10/1974 (total 26 = 8), and my name number as we have seen is 4. Adding 7+8+4 we get 19. Going on from that, 1+9 = 10, and 1+0 = 1, so the key number for me for today is 1, a number that stands for opportunity and action. The significance of the numbers in relation to the days corresponds with significances for personality analysis, as follows:

1 indicates a day for definite, direct action, for tackling problems; a day of opportunity

2 indicates a day for planning and for weighing problems, but not a good day for entering into commitments

3 indicates a day when many things can be done and achieved; a lucky day, and a good one for having fun

4 indicates a day for doing dull, routine things, for being practical

5 indicates a day for excitement and adventure; a good day for taking risks; a day to expect the unexpected

Above: the Duke of Wellington, English military chief who defeated Napoleon at Waterloo. The big battle fell on a 1-day for him—a day for decisive actions.

6 indicates a day for establishing harmony, reconciling conflicts, holding conferences, being sociable

7 indicates a day for meditation, study, research, for thinking things out

8 indicates a day for constructive effort, big undertakings, and financial dealings

9 indicates a day when ambitions might be fulfilled; a day of achievement, of personal fulfillment.

On the day of the Battle of Waterloo, one numerologist has pointed out, Napoleon's personal analysis would have indicated that it was a 6-day, a day for harmony and avoidance of conflict. For Wellington it was a 1-day, a day for decisive action.

Of course, many such examples of successful analyses can be put forward by numerologists to prove that theirs is a genuine psychic science and a key to occult knowledge. And anyone who tries it is likely to make some convincing hits. However, when we use numbers for fortune telling and for determining good and bad days in our personal lives, we have come a long way from the Pythagorean idea of the universe as a pattern of mathematical correspondences. It is also a far cry from the basic Cabala concept of numbers as the key to the secrets encoded in sacred texts on the nature, origins, purposes, and ultimate destiny of human life on earth.

大宅太郎光國

Chapter 6 Ritual Magic

It is like a stage setting: the circle with its symbolic drawings, the special robes, the smell of incense. Elaborate and exact preparations, pageantry and ceremony—all go into ritual magic. The purpose? To invoke the spirits in order to gain knowledge or help from them. Can magicians really do it? There are many testimonials that they can, from those who undergo the ascetic discipline of fast and prayer to prepare themselves to those who believe in ritual sex as a means of attaining magical power. All agree that there is a danger in trying to conjure up demons, whatever the rewards.

A strange account of an act of ritual magic is given in the autobiography of the swashbuckling 16th-century artist-adventurer Benvenuto Cellini. The tale goes that Cellini, his 12-year-old apprentice Cenci, and two friends one night went to the empty Coliseum in Rome with a Sicilian priest who was also a sorcerer. Their purpose was to summon up demons. The sorcerer, clad in his wizard's robes, ceremonially drew his magic circles on the ground, and the whole group stepped inside the main one for protection. Cellini's friends, Romoli and Gaddi, were instructed to tend a fire and feed it with perfumes. Cellini himself was given a pentacle or magical five-sided symbol, and told to point it in whatever direction the sorcerer indicated. The little apprentice stood under it.

When the elaborate ceremonial preparations had been completed, the sorcerer began calling on a vast multitude of demons by name, in Hebrew, Greek, and Latin. Almost at once the amphitheater was filled with them. Cellini, encouraged to put a request to them, asked to be reunited with his Sicilian mistress, Angelica. "Do you hear what they have told you?" the sorcerer said. "Within the space of a month you will be where she is."

Soon the magician began to get worried because there were a thousand times more fiends than he had summoned, and they were dangerous. He asked Cellini to be brave and give him support while he tried to dismiss them as civilly and gently as possible, as was required by the ritual. Meanwhile young Cenci

Opposite: Mitsukuni, a Japanese sorceress, summons a spirit to frighten her enemies. It appears as a gigantic skeleton.

Above: Benvenuto Cellini, the 16th-century Italian goldsmith-sculptor who had a terrifying experience with demons in Rome. The story comes from his autobiography, recording his often swashbuckling life in a surprisingly frank manner.

was cowering with terror, declaring that he saw a million fierce men menacing them, and four armed giants trying to force a way into the circle. The sorcerer, quaking with fear at this, tried all the soft words he could think of to persuade them to go. Cellini did his best to encourage the others but Cenci, with his head between his knees, began to moan that they were doomed. Cellini tried to convince him that the demons were all under control, and assured him that he would only see smoke and shadows if he looked up. Cenci looked up—and then cried out in terror. He said that the whole Coliseum was on fire, and that the flames were coming toward them.

The sorcerer tried one last desperate remedy. He burned some asafetida, a stinking substance obtained from the root of a certain plant. This—and perhaps the petrified Gaddi's involuntary contribution to the foul smell—broke the spell. Soon Cenci reported that the demons had started to withdraw in fury. The group remained in the safety of the circle until dawn, however, and the magician meantime repeated ceremonial exorcisms. Even when they had packed up and were returning home, Cenci insisted that two of the fiends were still accompanying them, gamboling along the roofs and the road. The adventure had been a little more than anyone had bargained for.

Right: a Japanese screen depicts the legendary hero Raiko lying sick and unaware of the horde of demons being set against him. His inattentive guards are no help.

How many Kinds of Reality Exist?

Whatever may actually have happened at the Coliseum, it is clear that Cellini and his friends were convinced that they were surrounded by demons, and they were scared out of their wits. Today psychologists would be inclined to say that they were all hallucinating, the boy more vividly than the rest. This may be true, but the question then arises: what degree of reality do hallucinations have? The 19th-century poet Coleridge put the question another, more gripping, way. He asked: what if you had a dream in which you went to heaven, and there plucked a flower—and upon waking you found the flower in your hand?

Are the subjective and objective worlds as separate as we usually think? Neither the modern physicist nor the psychologist would claim that the world revealed to us by our normal senses is the whole of reality. Drawing on the insights gained into the physical world by relativity and quantum theory, the psychologist Lawrence Leshan has recently put forward the theory that two kinds of reality exist. He calls one Sensory Reality and the other Clairvoyant Reality. He suggests that both are equally real, and both complement each other and shade into each other like the colors of the spectrum. We conduct our normal lives at one end of the spectrum, that of Sensory Reality, but gifted mystics and poets move easily to the other end. Controlled laboratory

Circles of Safety

Right: a miniature from a medieval account of a pilgrim's journey, showing his encounter with the messenger of Necromancy. The messenger, standing within his magic circle, shows the pilgrim how he can raise spirits. Around the circle are the suitable mystic symbols. The story tells of the various adventures the pilgrim falls into in his search for the true joy. Necromancy and his messenger are obviously one of the false joys the pilgrim sees.

experiments have shown that subjects under hallucinogenic drugs can also make the transition. Traditional ritual magic may be regarded as another technique for making this shift to levels of the mind where individuality can become merged in totality, and where the concepts of subjective and objective no longer apply. The powers of the mind at these levels are not fully understood, though science is beginning to take them seriously. It is not completely inconceivable that they might include the power of materialization, of plucking flowers from heaven, or of summoning fiends from hell.

Ritual magic is an elaborate and impressive use of ceremony carried out by magicians in order to conjure up spirits. The magician's aim is usually to gain some kind of knowledge from the evoked spirit, or to force the spirit to help.

Eliphas Lévi, the well-known 19th-century French writer on the occult, was perplexed by the problem of the reality of the phenomena produced in ritual magic. Although he wrote volumes on magic and taught the subject, he never actually practiced it much. But on one occasion circumstances so conspired that he could not resist the temptation to take a stab at it. His curious story was later used by the English writer Somerset Maugham as the basis for one of his short stories, "The Magician."

Lévi was staying in London at the time. One day he returned to

Left: the magician Doctor Faustus, here in a 17th-century English drawing, stands within his protective circle and controls a demon that he has invoked. On the magic circle are written zodiacal signs.

Below: Eliphas Lévi (1810–1875). He was the son of a poor shoemaker in Paris. His real name was Alphonse Louis Constant, but he adopted the pseudonymn Eliphas Lévi when he began to write about magic and other occult subjects in the 1850s. The taken name was the Hebrew equivalent of his first two names.

his hotel and found an envelope addressed to him. It contained half a card cut diagonally, with the Seal of Solomon, a six-sided figure, drawn on it. A note with it read: "Tomorrow, at three o'clock, in front of Westminster Abbey, the second half of this card will be given to you." Of course he felt compelled to keep the mysterious assignation. He was met by a footman who ushered him into a carriage in which a veiled woman dressed in black showed him the other half of the card. She knew of Lévi through a friend, she said, and she wanted to offer him facilities for the practice of a ritual of spirit evocation. They drove to her house where she showed him a complete magical cabinet and a collection of vestments, instruments, and rare books on magic. Lévi accepted her offer.

He decided to try to call up the spirit of one of the great legendary magicians of antiquity, Apollonius of Tyana. For this the prescribed ritual required a month of continued meditation on the dead person's life, work, and personality. The preparation also included a three-week vegetarian diet and a week of severe fasting. This was no small sacrifice for Lévi, who like most Frenchmen was fond of his food. But he suffered the ordeal, and the night chosen for the attempted evocation duly arrived.

Lévi tells how he prepared the ritual, uttered the prescribed invocations, and then—as smoke floated around the altar—felt the earth shake. A huge figure of a man appeared. But before Lévi could put the two questions he had wanted to ask of Apollonius, he fell into a dream-filled swoon. When he came to it seemed that the questions he had intended to ask were answered in his mind.

"Am I to conclude from all this that I really evoked, saw, and touched the great Apollonius of Tyana?" Lévi asks. He realizes that the circumstances he had created had put him in what psychologists today would call an "altered state of consciousness." "The effect of the preparations, the perfumes, the mirrors,

Let Apollonius Appear!

Eliphas Lévi, the 19th-century writer on theories of magic, seldom practiced what he wrote about. But when he was offered a complete magical chamber, he decided to try to evoke Apollonius of Tyana. Lévi made his circle, kindled the ritual fires, and began reading the evocations of the ritual. A ghostly figure appeared before the altar. Lévi found himself seized with a great chill. He placed his hand on the pentagram, the five-pointed symbol used to protect magicians against harm. He also pointed his sword at the figure, commanding it mentally to obey and not to alarm him. Something touched the hand holding the sword, and his arm became numb from the elbow down. Lévi realized that the figure objected to the sword, and he lowered it to the ground. At this, a great weakness came over him, and he fainted without having asked his questions. After his swoon, however, he seemed to have the answers to his unasked questions. He had meant to ask one about the possibility of forgiveness and reconciliation between "two persons who occupied my thought." The answer was, "Dead." It was his marriage that was dead. His wife, who had recently left him, never returned.

Above: the *Awful Invocation of a Spirit*, an illustration to a lurid romance, *The Necromancer*, published in England in 1825. It appeared in *The Astrologer of the 19th Century*, a collection of popularized pieces on magic and astrology. At this point in the narrative, the sorcerer, called "the sage," strikes the boundary of the magic circle with his wand to remind the spirit that she may approach no closer.

the pentacles, is an actual drunkenness of the imagination, which must act powerfully upon a person otherwise nervous and impressionable," he writes. But he did not believe that the apparition had only been an insubstantial figment of his imagination. "I do not explain the physical laws by which I saw and touched; I affirm solely that I did see and I did touch, apart from dreaming, and this is sufficient to establish the real efficacy of magical ceremonies."

If this sounds incredible, consider some of the accounts of Tibetan ritual magic given by Alexandra David-Neel in her book *Magic and Mystery in Tibet.* Alexandra David-Neel was one of those extraordinary British women of the late 19th and early 20th century who traveled alone in the East in quest of adventure and knowledge. Her courage, intelligence, and fortitude led to her being honored as a lady lama. She was tough-minded and had a sharp eye for charlatanism, but she was not so conditioned by the Western way of thinking as to dismiss anything that didn't fit into its idea of reality. Living among one of the most mysterious and religious races in the world, she remained open-minded,

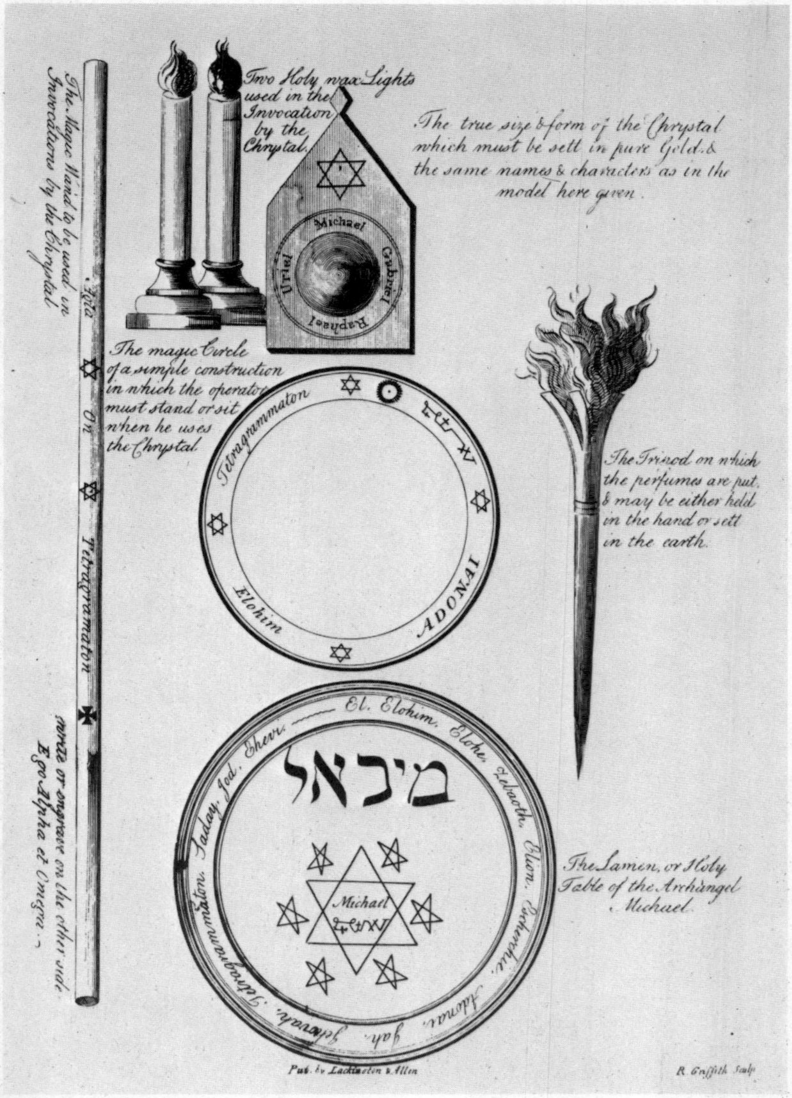

The Magician's Equipment

Left: the equipment of the magician—the magic wand, the candles, the crystal, the tripod, the magic circle, and the "Laman, or Holy Table of the Archangel Michael." This illustration appeared in a handbook on magic by Francis Barrett, published in 1801.

observant, and ready to test for herself the rituals and disciplines by means of which the Tibetan lamas and magicians acquired and exercised their strange powers.

One of these powers was the ability to create a phantom being from their own mind. They called this phantom a *tulpa*. Despite a lama's warning that these "children of our mind" can get out of their maker's control and become mischievous or even dangerous, Alexandra David-Neel decided to try the creation of a tulpa for herself. She took the precaution of choosing for her experiment a harmless character, a short fat monk "of an innocent and jolly type."

Preparations required her to shut herself away for several months, concentrating her thoughts and practicing certain prescribed rituals. At the end of this time she succeeded in creating the phantom monk. She came to regard him as a guest living in her apartment. She then decided to go on a journey on horseback, taking her servants, tents, and the phantom monk. In the course of the journey she would sometimes turn and see him performing "various actions of the kind that are natural to travelers, and

OF ZOS
GREAT CATS:

that I had not commanded." On one occasion a herdsman brought a present of butter to her tent, saw the monk, and took him for a live lama.

Then, as Alexandra David-Neel had been warned, her creation began to escape her control. He grew leaner and his face developed a mocking, malignant look. She decided to get rid of the phantom, but it took her six months of hard struggle to do so. Reflecting on the experience afterward she said, "There is nothing strange in the fact that I may have created my own hallucination. The interesting point is that in these cases of materialization, others see the thought-forms that have been created."

According to Tibetan beliefs, it is not only human beings and animals that can be visualized and animated by mental energy, but also objects. Sorcerers are reputed to be able to animate a knife so that when a man picks it up, it can move, give a sudden impulse to his hand, and make him stab himself. The preparation for this act of murderous sorcery requires months of seclusion, concentration, and performance of rituals—including the calling up of demons to assist with the work—before the knife is considered to be charged with sufficient psychic energy to accomplish its purpose. Commenting on this phenomenon, Alexandra David-Neel suggests that the victim must have fallen under the influence of occult "waves" generated by the sorcerer. In other words, he falls victim to powerful forces of suggestion that annul his own will. It is a more plausible explanation than the knife itself becoming animated. However, it implies that ritual magic can be used to evolve mental powers which are, at present, outside our comprehension.

The talented and original 20th-century English artist Austin Spare not only evolved his own magical rituals, but also painted them and the materializations he evoked through them. Once he was pressed by two dabblers in the occult to demonstrate to them the materialization of an elemental.

Elementals are minor spirits of the lower astral regions, dedicated solely to representing certain elements. The main elementals are associated with the four elements of earth, air, fire, and water, which have been known through the ages. But there are hundreds more. These others are derived from the primitive belief that everything in Nature had a spirit—hills, trees, rocks, streams, and clouds, to name but a few. Like Nature, the elementals are unpredictable and changeable, more often cruel and hostile than kindly. Even more malignant are artificial elementals, which can be created by magicians out of their own violent emotions such as hate, lust, and vengeance. Artificial elementals have only a short life span, but can usually accomplish much evil in the time given them. They appear as hideous animals or horrifying part humans.

Spare warned his friends that it might be dangerous to summon an elemental, but they insisted, and he allowed himself to be persuaded. His ritual preparations and evocations took some time, and at first it seemed that nothing was going to happen. Then a greenish vapor began to materialize in the room, to get thicker and thicker, and to concentrate itself gradually into a definite though amorphous shape. The phenomenon was accompanied by an overpowering stench, and the greenish mass became

Created Phantom or Hallucination?

Opposite: *This is my wish, to obtain the strength of a tiger*, a painting by the English magician-artist Austin Osman Spare. It records Spare's experience when he needed to lift an immensely heavy weight. To do so he magically summoned the strength of a tiger from his subconscious, so that he could command it. The operation worked; he reported that he felt a surge of great strength rush through him, and he easily moved the heavy weight.

Below: a self-portrait by Spare, who died in 1956. His unconventional paintings express and illustrate his own system of magic, which he developed using elements of Cabalism and ritual traditions derived from the Golden Dawn.

Solomon's Seal to Control Spirits

Below: Lévi's interpretation of the Great Seal of Solomon, with which Solomon, in Jewish tradition, controlled the legions of demons. For Lévi the universe was entirely dualistic, with the polarities of light/dark, mind/matter, good/evil existing as absolutes and all manifestations a result of the interplay between these absolutely opposed qualities.

an immense face with two points of fire in it glowing like eyes. It filled the room. The terrified would-be occultists begged Spare to get rid of the thing, and he did so. Within weeks one of the dabblers was dead of no apparent cause, and the other had been committed to an asylum.

In his book *The Magical Revival*, Kenneth Grant, another modern magician, tells a story that sounds like an episode from a stereotyped horror-movie. It differs notably from Lévi's account of his evocation of Apollonius of Tyana, and from Alexandra David-Neel's creation of the jolly monk in that no prolonged ascetic discipline preceded the ritual. From Grant's story, it appears that an elemental may be fairly easily invoked, but not easily gotten rid of.

In the 1920s a group of magicians formed a lodge in north London. Its members were greatly annoyed when a rival lodge was established in the district, and they decided to punish the upstarts by plaguing them with the attentions of an invoked elemental. The newcomers got wind of the plot and performed a ritual designed to turn the malevolent force back on its creators. Unfortunately for the original group, this ploy was successful. Their own elemental disrupted a cosy tea party, sent cups, plates,

Right: a witch driving off evil spirits she has conjured up. Apparently she had raised the elementals to obtain the gold and jewels that are seen bulging out of her apron. Like magicians the world over, she faces the problem of dispersing the spirits.

and sandwiches flying around the room, smashed ornaments and pictures. For weeks—day and night, at home and at work—all the members of the original group were tormented by the treacherous elemental, their own creation, which was said to look like a giant sea anemone with long spindly legs. They only got rid of it after several long ceremonies of exorcism.

Lévi said of ritual magic, "I regard the practice as destructive and dangerous." The foremost contemporary historian on the subject, A. E. Waite, makes it clear in the opening pages of his *Book of Ceremonial Magic* that he also deplores the practice as "the hunger and thirst of the soul seeking to satisfy its craving in the ashpits of uncleanness, greed, hatred, and malice." Waite calls the grimoires "little books of wicked and ultra-foolish secrets." He justifies the publication of his own *Complete Grimoire* only as a definitive act of scholarship and "a contribution of some value to certain side issues of historical research." The examples we have given seem to illustrate his objection to ritual magic as normally practiced for trivial or ignoble purposes. Yet even if all the "ultra-foolish secrets" of the grimoires are dismissed as charlatanism or superstition, and their elaborate rites as so much mumbo-jumbo, there remains a fascination about

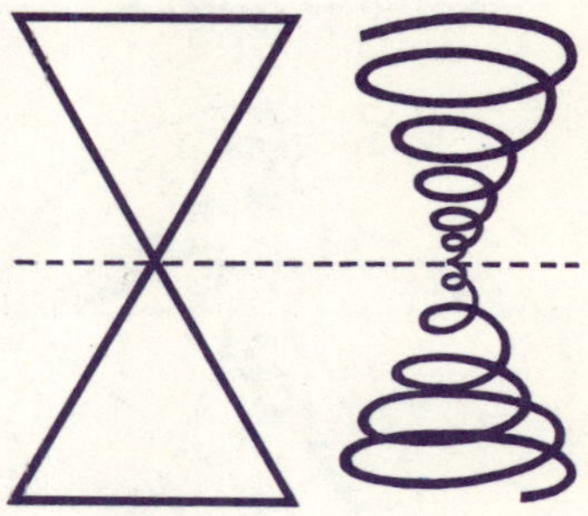

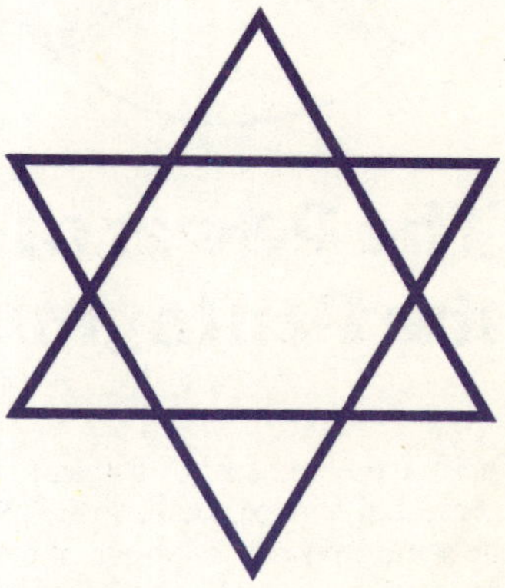

Above: within Solomon's Seal are these elements, each carrying a particular significance. The triangles symbolize heaven and earth, meeting only at a tiny point. Man's role is to connect and balance them. The descending spiral is the creation of matter from spirit, the ascending spiral man's return path. Therefore the intersecting of all these symbols, as in the Seal of Solomon, shows man in a state of balance.

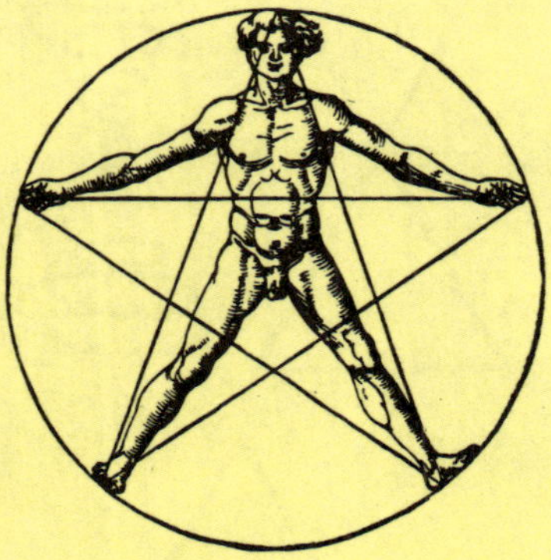

The Power of the Pentagram

The five-pointed star of magical ritual is a symbol both of good and evil. With one point upward, as above, it can be visualized as a man's body, and is a representation of the dominance of the divine spirit over the material world. Reversed, as below, the pentagram becomes the symbol of evil with the two upward points representing the horns of the Devil. It is used in the reverse position if there is a strong necessity for dealing with evil in a ritual.

The power of the pentagram comes mainly from its association with the number 5, which in number magic stands for the living world of Nature; the four directions and the center; the senses and union of the sexes; and man as microcosm.

Pentagrams are drawn in the rim of the magic circle to protect the magician, who usually wears the symbol embroidered on his or her ceremonial robes, or carries it in one hand as a further guard against hostile spirits.

ritual magic. It is not merely the fascination of the outlandish and grotesque. It is our constant fascination with the strange powers and hidden potentials of our own minds.

Laboratory research by parapsychologists has clearly established the existence of psychic energy. It has been demonstrated that material objects can be moved in space by the power of thought. The Russian woman Nelya Mikhailova appears to have this power, called psychokinesis. Reports of laboratory experiments with her state that she takes from two to four hours to work up her powers, and that after a successful exercise in moving things by psychokinesis, she is exhausted and has lost weight. The Israeli psychic Uri Geller is said to be able to produce similar effects without such effort. He has also been studied under laboratory conditions. Many scientists have now become convinced that psychic energy exists, and are anxious to find out what it is and how it works. Some have pointed out that electricity, the energy on which the modern world is virtually dependent, has always existed as a hidden potential in the laws of nature. Yet we have only known how to harness it for about a century. From this, some scientists have suggested that psi energy might be as little understood and exploited as electricity was a hundred years ago.

A practitioner of ritual magic would say that he or she holds the secret the psychic researchers seek, and would find the analogy with electricity particularly apt. Before we could use electrical energy, we had to learn how to generate it, how to control and conduct it, and how to protect ourselves from it. Ritual magic claims to have this knowledge in respect of psychic energy. It is generated by the right ceremonies, and it is controlled and conducted by the techniques for binding spirits to do the operator's will. Magicians protect themselves from the danger inherent in forces they unleash by means of the magic circles and the ritual sword, pentacles, and so on.

The revival of interest in magic and the psychic sciences in recent years has contributed to the creation of a mental climate in which serious research into the supernatural powers of the mind can be conducted. It is difficult to imagine how a magic ritual could be monitored under laboratory conditions, but it is possible that something of value might be learned from the study of the ancient texts and methods. Alexandra David-Neel made the point in the introduction to her book on magic in Tibet, saying: "Psychic training, rationally and scientifically conducted, can lead to desirable results. That is why the information gained about such training—even when it is practiced empirically and based upon theories to which we cannot always give assent—constitutes useful documentary evidence worthy of our attention."

Anyone who studies the texts of the grimoires will be struck by the contrast between the grandeur and solemnity of the ritual itself and the triviality, preposterousness—and sometimes wickedness—of the ends it seeks to achieve. The grimoires are curious evidence of the coexistence in the human mind of sublime and mundane aspirations. But they are essentially documents based on a system of religious beliefs, and it is this aspect of them that is worthy of serious study.

Because magical power is not generated in normal conditions

Invoking Demons

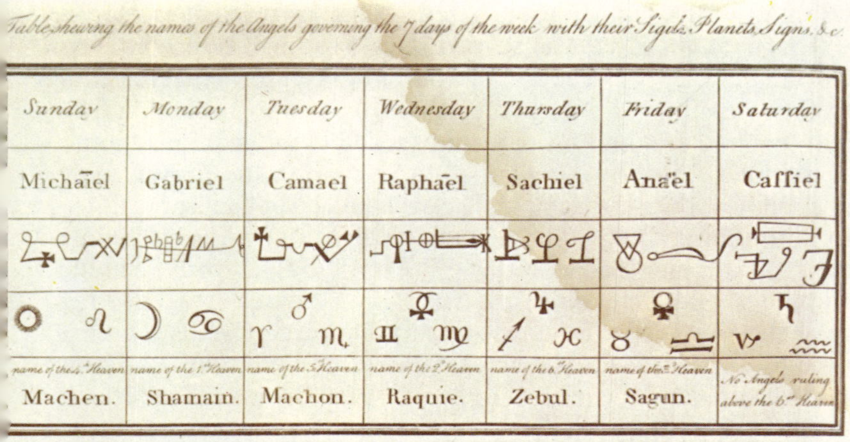
Table shewing the names of the Angels governing the 7 days of the week with their Sigils, Planets, Signs, &c.

Sunday	Monday	Tuesday	Wednesday	Thursday	Friday	Saturday
Michaël	Gabriel	Camael	Raphaël	Sachiel	Anaël	Cassiel
☉ ♌	☽ ♋	♂ ♈ ♏	☿ ♊ ♍	♃ ♐ ♓	♀ ♉ ♎	♄ ♑ ♒
name of the 4th Heaven Machen.	name of the 1st Heaven Shamain.	name of the 5th Heaven Machon.	name of the 2nd Heaven Raquie.	name of the 6th Heaven Zebul.	name of the 3rd Heaven Sagun.	No Angels ruling above the 6th Heaven

Above: Francis Barrett, the Englishman who wrote *The Magus*, subtitled *A Complete System of Occult Philosophy* and published in 1801. It was a magic textbook.

Left: a table showing the days of the week with their governing angels and two pages from the Book of Spirits, from Barrett's *The Magus*. Each planet had its own angel, which the magician could invoke to attain mastery over the areas of life that that planet controlled. Barrett maintained he only practiced white magic, and the Book of Spirits shows an invocation to Cassiel, "chief of the spirits," urging him to "only swear in future by him who has created everything with one word and to whom all creatures are subject."

of life or states of consciousness, magicians operate on the assumption that it has an external source. Whether this is so, or whether it is really self-induced, is a question that we cannot answer. However, the various external frameworks that magicians use in their magic ritual enable them to give some kind of order and coherence to psychic forces. The cabalistic Tree of Life is one such framework and, on a far less profound level, the system of demonology found in the grimoires is another. But whereas magicians using the Tree of Life will seek to harmonize and tune in with the external forces, magicians using the demonology will aim to coerce certain spirits into performing certain well-defined tasks. The idea that spirits or demons can be called up and compelled to give assistance to magicians is believed to have its origin in various documents attributed to King Solomon. The first, the *Testament of Solomon*, is Solomon's own story of his acquisition of magical powers. The second, the *Key of Solomon*, is the original and most celebrated grimoire, allegedly

Above: Abraxas, a fat-bellied demon whose name seems to have been the origin of the word "abracadabra," which was thought to be a spell of great power. His name adds up to exactly 365.

Below: the demon Belphegor, wno was originally the Moabite deity called Baal-Peor, worshiped in the shape of a phallus. He was supposed to be very difficult to summon, although once there he distributed goods with great generosity if he liked the magician. One legend says that Belphegor came to earth to investigate rumors about the unhappiness and misery of married couples, and retreated to hell gratefully, happy that relationships between men and women didn't exist there.

written by Solomon himself based on his knowledge of magic.

The *Testament* tells a story about a young boy who was working on the construction of Solomon's temple. He fell victim to the attentions of a demon called Ornias, who robbed him of half his food and half his pay, and sucked blood from his thumb every night. The boy complained to Solomon, who prayed to be given power over the demon. The archangel Michael came down to Solomon and gave him a small ring with an engraved stone on it, telling him that with this gift from God, he would be able to bind all the demons of the world into his service. The king gave the ring to the boy, who with it captured Ornias the next time he appeared. Ornias was taken before Solomon, who sent him to command the presence of the chief of demons, Beelzeboal. Beelzeboal in turn was forced to bring before Solomon all the other demons. The king interrogated the demons as to their names, powers, and functions, and set them to work on the building of the great temple.

The engraving on the ring of Solomon was a pentacle, the five-sided mystic sign of power used by magicians for centuries. There is no mention of the magic circle in the *Testament of Solomon*, though it has been suggested that the ring itself was symbolical of the circle. In magic it is the circle that protects the magician during the ceremony, and he steps outside it at his peril. To the East of the circle he draws a triangle to confine any spirit that he might evoke.

In the *Key of Solomon* detailed instructions for the conduct of magical rituals are given. From it aspiring magicians may learn how they must prepare themselves for the ritual with a period of fasting, celibacy, and meditation; what they must wear and what symbols they must have embroidered on their robes, shoes, and crown; how they should make and consecrate the pentacles; and how to draw the magic circle and inscribe it with words of power. The preparations are elaborate, but according to the *Key*, every detail is essential to the safe and successful conduct of an invocation.

There is great emphasis in the *Key of Solomon* on the spiritual preparation of the magician. By means of fasting, continence, and prayer, he puts himself firmly on the side of the angels before venturing to deal with the demons. The ritual itself is preceded by long prayers of a most solemn and exalted kind, consisting of profound adoration of the Almighty, abject confession of the magician's own sins, ignorance, and unworthiness, and a humble petition for God's help in pressing the demons into the service of the magician's will. After all this solemnity, it can be disappointing to think that the object of the ritual may turn out to be the finding of treasure, the persecution of an enemy, or the conquest of a woman.

Invested with power in God's name, the magician is able to command the presence of any of the demons. The *Lemegeton*, another work attributed to Solomon, gives a series of invocations for making a spirit appear, each one more eloquent and terrible in its threats of eternal damnation and fire than the one before. The desired demon is made to appear in the triangle drawn outside the magic circle in "invisible and pleasant form"—an important phrase in the conjuration because some demons can

A Variety of Demons

Left: Behemoth, who according to Islamic tradition was placed by God under the earth to hold it firmly in place. The demon was probably derived from the Egyptian hippopotamus goddess Taueret. In medieval demonologies he is mainly described as a fat and rather stupid demon, with duties as a headwaiter in hell. But his description in the Book of Job in the Bible is truly awe-inspiring—"He is the first of the words of God; let him who made him bring near his sword!"

Below: Asmodeus, a demon who belonged to the order of the Seraphim, the highest order of angels, before he fell. Asmodeus inspires men with such lust that they eagerly betray their wives. He plotted against those newly wed, and during the medieval period he was greatly dreaded.

assume terrible and monstrous forms. The magician then negotiates with the demon for the performance of the service that he was summoned for, and afterward dismisses him with due ceremony.

Because the powers and functions of the demons vary greatly, it is essential for magicians to know which one will best serve their purpose. They also need to know the demon's seal, which they inscribe within the circle. All this information is given in the *Lemegeton*, which catalogs 72 prominent demons, each of them a leader of legions of subordinates. Eighteen of them are classified as kings, 26 as dukes, and others as earls, presidents, princes, and marquises.

An idea of the variety of character and functions of the demons will best be conveyed by giving a few examples. Amon is a strong and powerful marquis who appears like a wolf with a serpent's head and vomiting flame. When so ordered he assumes a human shape, but with the teeth of a dog. He discerns past and future, procures love, and reconciles friends and foes. Buer is a great president who appears when the sun is in Sagittarius and teaches philosophy, logic, the virtues of herbs, etc. He heals all diseases and provides good familiars—that is, spirits meant to serve a single individual, usually a witch. Sytry: a great prince who appears with a leopard's head and the wings of a griffin, but assumes a beautiful human form at the magician's command. He provides sexual services.

Right: the Hermetic Order of the Golden Dawn, set up in London in 1888, developed what could almost be called a university degree course in the occult. The members were given great masses of occult texts to master, and tested on them in a series of examinations that were graded. In addition, the novice passed through a succession of magical rituals initiating him into new areas of mystic understanding. Here is the certificate awarded to Alan Bennett—who later became a Buddhist monk—as Adeptus of the Golden Dawn. I.A. stands for Iehi Aour, Bennett's special name as a Golden Dawn member.

Above: the Rosicrucian symbol of the Golden Dawn. Many of the Golden Dawn rituals developed from the rituals and literature of the Rosicrucian Society.

Glasyalabolas: a mighty president who comes in the form of a dog, but winged like a griffin. He teaches all arts and sciences instantaneously, incites to bloodshed, is the leader of all homicides, discerns past and future, and makes people invisible. Astaroth: a great and powerful duke who appears as a beautiful angel riding on a dragon and carrying a viper in his right hand. He must not be permitted to approach on account of his stinking breath, and the magician must defend his face with the magic ring. Astaroth answers truly concerning the past, present, and future, discovers all secrets, and gives great skill in the liberal sciences.

Shax: a great marquis who comes in the form of a wild dove speaking with a hoarse voice. He destroys the sight, hearing, and understanding of any man or woman at the will of the magician. He will transport anything, but must first be commanded into the triangle or else he will deceive the magician. He discovers all hidden things that are not in the keeping of wicked spirits, and provides good familiars.

Between them the 72 demons of the *Lemegeton* have the power

Magicians of The Golden Dawn

to gratify just about every conceivable human desire or hope. However, the book itself is probably more interesting as a literary curiosity than as a practical guide for the modern magician. Not only are its procedures extremely complicated, but also it demands too much by way of piety, credulity, and suspension of common sense to appeal to the modern mind. Apparently much more appealing for today's practitioner of supernatural arts is ritual sexual magic.

In Germany at the beginning of the present century, Karl Kellner, a high-grade member of the Freemasons, founded his own occult organization. He named it the Ordo Templis Orientalis, which became known as the OTO. In founding the organization, Kellner declared boldly that: "Our Order possesses the KEY which opens up all Masonic and Hermetic secrets, namely, the teaching of sexual magic, and this teaching explains, without exception, all the secrets of Freemasonry and all systems of religion."

The OTO had nine grades, the last three of which were concerned with the practice of sexual magic. Initiates of the ninth

Top and above: Golden Dawn paraphernalia. Each detail of symbolism used on the ritual equipment was described in the Golden Dawn manuscripts, copied by hand to guarantee secrecy, and accepted as chosen by the Secret Chiefs. (They were invisible supermen who had given the original authority for the magical order to be founded.) The society eventually fell apart when more than one member claimed to be in contact with these mysterious Secret Chiefs.

Above left: Golden Dawn magical wands. When novices passed the rite of initiation for the grade of Adeptus Minor, their first major task was to make their own seven pieces of personal ritual equipment, using the color symbolism which was supposed to have been learned from the Secret Chiefs. In addition there were the wands, badges, and banners that belonged to the Order and were used in the initiation rituals and other ceremonies.

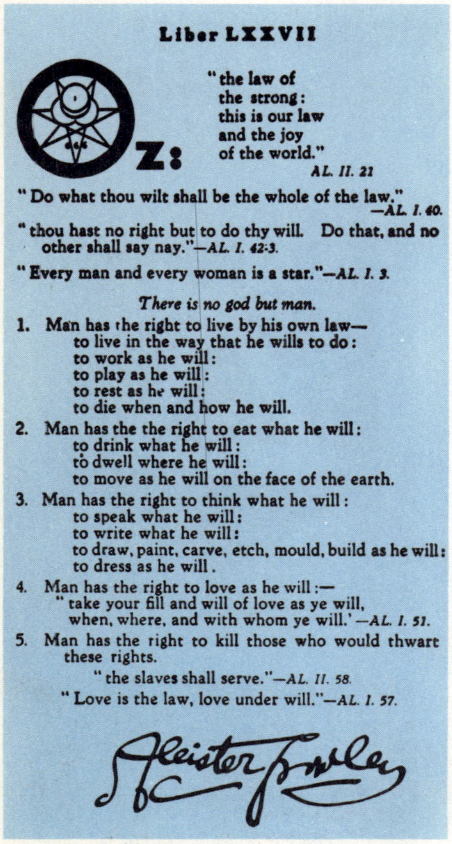

Liber LXXVII

OZ: "the law of the strong: this is our law and the joy of the world." *AL. II. 21*

"Do what thou wilt shall be the whole of the law." —*AL. I. 40.*

"thou hast no right but to do thy will. Do that, and no other shall say nay."—*AL. I. 42-3.*

"Every man and every woman is a star."—*AL. I. 3.*

There is no god but man.

1. Man has the right to live by his own law—
   to live in the way that he wills to do:
   to work as he will:
   to play as he will:
   to rest as he will:
   to die when and how he will.
2. Man has the the right to eat what he will:
   to drink what he will:
   to dwell where he will:
   to move as he will on the face of the earth.
3. Man has the right to think what he will:
   to speak what he will:
   to write what he will:
   to draw, paint, carve, etch, mould, build as he will:
   to dress as he will.
4. Man has the right to love as he will:—
   "take your fill and will of love as ye will, when, where, and with whom ye will.'—*AL. I. 51.*
5. Man has the right to kill those who would thwart these rights.

"the slaves shall serve."—*AL. II. 58.*

"Love is the law, love under will."—*AL. I. 57.*

Aleister Crowley

Above: Aleister Crowley's brief summary of the doctrines of Thelema, which was to supersede Christianity as the gospel of the coming Aeon of Horus. It is taken from the Book of the Law, which Crowley said was dictated to him by the spirit Aiwass on three consecutive days in April 1904 when he was in Egypt. This postcard summary appeared in 1943, long after Crowley had been expelled from Italy to close the Abbey of Thelema, which he had established in Cefalu, Sicily.

grade claimed that, by employing the appropriate sexual technique, any magical operation would be successfully concluded, from the invocation of a god to the acquisition of a great treasure. The techniques were, in fact, similar to and probably derived from Tantra, the Indian sect that uses ritual sexual intercourse both as a means of heightening consciousness and a way of worship.

Aleister Crowley was a lifelong devotee of the methods of sexual magic, and he engaged in autosexual, homosexual, and heterosexual ritual practices with equal enthusiasm. In 1912 he published material that enraged the leaders of the OTO, who accused him of betraying the secrets of their ninth grade. Crowley replied that since he was not a member of their ninth grade, he was in no position to know their secrets, and what he had published was entirely his own work. They saw his point, marveled at his work, and promptly appointed him leader of a British subsidiary of the OTO with the splendid title of "King of Ireland, Iona, and all the Britains within the sanctuary of the Gnosis."

The fundamental idea behind ritual sexual magic is that at the moment of orgasm a tremendous psychic force is released which can be directed to accomplish any magical purpose. The practice demands the same training in visualization that is involved in rituals based on the Cabala or the grimoires. The participants must be able to prolong intercourse and defer orgasm at will until a subjective reality of such intensity has been built up that at the moment of orgasm it is projected as an objective reality and produces a magical effect in the real world. Alcohol or drugs may be used to assist the process and, if the invocation of a demon or a planetary spirit is intended, the appropriate defensive symbols, incenses, and other essentials to the ritual are usually employed as well.

In *The Magical Revival* Kenneth Grant tells the inside story of the influence of Crowley on American disciples. It is a harrowing story of a series of personal tragedies, and it shows that the dangers traditionally involved in ritual magic are by no means minimized for those who choose the sexual practice. Few stories are more tragic than that of Jack Parsons, a brilliant scientist who became leader of the Agape Lodge, the successor of the OTO in California.

Parsons adopted the magical name of Belarion and named his partner, who was his second wife, Babalon (the Scarlet Woman). In the course of ritual sexual intercourse with her, Parsons contacted an Intelligence which gave him what he claimed was the missing conclusion of Crowley's *The Life of the Law*. He called his work the *Book of Babalon*. His life became obsessive, and his writings wild and paranoid. Crowley himself, dying in obscurity in England, was moved to reply to one of his letters: "I thought I had a most morbid imagination, as good as any man's, but it seems I have not. I cannot form the slightest idea of what you can possibly mean." To another disciple in California Crowley wrote: "Apparently he [Parsons] is producing a Moonchild. I get fairly frantic when I contemplate the idiocy of these louts." Parsons nonetheless remained loyal to Crowley and his doctrines, and declared, "In His Law I shall conquer the world."

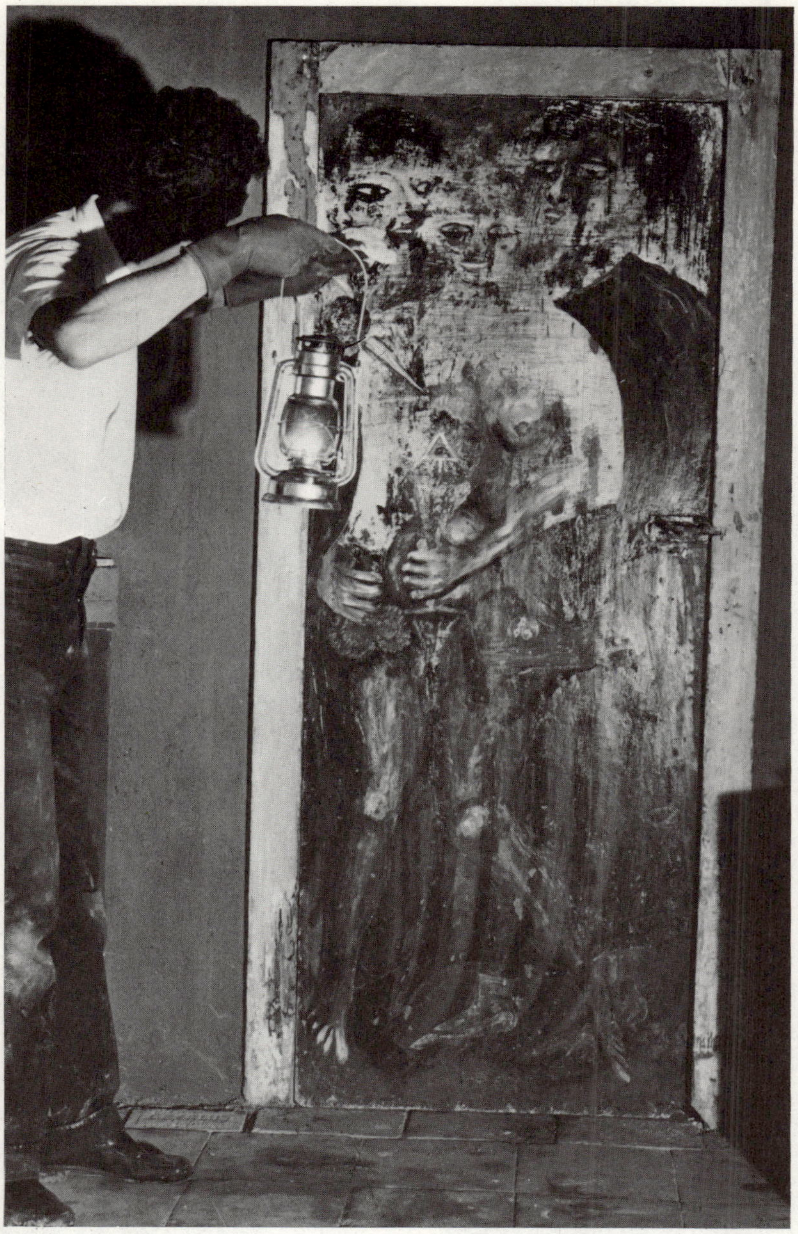

Aleister Crowley and Sexual Magic

He didn't. In 1952 while working in his laboratory, Parsons dropped a phial of fulminate of mercury, and was instantly enveloped in a sheet of flame. Shortly before his death he had written, or transcribed from his spirit Intelligence, the following passage in the *Book of Babalon*:

"She is flame of life; power of darkness; she destroys with a glance; she may take the soul. She feeds upon the death of men. Concentrate all forces and being in Our Lady Babalon. Light a single light on Her altar, saying Flame is our Lady; flame is Her hair. I am flame."

These were prophetic words. Who would not rather undergo Cellini's harrowing night in the Coliseum than suffer Jack Parson's eclipse in derangement, paranoia, and flame? Both men's experiences may be read as warnings of the consequences of ritual magic gone wrong.

Above left: American film-maker Kenneth Anger explored the Abbey of Cefalu and discovered under the whitewash murals painted by Crowley during his time there. The paintings were covered over because of their erotic content when Crowley was expelled from Italy after the death of a young disciple under mysterious circumstances.

Above: Aleister Crowley. For all his showmanship, he obviously believed firmly in his message.

Chapter 7
Books in Stone

It has been shown that the natural features in the environs of Glastonbury—holy site of the first Christian Church in England—form a giant zodiac. The ancient stone monument of Stonehenge and other prehistoric megaliths in Britain have also been seen to relate to the planets. Can this be evidence of great knowledge of astronomy by prehistoric peoples? Belief that the ancients could fly has roots both in the East and West, and has given rise to the theory of ley lines of magnetic force in the earth. Do ley lines exist and can they be used for self-generated flight?

There is a legend that, shortly after the crucifixion, the apostle St. Philip sent 12 missionaries to England. Among them was Joseph of Arimathea, who had been responsible for the burial of Christ. In the West of England, in an area of peat bog and winding water courses, these missionaries were granted some land. In what later became known as Glastonbury, they built a simple church of timber and wattles, supposedly the first Christian church built in Britain. It was dedicated to the Virgin Mary.

Glastonbury became steeped in sanctity, and its church came to be considered a holy site. Lying as it does in the midst of the region of Arthurian legend, Glastonbury also had its share of myth. It was believed, for example, that Joseph of Arimathea had brought the Holy Grail to Glastonbury, and that King Arthur was buried in the church grounds. In the 8th century an abbey was built, slightly to the east of the old church, and later joined to it. When the church and abbey burned down in 1184, King Henry II ordered that both should be rebuilt. A new Chapel of St. Mary was constructed of exactly the dimensions of the original Church. The abbey flourished for many centuries, but had begun to decay by the mid-16th century. Its stones were removed for other buildings and it quickly became a ruin, as it is today. But growing there still is a flowering thorn bush said to be a cutting from the original thorn bush which sprang up when the holy Joseph of Arimathea stuck his staff in the ground.

Opposite: prehistoric monuments—like Stonehenge, shown here—present a continuing challenge to modern man. They were obviously built for some specific purpose, but the last person to understand died centuries ago and the secret is lost. What could it have been?

The Zodiac of Glastonbury

Below: Glastonbury Tor from the air. The tor is a hill rising to 500 feet above sea level, dominating the surrounding countryside. The nearby abbey is thought to be the oldest Christian establishment in Britain, and its traditions go back, with no break in continuity, to King Arthur, to the Romans, and even to the apostolic period. There is also a tradition that it was a pagan holy place before Joseph of Arimathea and his companions arrived and built the Old Church chapel of wattle.

In 1921 Frederick Bligh Bond, the architect in charge of maintaining the Glastonbury abbey ruins, published a remarkable account of a communication he had received through a medium. The message was alleged to have come from a monk who had been a member of the Glastonbury community in the 15th century. Part of it went as follows: "That which the brethren of old handed down to us, we followed, ever building on their plan. As we have said, our Abbey was a message in ye stones. In ye foundations and ye distances be a mystery—the mystery of our Faith, which ye have forgotten and we also in ye latter days."

Bligh Bond believed that in the measurements and proportions of what is possibly Britain's most sacred site, he had discovered evidence of the survival of a religion and a mystery more ancient than Christianity. However, whether his spirit communication was genuine or not, Bligh Bond paid dearly for publishing it. He was abruptly dismissed from his post, and the archeological investigations he had initiated were halted. The Church authorities in reaching their decision may have been influenced by the fact that Bligh Bond was not only a dabbler in Spiritualism, but also an expert on the Cabala and gematria.

The 12th-century monk and historian William of Malmesbury lived in Glastonbury before the original church had burned down. He wrote of it: "This church, then, is certainly the oldest I know in England . . . in the pavement may be seen on every side stones designedly inlaid with triangles and squares, and figured with lead, under which, if I believe some sacred enigma to be contained, I do not injustice to religion." This design was later completely erased, and no record left of it. However, according to Bligh Bond's spirit monk, "All the measures were marked plain on the slabs in Mary's Chapel, and you have destroyed them . . . In the floor of the Mary Chapel was the Zodiac, that all might see and understand the mystery."

A zodiac design might well have been incorporated in the mosaic pavement of the old church, but whether or not it was, the zodiac was linked to Glastonbury in a peculiar way. This link was discovered by the extraordinary Elizabethan scholar-magician Dr. John Dee on a visit to the Glastonbury area in about 1580. He noticed the unusual arrangement of the prehistoric earthworks in the district, and was curious enough about the phenomenon to make his own map. The intuition that had prompted him to do so was proved correct: he discovered that the earthworks and natural features of the landscape were laid out in a pattern that corresponded with the zodiac. He wrote: "This is astrology and astronomy carefully and exactly married and measured in a scientific reconstruction of the heavens which shows that the ancients understood all which today the learned know to be facts."

Dr. Dee's discovery was forgotten, however, and was only exhumed from the mass of his papers after Glastonbury Zodiac had been rediscovered in 1920 by Mrs. K. E. Maltwood. Mrs. Maltwood, an occultist, was well acquainted with all the legends about Glastonbury and the surrounding countryside, including the belief that Christianity and the Holy Grail had been brought here by Joseph of Arimathea, and the tradition that King Arthur had held his court at nearby Camelot, and was not dead but sleeping forever in the hills. Standing on one of these hills one summer afternoon, Mrs. Maltwood saw in a flash the mystic landscape, the figures of giants sleeping, and the twelve signs of the zodiac. Each sign was in order beneath its appropriate constellation, and was formed by natural features of the landscape plus artificial banks, paths, and ditches. Aerial photography later confirmed Mrs. Maltwood's discovery, and scholars subsequently dug up Dr. Dee's anticipation of it. It would seem that the "sacred enigma" of Glastonbury mentioned by William of Malmesbury has something to do with the zodiac and the correlation of the heavens and the earth. To establish this fact is only to arrive at a further puzzle, however. Why should the ancients have gone to such trouble to mirror the patterns of the heavens in the features of the earth?

In 1967 a retired Scottish engineer, Professor Alec Thom, published a book called *Megalithic Sites in Britain*. It was the product of many years of independent work surveying most of the stone circles in the British Isles. His patient work was rewarded by two remarkable discoveries, both indicating that the people who constructed these stone circles were more than competent geometricians and astronomers.

Professor Thom's breakthrough came with his discovery of the principle unit of measurement of antiquity, which he called the megalithic yard (MY), and which is equivalent to 2.72 feet. Subsequent studies have shown that this unit of measurement is to be found in the proportions of ancient buildings all over the world. Applying this unit to the British stone circles, Thom discovered that lines drawn joining the seemingly randomly placed stones form precise Pythagorean triangles. From these triangles, circles and ellipses can be constructed, the perimeters and diameters of which can be expressed in multiples of the megalithic yard.

That the ancient Britons applied Pythagorean principles long before Pythagoras was born was a remarkable discovery, but even more so was Professor Thom's second conclusion. He found that the stones not only formed geometric patterns within and immediately around the circle, but that they also defined patterns in relation to features in the surrounding landscape with which they were aligned—and beyond that, in relation to the position occupied by the sun, the moon, or a prominent star on the horizon at a particular time. A stone placed outside a circle would be in exact alignment both with a geometrically fixed point within it and some feature on the skyline marking the spot where the sun appeared or disappeared at the equinox or one of the solstices, or the spot where the moon occupied one of the extreme positions in its cycle. Sometimes these features on the skyline were natural ones, like a hill or mountain peak. Where a natural feature was lacking, however, there would be a man-made one—a mound, a pile of stones, or a notch cut into a ridge. So consistent are these characteristics in so many of the remaining stone circles of Britain, it would not seem unreasonable to assume that at one time the whole land was constructed in terms of a symmetry bearing a direct

Above: the 14th-century Great Seal of Glastonbury, showing the Holy Thorn that sprang from a saint's staff. The thorn blooms just after Christmas. The original thorn was cut down by Puritans, but its descendants still flourish.

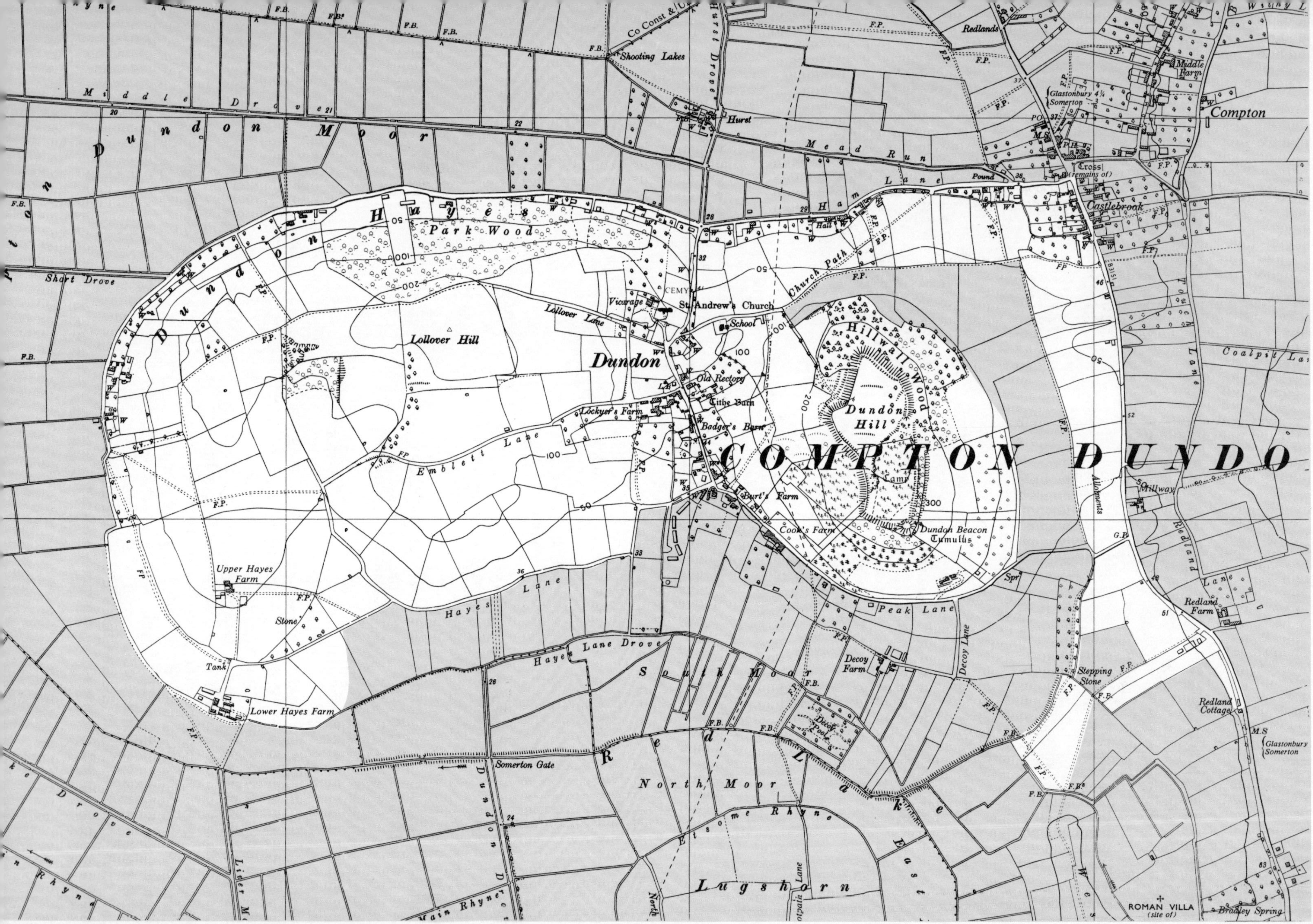

COMPTON DUNDON
Dundon
Compton
Castlebrook
Dundon Hill
Hillwall Wood
Dundon Beacon
Tumulus
Camp
Lollover Hill
Lollover Lane
Park Wood
Hayes
Dundon Hayes
St Andrew's Church
CEMY
Vicarage
School
Old Rectory
Tithe Barn
Badger's Barn
Lockyer's Farm
Burt's Farm
Cook's Farm
Emblett Lane
Church Path
Ham Lane
Mead Run
Pound
Cross (remains of)
Middle Farm
Redlands
Hurst
Hurst Drove
Shooting Lakes
Dundon Moor
Middle Drove
Short Drove
Upper Hayes Farm
Lower Hayes Farm
Stone
Tank
Hayes Lane
Hayes Lane Drove
South Moor
Peak Lane
Decoy Farm
Decoy Lane
Decoy Pool
Redland Lake
North Moor
Etsome Rhyne
Lugshorn
Somerton Gate
Dundon Drove
Main Rhyne
Touch Lane
Coalpit Lane
Allotments
Millway
Redland Lane
Redland Farm
Redland Cottage
Stepping Stone
Glastonbury 4¼ Somerton
Glastonbury Somerton
ROMAN VILLA (site of)
Bradley Spring
Co Const & UD

relation to the patterns described by the heavenly bodies in their seasonal cycles.

So the Glastonbury Zodiac was not unique as a pointer to the prehistoric existence of a precise observational science of the heavens, a science presumably linked up with a belief in its relevance for life on earth. But what was that relevance? At the moment we know very little about what life was like when the Glastonbury Zodiac was conceived. All we can say is it seems most unlikely that a people who possessed such a refined observational science, such sophisticated mathematical and geometrical expertise, and such engineering genius, were at the same time ignorant and superstitious barbarians, as the ancient inhabitants of Britain are popularly believed to have been.

Let us look more closely at Stonehenge, the huge stone monument in southern England, through the eyes of Gerald Hawkins, Professor of Astronomy at Boston University. In 1966 Hawkins published a book entitled *Stonehenge Decoded*. The title was perhaps ahead of itself, but Hawkins significantly contributed to our knowledge of Stonehenge. His findings corroborate those independently arrived at by Professor Thom and published in the following year.

Professor Hawkins' discoveries had an extra element of glamor and prestige in that they were obtained with the help of one of the marvels of modern technology, an IBM computer. The Stonehenge complex has 165 significant features consisting of stones, holes, and artificial mounds. From these features 27,060 possible alignments can be formed. The task programed into the computer by Hawkins and his assistants was to determine whether lines extended through significant Stonehenge alignments into space would coincide with significant positions of the heavenly bodies. Due allowance was made for the slight difference between what those positions are today and what they would have been in about 1500 B.C. The results were astonishing. Among the figures that the machine produced were some that occurred frequently. These were found to correspond to a fraction of a degree in accuracy with extreme positions that the sun and moon would have occupied in prehistoric times.

It is well known that on the day of the summer solstice an alignment taken from the "altar stone" to the "heel stone" at Stonehenge will pinpoint the position of the sunrise, and every year tourists gather to witness the phenomenon. What is not so well known is that no less than 12 significant extreme positions of the sun, and 12 of the moon, are accurately pinpointed by Stonehenge alignments. The astronomical, geometrical, and engineering ingenuity involved in establishing and preserving these alignments is astonishing enough in itself. It is even more so when it is considered that the Stonehenge complex was developed in three distinct stages over three centuries, and the later engineers and builders managed to place their stones so skillfully that the alignments established in the original structure were never obscured.

According to Professor Hawkins, who was supported by the famous British astronomer Professor Fred Hoyle, Stonehenge was a gigantic and complex astronomical clock with a built-in

Constellation – or Coincidence?

Opposite: the figure of Aquarius in the Glastonbury Zodiac as it appears on an official Ordnance Survey map. Mrs. K. E. Maltwood, modern rediscoverer of the Glastonbury Zodiac, wrote that it is much easier to follow the figures on these maps than to try to pick them out from the top of Glastonbury Tor, for woods, roads, and modern buildings make them difficult to follow. Half the outlines of seven giant figures are drawn by natural water courses, she says, and can be taken as an indication that "Mother Earth first suggested the design." Skeptics point out that although she discarded many features as being of modern origin she included others, still more modern, which substantiated and rounded out her theory of design.

Below: the constellation of Aquarius according to Mrs. K. E. Maltwood's Glastonbury theory.

Stonehenge as a Computer

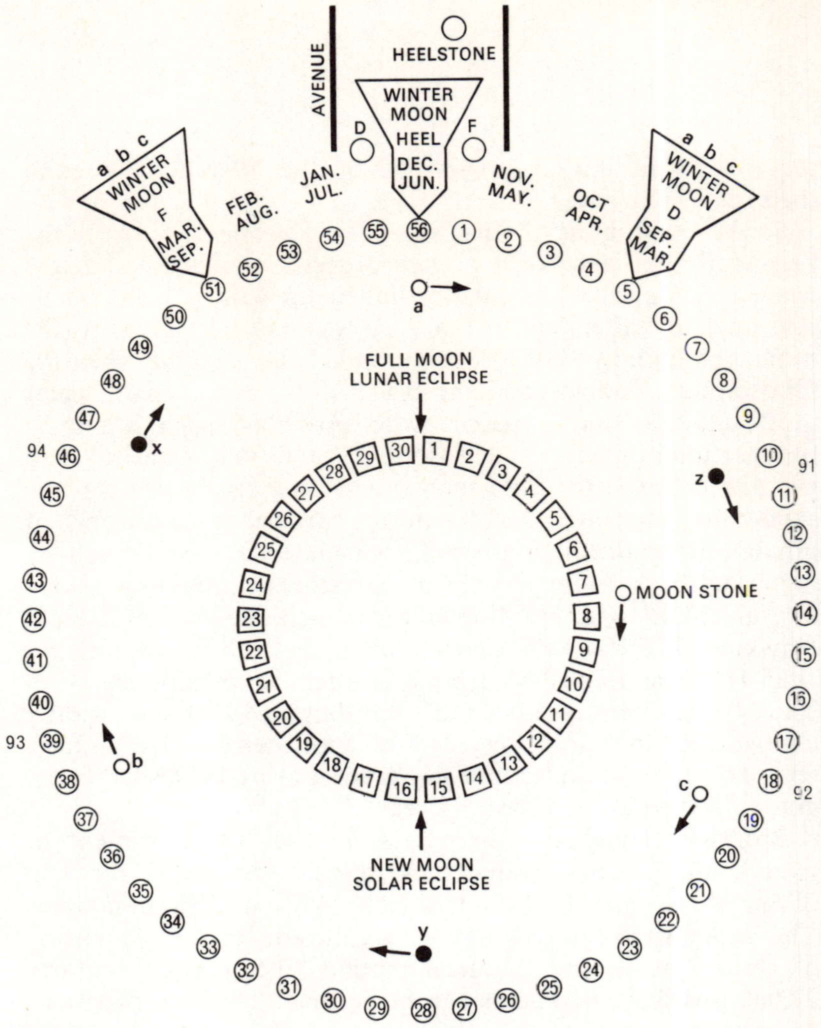

Right: Stonehenge as a computer—schematic plan by Gerald Hawkins. According to Hawkins, one method for operating the computer is to place three white stones (a, b, c) in holes numbered 56, 38, and 19; place three black stones (x, y, z) in holes 47, 28, and 10; and then move each stone one place around the circle each year. He suggests this be done at the winter or summer solstice. He points out that this will then predict every important lunar event for hundreds of years. For example, when any stone is at hole 56, the full moon will rise over the heel stone at the winter solstice. It can also be used to predict eclipses of the sun or the moon.

computer capable of accurately predicting lunar eclipses. This was achieved by the positioning of six stones, three black ones and three white ones, in the 56 holes now known as the Aubrey holes and dug by the first builders of Stonehenge. But why should succeeding generations of brilliant mathematicians and engineers over a period of 300 years have bent all their efforts on the task of constructing an astronomical clock? Various tentative suggestions have been put forward. One is that the astronomical clock served the need of a farming community to determine the right time for the planting of crops. Another is that it served to maintain and enhance the power of a dominant priesthood over an ignorant and subdued populace. A third is that it was an intellectual exercise engaged in by men seeking ever more complex mathematical and engineering problems to test their powers.

A still different explanation is given by the best-selling English author John Michell. In *The View over Atlantis* published in 1969, and *City of Revelation* published in 1972, he has developed a theory that the Temple of Jerusalem, the Great Pyramid, Stonehenge, and Glastonbury all incorporate the same principles and proportions in their construction, and that these and other structures throughout the world are evidence of the existence of a worldwide prehistoric civilization. In that civilization according to Michell, religion, magic, astronomy, and a technology that he calls "sonic engineering" belonged together in a grand design that harmoniously united

Above: for the tourist Stonehenge appears abruptly, an improbable circle of massive stones set in the midst of the calm English farming country. For scientists like Hawkins, Stonehenge is not a peculiar heap of stones but a precise instrument that can be readily and accurately deciphered.

the heavens and the earth, humankind and Nature. Michell reads the riddles of the stones as clues that could lead to the recovery of the lost arts and sciences of the bygone Golden Age he described.

Basing his ideas on numerology and gematria, Michell puts forward the suggestion that both Stonehenge and Glastonbury were structures designed with incredible subtlety on principles accredited to traditional magic for the purpose of collecting, storing, and transmitting solar energy. He quotes the work of a Scottish psychic, Foster Forbes, who visited numerous prehistoric sites to try to describe their history and meaning through his sense of touch. The ability to do this is called psychometry, and its existence is scientifically acknowledged. In 1938 Forbes published the book *The Unchronicled Past*. In it he asserted that stone circles were erected "not only in conjunction with astronomical observation by the advanced priesthood"—a discovery later confirmed by both Thom and Hawkins—"but that the actual sites should serve in some measure as receiving stations for direct influences from heavenly constellations that were known and appreciated by the priesthood—especially at certain seasons of the year." This view immediately brings us back from cautious, rational speculation based on known scientific principles to magic, to the hermetic idea of "as above, so below," to Marsilio Ficino's idea of the *spiritus mundi*, and even to gematria and numerology.

One of the more arcane traditions of number magic is that there is associated with each planet a numerological magic square, which is the key to the control of the planet's influence and power. The magic squares were believed to express mathematically the motions of the planetary orbits, and to contain a formulation of a pattern of natural growth. For example, the magic square of the sun consists of 36 figures and is as follows:

6	32	3	34	35	1
7	11	27	28	8	30
19	14	16	15	23	24
18	20	22	21	17	13
25	29	10	9	26	12
36	5	33	4	2	31

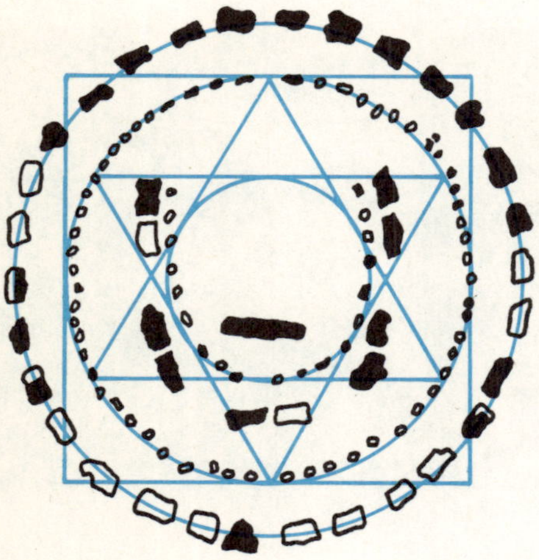

Above: the cosmic temple of Stonehenge by John Michell. Again the figure of St. John's New Jerusalem is superimposed over the reconstructed ground plan of Stonehenge. As the Jerusalem square and the outer circle have exactly the same perimeter (316.8 feet), and the inner square exactly contains the bluestone circle, "The New Jerusalem is Stonehenge with the circle squared," Michell writes.

This may look like a random jumble of figures, but a closer study will reveal that if one figure were altered, or if two were made to change places the symmetry of the whole square would collapse. Add together any row, column, or diagonal: the total is always 111. Add together the corner numbers of the square, 6, 1, 36, 31: they total 74. Move inward toward the center and add the corner numbers of the smaller square formed by 11, 8, 29, 26: again the total is 74. Add the total of the four numbers at the very center, 16, 15, 22, 21: it is also 74. Add together the numbers around the perimeter: the total is 370. The total sum of all the 36 numbers in the square is 666.

From this are drawn the potent magical numbers of the sun: 36, 111, 74, 370, and 666. Whole multiples of the magic numbers are taken to be as potent as the numbers themselves. According to Michell's analysis Stonehenge was laid out on a plan that incorporated these numbers, so functioning as a magical instrument for the control of solar power. The perimeter of the circular earthwork surrounding Stonehenge measures 370 MY. A hexagon drawn within this circle has an area of 66,000 square feet or 7400 square yards. The circle formed by the Aubrey holes has an area of 6660 square yards. A line drawn through the center of the inner ring would form the axis of two intersecting circles of 666 feet circumference, or alternatively a side of an equilateral triangle of area 44,400 feet (6 times 7400). The bluestone circle has an area of 666 square MY. Furthermore, if two triangles are placed within the circle of the outer earthwork in the form of Solomon's seal—that is, overlapping to form a six-sided star—each of their sides will measure 3330 inches (half of 6660 and 3 times 1110) or 277.5 feet. This latter number is held to be significant because 2775 is the sum of all the numbers from 1 to 74, and 277.5 is also the radius of a circle with a circumference of 1746. This number, 1746, is "the cabalistic number of fusion," and Stonehenge, according to this theory, was constructed in order to bring about a fusion of solar and terrestrial forces.

Assuming that Michell's measurements are accurate, the mathematic and geometric calculations based on them can be checked and found to be correct. A valid objection might be made that Michell proves his point by skipping from one unit of measurement to another, using the inch, the foot, the yard, and the MY to suit his purpose. But let us suspend skepticism for the time being and follow his argument further.

Glastonbury, according to Michell, was also designed on a pattern dictated by the principal numbers of the magic square of the sun. The authority for this information is none other than the controversial Bligh Bond, cabalist and former architect in charge of work on the abbey ruins. Bligh Bond laid out a ground plan of the abbey in the form of a rectangular grid of 36 squares, 36 figures comprising the square of the sun. A side of each of these squares measures 74 feet or 888 inches, and the whole rectangle measures 666 feet by 296 feet (4 times 74). The area of each of the 36 squares is 74 square MY, and the area of the whole rectangle is 26,640 square MY (666 times 40) or, to bring in another of the units of measurement of antiquity, 666,000 square cubits (1 cubit = 1.72 feet).

According to these calculations it appears that Glastonbury was founded on identical principles to those employed by the people who built Stonehenge between 1500 and 2000 years before the first Christian church was erected. The theory is that Glastonbury was conceived not only as a place of Christian worship, but also like Stonehenge to attract solar energy.

There might seem to be a contradiction in the idea that prehistoric man and the early Christian saints applied the same principles of building, but John Michell believes that early Christianity embraced a magical tradition based on numerology and "sacred geometry" which had been handed down from remotest antiquity. Furthermore, the tradition survived into the Middle Ages, and Gothic cathedrals all over Europe were expressly designed on magical principles to attract some specific celestial power. The ancient secrets were preserved by members of the medieval guilds, particularly the masons, and were applied without the consent or knowledge of the Church.

For good measure, Michell also demonstrates that the Great Pyramid was constructed according to an identical system and for a similar purpose as Stonehenge, but in relation to the planetary influence of mercury instead of the sun. This is how his theory emerges of an ancient worldwide civilization founded on a science that involved numbers, proportions, and a belief in the possibility and usefulness of focusing celestial forces and influences. The belief was carried out by means of stone structures arranged in certain patterns, and often situated in calculated relation to features in the surrounding landscape.

That isn't the whole story. In fact it is little more than half the story. The rest of it concerns terrestrial forces and influences as well.

Alfred Watkins and the Ley Lines

In the early 1920s a 65-year-old English merchant and amateur archeologist, Alfred Watkins, was out riding in the hills in his native Herefordshire. He pulled up in order to view the familiar landscape, and suddenly saw it as he had never seen it before, criss-crossed by straight lines that intersected at churches and at points marked by ancient stones. It was a visionary experience and, as often happens with sudden revelations, it determined the course of the rest of his life's work. He was convinced that he had seen in a flash the landscape of ancient Britain, a landscape covered with a vast network of straight tracks, many of them aligned either with the sun or with the path of a star. He called this network the "ley system."

Working on a special ordnance survey map, Watkins confirmed his vision. He found that straight lines extending many miles could be drawn to pass directly through churches, ancient sites, and man-made landmarks. It seems that for some reason not yet understood by us, but possibly for trade, straight roads were planned long before the Romans. However, because many of these tracks pass through difficult countryside with no attempt to skirt lakes, bogs, or mountains, one is tempted to think there is a deeper significance to them than a system of trade routes. The routes are marked by man-made landmarks such as cairns built on mountain slopes or notches cut in ridges, and various ancient sites.

Watkins was ridiculed for his theory because the prevailing

Below: Alfred Watkins was a retired English businessman who had a sudden vision in which the countryside was crossed by a system of lines linking ancient sites. He called them ley lines.

The Old Straight Tracks

Alfred Watkins was a down-to-earth businessman. He had lived his entire life in Herefordshire, England, as generations of his ancestors had before him. He was more familiar than most with the look of the land around him, for he had spent his working life as a representative for a brewery, traveling from village to village and town to town in his daily work. One day as he was riding across the hills, he pulled up his horse to look out over the familiar landscape stretched out below him. Suddenly, in a vision like a lightning flash, he saw a network of lines standing out like brightly glowing wires across the surface of the countryside. They met at the sites of churches, ancient stones, and castles. Watkins embarked upon an intensive study of the line system. He found that ancient sites throughout the countryside could be connected on Ordnance Survey maps by absolutely straight lines. He named them "ley" lines because many ancient places with names ending in -ley, -ly, and -leigh were found along these straight tracks. For the rest of his life he maintained that his first unexpected glimpse of the line network had been complete and accurate. His studies only verified his vision.

Above: the Long Man of Wilmington, a figure that appears in the chalky white ground when the turf is cut away. It is in Sussex, England where the hills, called "downs," are of chalk composition. Watkins believed that the staves held by the Long Man were for surveying. It is thought that this figure dates from pre-Roman times.

version of ancient history at that time was that prehistoric Britons were little more than painted savages. But he stuck to his view and amassed a great deal of evidence which he published in 1925 in *The Old Straight Track*. Gradually other antiquarians became convinced, and began to investigate too.

One of these was Guy Underwood, another amateur archeologist who learned dowsing, or water divining, in order to carry out his investigations. His research with his divining rod took him to old churches and ancient sites of traditional sanctity all over the country. He found that at the center of every circle of stones, and at a key point in every church he examined, there was an underground source of energy. A number of water lines converged in a radiating pattern to this spot. He called the spot a "blind spring." But he also found two other underground lines of force, not necessarily connected with the water line, which responded to the divining rod. One of these lines, which he called an "aquastat," seemed in some way to govern the layout of religious monuments and determine the positioning of stones, ditches, or buildings. The other, which he called a "track line," seemed to govern the route of roads and tracks. Underwood called all these subterranean lines of force "geodetic" lines. He believed that the main use early man had made of them was to mark out and divide the surface of the Earth. His research led him to the conclusion that both prehistoric and medieval builders had placed sacred sites and aligned the buildings they erected on them in observance of geodetic laws. In other words, they knew of the existence of lines of force running through the earth and, in some way, they had attempted to harness them for beneficial ends. Incidentally, Underwood found that Watkins' surface leys were often paralleled beneath the surface of the earth by a line of force.

In his book *The Pattern of the Past*, published in 1969, Underwood writes ". . . the three geodetic lines, the water line, the aquastat, and the track line appear to have much in common: they appear to be generated within the Earth; to involve wave motion; to have great penetrative power; to form a network on the face of the Earth; to affect the germination and manner of growth of certain trees and plants; to be perceived and used by animals; to affect opposite sides of the animal body, and to form spiral patterns." From these observations he goes on to say that they seem to be controlled by mathematical laws that involve the number 3 in their construction and the number 7 in their spiral patterns. These two numbers have been accorded arcane meaning from the earliest times. Underwood sees these geodetic lines as manifestations of an Earth Force, an idea which was central to many ancient religions. Traces of this belief can still be found throughout the world today.

When the bustling, expansionist, industrialized civilization of Western Europe tried to carry its influence into China about a century ago, its pioneers suffered a great deal of frustration and exasperation. For example, a proposal to cut a railway tunnel through a hill would be met by a polite refusal from the Chinese authorities. Their explanation would be that that particular range of hills was a terrestrial dragon, and that to cut through its tail was forbidden. Proposed sites for factories were firmly rejected for reasons that seemed to Europeans equally superstitious and nonsensical. They had not understood that in China there was an ancient and important belief in lines of force, known as "dragon current," running all over the surface of the Earth. Before any building was erected, or any tree planted, an expert known as a geomancer had to be consulted as to how the current would be affected. The Chinese were amazed on their side that the technologically advanced Europeans had no conception of this venerable science.

As everything else in Chinese philosophy, the dragon current was divided into yin and yang. The yin, or female current, was supposed to flow along gentle undulating countryside, and the yang, or male force, through steep high peaks. The most favorable position was felt to be where the two currents of yin and yang met. This was therefore often selected by a geomancer as a site for a tomb because the Chinese believed that the influences surrounding their dead ancestors played a decisive role in the future of their family.

Geomancers interpreted the earth in terms of the sky, rather like the principle of "as above, so below" that recurs so many times in ancient philosophy and magic. Mountains were thought of as stars, and large rivers as the Milky Way. Each main dragon current had small tributaries or veins, and every small vein had its own astrological interpretation. Different parts of the Earth were thought to come under the influence of the different planets then known—Jupiter, Mars, Venus, Mercury, and Saturn. These planets in turn had correspondences with colors, materials, landscape characteristics, animals, parts of the body, and so on. Between the planets and the various correspondences was a complex system of harmony and discord. As John Michell writes in *The View over Atlantis:* ". . . Venus can go with Saturn but not with Mars. Thus a high rounded hill will harmonize with one with a flat top but not with a sharp mountain peak. The two could not therefore stand together. Where nature had

Long Men and White Horses

Below: an aerial view of Britain's most famous below-the-turf figure—the White Horse of Uffington. The green area is the chalk ground that, when the turf is cut away, appears as white both in actuality and in the photograph. It is 350 feet long, and on clear days is visible for 15–20 miles. There is an old superstition that a wish will come true if someone stands on the Horse's eye and turns around three times.

Mysteries Remain

placed two hills in discord, Chinese geomancers had the shape of one altered. The top of the peak would be cut off or the rounded hill sharpened with an earthwork or flattened into a high plateau. In this way the paths of the various influences across the country were visibly defined, the very bones of the landscape altered to reflect the celestial symmetry."

On the Nazca plains of Peru a remarkable network of straight lines, together with various figures of men, animals, and symbols, has been etched. The paths and figures were created by removing stones and pebbles to expose the dark earth beneath. It was first discovered by pilots flying over the region. One of the many interpretations is that they are sun paths, so arranged that a person moving along a certain path at the solstice or equinox would see the sun rising or setting on the horizon, straight ahead.

In the course of her travels in Tibet, Alexandra David-Neel saw several "lung-gom-pas runners." These men travel for days across the country without stopping, maintaining an extraordinary speed and proceeding by leaps so that they seem to rebound from the earth each time their feet touch it. They always pursue exactly straight tracks, even when these lead over mountains. Alexandra David-Neel supposed that the runners' strength must be the result of prolonged physical and spiritual training. No doubt this was a part of it, but the fact that they pursued straight tracks even when these led over difficult terrain suggests, in the light of what we now know, that they might have possessed the secret of harnessing the earth force. Really advanced lung-gom-pas, it is said, could glide through the air without ever touching the ground with their feet.

In other words they could fly. There are many legends of feats of magical flight performed by the ancient Britons. Bladud, an ancient magician said to fly using stones, crashed where St. Paul's Cathedral now stands in London. But another British magician, Abiris, is said to have flown all the way to Greece without mishap. Fairy tales? Perhaps. But John Michell has a theory about magical flight. He believes that flying on a stone or other conveyance was made possible by using the magnetic force of the leys, which harnessed celestial energy. Many of the mysterious buildings of antiquity, he believes—notably Stonehenge and the Pyramids—were constructed in order to effect this fusion of terrestrial and celestial forces. This is why the cabalistic number for fusion, 1746, is to be found in their proportions. Furthermore, the energies thus generated could be employed for numerous other purposes, especially the construction of the huge monuments that survive today.

Some would say that to speculate so wildly is irresponsible. But the mysteries remain. There is no doubt that the impressive achievements of our technological civilization have been bought at a price and have resulted in a loss of coordination between human beings and their environment. Both are in jeopardy today. Perhaps we should no longer dismiss the magical and psychic sciences of our remote forebears as nonsense and superstition. In the present plight of the world, perhaps we could do with a little magic—which might just be another name for a long-lost science.

Opposite: a long perfectly straight ley line cuts sharply through the English countryside. Could it possibly be purely chance, or is there a message waiting there from some dimly perceived figure in the past, just waiting for the clues to be properly read?

Chapter 8
What is Alchemy?

The picture of the alchemist as a half-mad charlatan is more myth than truth. In fact, alchemists regarded their search for the secret of making gold out of base metal as of secondary importance to their primary quest of attaining spiritual perfection. The process of transmuting ordinary metal into precious gold was merely the outward symbol of the inner transformation. Yet they searched long and hard for the mysterious Philosopher's Stone, which was essential for making gold and which was also a miracle cure. In doing so they established processes and created apparatus that led to modern chemistry.

It is late at night. In a room hidden away from prying eyes, an old man bends over a flask of bubbling colored liquid. All around is a clutter of jars, bottles, and apparatus that looks somewhat like the equipment in a modern school chemistry laboratory. The walls are hung with animal skulls and astrologers' charts. A stuffed owl sits amid a jumble of thick leather-bound books with iron clasps. From time to time he stirs the liquid, muttering strange words to himself. His fur-collared cloak is in tatters, and he shivers slightly from the chill draft leaking through a broken window. His supper, entirely forgotten and long cold, lies untouched on a nearby bench. Nothing disturbs his concentration as he patiently watches the liquid evaporate. Then disappointment clouds his face. Something has gone wrong. He pores over an old manuscript, puzzling at the strange language and symbols. With a sigh, he sets up some more apparatus. Perhaps a grain more of this and a grain less of that? His excitement returns. The years have slipped by unnoticed. His whole life has been dedicated to one task. He is determined to discover the secret of turning ordinary metals into gold.

Although there is some truth in this popular description of an alchemist, it is by no means the whole story. There is far more to alchemy than a desire to make gold, and serious alchemists were not crazy old men. They were often among the leading scientific and religious thinkers of their time.

The word *alchemy* is an Arabic one, but no one is wholly sure

Opposite: *Explosion in the Alchemist's Laboratory*, a painting that shows the dangerous result of a sudden and violent chemical reaction. The alchemist pursued his involved experiments, laying the foundations for the science, then still unborn, that we now know as chemistry. Often his experiments had unexpected results: sometimes a new element would be isolated, sometimes a mixture went up with a bang.

The Ancient Quest

where it came from. The most popular explanation is that it originally meant "the art of the land of Khem." *Khem* was the name the Arabs gave to Egypt, and it was from Egypt that they acquired their knowledge of this strange science, which they later transmitted to the West. Another possibility is that the word derives from the Greek *chymia*, which means the art of melting and alloying metals.

Alchemy is extremely complicated. It is based on the practical skills of early metalworkers and craftsmen, on Greek philosophy, and on Eastern mystic cults that sprang up in the first centuries after Christ and influenced so much of magic and occult thought. It must be remembered that when alchemy flourished there was no dividing line between science and magic. Ideas such as the influence of the planets and the effect of certain numbers or letters on people's lives might today be regarded as superstitions. At that time they were perfectly acceptable to those who were making the kind of accurate observations about the material world that paved the way for modern science.

Long before the beginning of alchemy gold was regarded as the most valuable metal. Its possession indicated wealth and power, and it was prized for its beauty. Known as the most perfect metal, it soon acquired symbolic meaning. It came to stand for excellence, wisdom, light, and perfection. For serious alchemists gold had both a real and a symbolic significance, which at first seems confusing. The reason is that alchemists embarked on two different and difficult quests at the same time, and success in one meant success in the other. The first aim is the one that most people know about. The alchemist was attempting to find a way of transmuting, or changing, ordinary metals into the most perfect metal, gold. The second aim is less well-known but was far more important. The alchemist was

Right: the Spanish mystic Ramón Lull, traditionally believed to have been an alchemist. Whereas the making of gold has been well remembered by posterity, the second, hidden part of the quest is mainly forgotten. The alchemist was also searching for a way to reach spiritual perfection, and believed that purifying base metals into the "perfect" metal, gold, was the outward symbol of transmutation of his soul from an ordinary state to a condition of union with God. In this illustration, Lull holds a newborn baby—the personification of the soul.

Above: the obvious goal of alchemy and the best-remembered one was the production of gold from base metal. Here in a 19th-century engraving, executed long after alchemy had lost its preeminent position as a respectable science, an alchemist displays a small nugget of gold to his patron.

trying to make the soul progress from its ordinary state to one of spiritual perfection.

For many centuries Western alchemists ceaselessly searched for the Philosopher's Stone. What was this elusive object? It was not some giant boulder on which ancient sages sat and meditated. Nor was it a closely guarded tablet inscribed with words of wisdom. It was a substance that alchemists were convinced they could make, with divine assistance, by subjecting certain raw materials to complex and lengthy chemical processes. The problem was to find the right raw materials and the correct chemical processes. It was a widely held belief that the Universe was permeated by a spirit that linked everything together. Alchemists thought that this spirit could somehow be reproduced and compressed into a magical substance which they named the Philosopher's Stone. Once discovered, a small quantity of this magical substance added to ordinary metal would change it into gold. Taken as a medicine, the Stone would act as a miraculous cure. It was even believed by some to confer immortality, and was often called the Elixir of Life.

All the patient experiments that alchemists carried out in their laboratories over the centuries were motivated by one overwhelming desire—to produce the Philosopher's Stone. In the

R.Lullo

course of their painstaking and dedicated work they established many important chemical facts which, even if they did not lead to the Philosopher's Stone, helped to form the basis of chemistry as we know it today.

The greatest alchemists were skilled in many fields. The scope of knowledge in those days was small enough that a person might hope to master all there was to know about subjects as diverse as medicine and religion, philosophy and alchemy, logic and magic. The seeker of knowledge would see nothing incompatible in the different fields of study. Magic would not conflict with medicine, or philosophy with religion. Knowledge was thought of as a unity, and all the different branches were different aspects of this unity. They all led toward a greater understanding of the Universe.

The greatest Arab alchemist, Jabir, who lived from about A.D. 722 to 815, was a widely read scholar who wrote treatises on an enormous variety of subjects including geometry, poetry, magic squares, and logic. Although his main concern as an alchemist was discovering how to convert ordinary metals to gold, he also recorded many important chemical observations, and his design of apparatus led to the development of the modern still.

Al-Razi, the celebrated Persian alchemist and physician who lived from about A.D. 866 to 925, wrote books on medicine, natural science, mathematics, astronomy, logic, philosophy, and theology, as well as many works on alchemy. For the first time in the history of chemistry, facts about chemical substances,

Searching for the Elixir of Life

Opposite: *The Alchemists* by Pietro Longhi, painted about 1757. The alchemist on the right points to the Philosopher's Stone, the gold-colored magical liquid that could be produced only by a series of mysterious, intricate processes.

Left: *The Elixir of Life* by the 19th-century caricaturist Phiz. Medieval alchemists believed that the transmuting agent—the Philosopher's Stone—would also act as a universal cure if taken as a medicine, ending disease and old age by conferring immortality upon the fortunate beings who drank the magical and elusive substance.

reactions, and apparatus are carefully observed and verified in his books.

When we come to 13th-century Europe we find Albertus Magnus among a distinguished selection of alchemists. He was one of the greatest scholars and teachers of the Middle Ages, and as recently as 1932 was canonized as a Catholic saint. Among his many works were treatises on alchemy, and he was the first to describe the chemical composition of such substances as cinnabar, white lead, and minium.

Paracelsus was one of the most notable scientific figures of the 15th century. From his knowledge of alchemy he was able to introduce a whole new range of medicines for medical treatment. Until that time remedies had been almost exclusively herbal.

One of the greatest difficulties encountered in exploring the development of alchemy is that the books and manuscripts describing the substances to be used and the chemical processes to be followed were written in such obscure, symbolic language. They were often open to many different interpretations, and were puzzling even to an experienced alchemist. An ordinary reader would be floundering after the first sentence. Because the books that the alchemists consulted are incomprehensible to all but an initiated few, most of our knowledge of alchemy is based on legends of transmutations. Many of these have been handed down and greatly embroidered in the course of time. At this distance it is impossible to gauge how much truth there might

The Scholar Alchemist

Roger Bacon was a medieval scholar of wide learning. Although some of his supposed inventions have been shown to be purely legendary—he did not, for example, invent gunpowder—he was certainly well ahead of his time in many ways. Two of his suggestions that show his many-sided brilliance were that imperfect sight could be aided by using suitably shaped lenses, and that the globe could be circumnavigated. It was perhaps this gift of thinking beyond others of his time which led to the idea that Bacon was aided by the Devil, and because of his willingness to oppose many of the notions current at the time, he suffered persecution.

In his alchemical work Bacon distinguished between theoretical alchemy and practical alchemy. He believed practical alchemy superior to other sciences, and more likely to produce material advantages. Like the other medieval thinkers, he thought experiments did not provide a basis for inferring general laws, but only gave confirmation of conclusions that are reached by deduction from already accepted general principles.

In this respect, Bacon was a man of his time. That reasoning lies behind much of the traditional alchemical work.

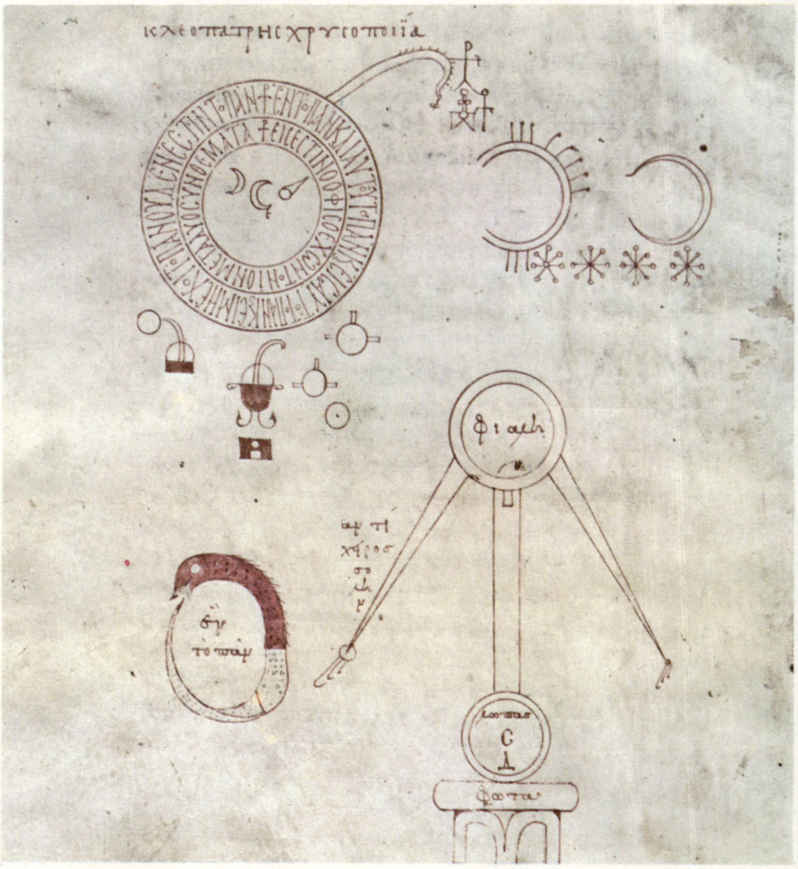

Right: even Cleopatra was considered by tradition to have been an alchemist, as shown in this illustration of her gold-making process, from a Coptic manuscript of the 3rd century A.D. Part of the inscription reads, "One is All, and through it is All, and by it is All" and "if you have not All, All is nothing."

Far left: Albertus Magnus, 13th-century scholar and churchman. His alchemical writings show his interest in a field of study that during his lifetime was considered fully worthy of investigation by the best and most pious thinkers.

Below: Saint Thomas Aquinas, who died in 1274, was a pupil of Albertus Magnus, and like his master believed in the possibility of making gold alchemically. But he held that the occult operations of a celestial virtue were needed.

The Alchemists' Need for Secrecy

Below: a symbolic synthesis of the Great Work, from a 17th-century French alchemical manuscript. The central figure is probably Nature, or Flora, uniting the powers of darkness and light (indicated by the dresses). The alchemist is sitting to the left under the tree with his scale beside him. The faces in the hollow tree behind him are probably past alchemists, whose accumulated wisdom helps him in his quest. The difficulty that the reader encounters in trying to unravel the symbolism of alchemy is largely intentional: it was meant to be obscure, to be deciphered only by those who had "eyes to see" and were capable of understanding the mystic message.

have been in these stories, and how much trickery. However, there are some accounts that appear convincing. These are ones in which the narrator has an established professional reputation and little to gain from deceiving others. One such man was the well-known Dutch physician Johann Friedrich Schweitzer, who lived in the 17th century.

Schweitzer, who was born in 1625, was a distinguished doctor. He numbered Prince William of Orange, the future King of England, among his patients. In the fashion of his day, he was generally known by the Latin version of his name, Helvetius. In 1666 when he was 41 years of age, Helvetius received a strange Christmas present: the ability to turn lead into gold. He later wrote down an account of what happened. On December 27, in the late afternoon, a stranger came to his house. He described him as being "of a mean stature, a little long face, with a few small pock holes, and most black hair, not at all curled, a beardless chin, about three or four and forty years of age (as I guessed) and born in North Holland." The stranger told Helvetius that he had read several of his pamphlets, and in particular one that was highly critical of an English experimenter who had claimed to have invented a universal medicine. Did

Left: the alchemist Leonhard Thurneysser being visited in his laboratory by his patron, the Elector Johann Georg. Fraud was hardly an unknown in alchemical circles, and Thurneysser had an interesting line of trickery. He would take an iron nail and offer to transmute half of it to gold. He dipped the nail into an oily liquid, and presto! as he withdrew it, half of it was golden. The secret was simply to start with a nail that was already half iron and half gold, paint it black, and then dip it into a solvent. The paint dissolved, and the rapt audience saw the "transmutation."

Above: the need—as alchemists saw it—to conceal their arts from all but each other led to a weird literature in which fantastic creatures were used as symbols only intelligible to the initiated. In this manuscript of 1572 a dragon resuscitated after death stands for one specific process.

Helvetius think, asked the stranger, that it was impossible?

The two argued in a friendly fashion for some time. Then the stranger took out of his inner pocket a carved ivory box and showed Helvetius its contents—three heavy pieces of stone "each about the bigness of a small walnut, transparent, of a pale brimstone color." This, said he, was enough to turn some 20 tons of lead into gold. Helvetius handled a piece greedily, and begged the stranger to give him just a little. When the stranger told him that this was impossible, he contrived to scrape a speck under his fingernail surreptitiously.

After telling Helvetius how he himself had learned the art, the stranger demonstrated "some curious arts in the fire," and

A True Story of Transmutation?

Below: Johann Schweitzer, known as Helvetius. He was a well-respected doctor of medicine, the physician to the Prince of Orange. His account of a transmutation is still one of the most circumstantial and puzzling alchemical reports, with apparently little opportunity and no motive for fraud.

promised to return in three weeks' time. As soon as he was gone, Helvetius excitedly got out a crucible and melted some lead in it. When he added the tiny crumb of stone, however, "almost the whole mass of lead flew away," leaving only a dull residue.

The physician impatiently awaited the return of the stranger, more than half convinced that he would not come again; but in three weeks exactly the man of mystery once more came to his house. "But," said Helvetius, "he was very sparing in speaking of the great elixir, gravely asserting, that was only to magnify the sweet fame of the most glorious God." Again the physician begged him for some of the stone, and at last the stranger relented. According to Helvetius: "He gave me a crumb as big as a rape or turnip seed, saying, receive this small parcel of the greatest treasure in the world, which truly few kings or princes have ever known or seen." Ungratefully Helvetius protested that this was hardly enough to transmute four grains of lead, whereupon the stranger took it back, divided it in half, and flung half in the fire saying, "It is yet sufficient for thee."

Helvetius confessed his former theft, and recounted his lack of success. The stranger laughed and said: "Thou art more dextrous to commit theft, than to apply thy Tincture; for if thou hadst only wrapped up thy stolen prey in yellow wax, to preserve it from the arising fumes of lead, it would have penetrated to the bottom of the lead, and transmuted it to gold." He promised to come again the next morning at nine to show Helvetius the proper procedure.

"But the next day he came not, nor ever since; only he sent an excuse at half an hour past nine that morning, by reason of his great business, and promised to come at three in the afternoon, but never came, nor have I heard of him since; whereupon I began to doubt of the whole matter. Nevertheless late that night my wife . . . came soliciting and vexing me to make experiment of that little spark of his bounty in that art, whereby to be more assured of the truth; saying to me, unless this be done, I shall have no rest nor sleep all this night . . . She being so earnest, I commanded a fire to be made (thinking alas) now is this man (though so divine in discourse) found guilty of falsehood . . . My wife wrapped the said matter in wax, and I cut half an ounce or six drams of old lead, and put it into a crucible in the fire, which being melted, my wife put in the said Medicine made up into a small pill or button, which presently made such a hissing and bubbling in its perfect operation, that within a quarter of an hour all the mass of lead was totally transmuted into the best and finest gold . . ."

The philosopher Spinoza, who lived nearby, came to examine the gold, and was convinced of the truth of Helvetius' story. The Assay Master of the province, a certain Mr. Porelius, tested the metal and pronounced it genuine.

What Helvetius implied in his story was that the strange visitor was an alchemist who had given him some of the Philosopher's Stone. Although we may find the idea incredible, and wonder whether Helvetius was the perpetrator of a giant hoax, none of his contemporaries saw it in that light. To them, alchemy was perfectly acceptable, and they saw no reason to doubt Helvetius' integrity.

Left: illustration from *Ordinall of Alchimy*, a 15th-century text by Thomas Norton. (Bodleian Library, Oxford, MS Ashmole 971, f.14v). It shows a pupil learning the mysteries of alchemy from a master, which was the usual way of becoming an alchemist oneself. The experience of Helvetius was startlingly different: he achieved success in alchemy without going through a long apprenticeship, having gained special powers and knowledge from a strange visitor.

What would an alchemist's laboratory have looked like at the time of Helvetius? We can gain a good idea from the many 16th- and 17th-century engravings and paintings of the subject. The walls of the room would probably be covered with strange symbols and alchemical inscriptions in Latin, Greek, Hebrew, or Arabic. Animal skeletons and bunches of medicinal herbs might hang from the ceiling. The tables would be piled high with books and parchments, jostling for space with retorts and crucibles and the odd human skull. There would be several different furnaces to provide different heats, and a bellows to fan the flames. There might be a glass mask for protecting the face, and there would be shelves filled with numerous jars, stills, and tripods. Of course, for the true alchemist, an altar for prayer and meditation was an essential feature. The room would probably be tucked away somewhere in the cellar or attic, where a gleam of light showing late at night would not attract too much attention. Alchemists were always anxious to preserve secrecy about their work. If too many people knew about their activities they might be persecuted by the Church for their strange beliefs, or hounded by greedy

IOÁNES
STRATENSÍS
FLANDRVS
1570

people hoping to amass a fortune.

Alchemists used a bewildering variety of ingredients in their search for the Philosopher's Stone. Copper and lead, sulfur and arsenic, urine and bile were but a few of them. Substances were combined and separated, heated and cooled, vaporized and solidified, and sometimes even just left to rot. The processes carried out in the laboratory were often fairly complex. Calcination, sublimation, and distillation are three of the better known ones. In *calcination* metals and minerals were reduced to a fine powder. In *sublimation* a substance was heated until it vaporized, and then returned to its solid state by rapidly cooling the vapor. In *distillation* a liquid was converted into a vapor by boiling, and then condensed back into a liquid by cooling. These and many of the other processes required heat, so furnaces were the most important equipment in the alchemist's laboratory.

Because the alchemist needed many different intensities of heat for his various operations, he had to have many furnaces of different sizes. Regulating heat was always a great problem. Thomas Norton, an English alchemist of the 15th century, is said to have invented dampers to regulate the heat of the furnace.

The fire of the furnace, which might be fueled with anything from charcoal and peat to rushes and animal dung, needed constant attention. Many alchemists believed that transmutation would be easier if very high temperatures could be obtained. They used the bellows to such an extent that they earned the nickname of "puffer." Now this term is used more appropriately to describe those who were searching only for gold, and not the true alchemist who also aimed at spiritual perfection.

Many chemical treatises give instructions on the use of different kinds of furnaces. Besides the calcinatory furnaces for reducing metals and minerals to a fine powder, there was the *athanor*. This contained a deep pan of sifted ashes. The material to be heated was placed in a firmly sealed container and covered with the ashes. This method is rather like a modern chemist's sand bath. Then there was the *descensory furnace*, which had a funnel with a lid. Liquid could flow down the stem of the funnel into a receptacle. Another sort of furnace was known as the *dissolving furnace*. It consisted of a small furnace supporting a pan full of water. In the pan were rings to hold glass containers. It resembles a modern water bath, and is thought to have been invented by a woman alchemist who lived some time in the early centuries after Christ. She is a shadowy figure who appears in much of the mystical alchemical literature, and is known as Mary the Prophetess. She is also sometimes wrongly referred to as the sister of Moses. The French water bath or *bain-marie* is named after her.

Distillation was an important process in alchemy, and required a large number of different stills. The earliest stills were fairly simple. They consisted of a flask containing the substance to be distilled, a lid or still head, and a delivery spout leading to another flask that would receive the distilled liquid. The Arabs greatly improved methods of distillation. The word *alembic*, which we use today for part of a still, derives from the Arabic. The Arabs perfected the art of distilling the essence of flowers, fruit, and leaves. The invention of more complex stills in the

Alchemists at Work

Opposite: a 16th-century alchemist at work as depicted by the Flemish artist Jan van der Straet. The scene shows a laboratory of the kind that Helvetius would have recognized, with the furnaces blazing and the assistants hard at work with a variety of elaborate and specialized bits of equipment.

Furnaces and Water Baths

12th and 13th centuries, which included cooling mechanisms, led to the distillation of comparatively pure alcohol, and the discovery of many new substances.

Alchemists subscribed to one strange belief that made their tasks even more time consuming. Even when they thought that they had found the right substance and the right method of treating it for any stage in their experiment, they were convinced that they must submit the same substance to the same process over and over again. A special still, known as a *pelican*, was especially useful in this respect because it enabled a substance that had been distilled to be returned to its residue, and then to be redistilled as often as the alchemist desired. In some cases this was hundreds of times.

One of the oddest named pieces of equipment was the *Philosopher's Egg*. It was a *retort*—that is, a vessel into which substances are distilled—but an especially important one. The alchemist hoped that it would eventually contain the substance that constituted the Philosopher's Stone. It could then be said,

Below: an alchemist's oven or athanor, from a fresco executed about 1400. The alchemist's furnace was the most important piece of equipment, for exact degrees of heat were considered crucial for the stages of transmutation.

Left: the alchemist's water bath or *bain-marie*, a woodcut of 1519. The substances in the glass vessels suspended in the water were warmed only gradually by the furnace below the bath.

Left: Mary the Prophetess, also known as Mary the Jewess, an early female alchemist who was credited with the invention of the water bath that still carries her name. Traditionally she was believed to be Miriam, the sister of Moses. This stylized portrait was published in the 17th century.

The Elaborate Equipment

Right: frontispiece of a treatise by Johann Rudolf Glauber, an alchemist who is now recognized as the greatest practitioner of practical chemistry of the 17th century. It shows a furnace with its parts, used for distillation.

A. the furnace itself, with an iron distilling vessel inside, fastened to a globular vessel that received the distillate.
B. the alchemist taking off the lid of the distilling vessel in order to spoon in some material.
C. the distilling vessel itself.
D. a cutaway view of the distilling vessel.
E. a second distilling vessel, not incorporated within a furnace.

Below: the Neapolitan alchemist Giambattiste della Porta, writing in the late 16th century, came up with the interesting theory that the maker of alchemical equipment should consider nature, "who hath given angry and furious creatures as the lion and bear thick bodies and short necks." Thus vessels to contain materials "of a flatulent nature and vaporous" should be large and low. Delicate spirits, however, should be drawn through long slender necks, like the ostrich—"gentle creatures and of thin spirits."

in the strange allegorical language of alchemy that so often mixed the symbolic and the mundane, that the Stone had hatched from the Egg.

An alchemist's laboratory was a fascinating place, and alchemy exercised a hold over a wide range of people from learned religious and scientific thinkers to humble smiths and tinkers. Even reigning monarchs could be included among its practitioners. Charles II of England, who might be thought to have been fully occupied with foreign and domestic affairs, had a laboratory constructed under the royal bedchamber. Access was by a private staircase. Herakleios I, the 7th-century emperor of Byzantium, neglected his duties in later years to pursue his studies of alchemy. And Rudolf II, who was Holy Roman Emperor from 1576 to 1611, was financially ruined by his expenditures on astrology and alchemy.

Why was alchemy such a compelling subject? At first sight it seems to be an odd blend of the bizarre and the practical. The stories of transmutations are incredible, bordering on fairy tales, but the equipment that the alchemist used in his laboratory was technically advanced for its time. Why were such sophisticated scientific methods used in the pursuit of such mystical ideas? What were the beliefs that lay behind this occult science?

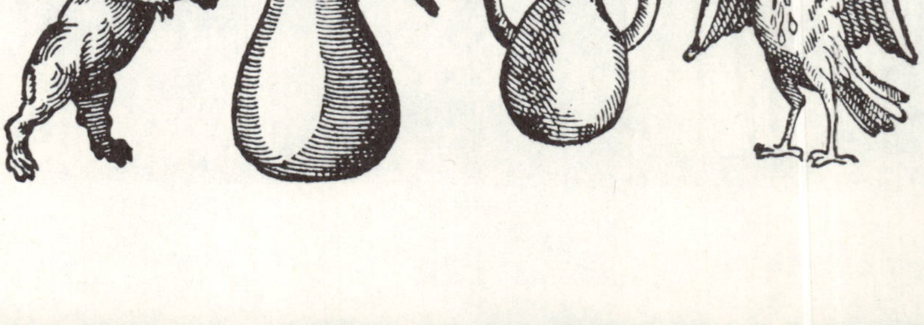

Other apparatus based on animal shapes and characters were (left to right): a sturdy alembic, part of distilling equipment, likened to an aggressively prancing bear; the pelican, with two necks for continuous distillation, named after the bird; the retort, another long-necked piece of equipment, likened to a kind of wild goose.

Above: *The Alchemist's Experiment Takes Fire*, by the 17th-century Dutch artist Hendrick Heerschop, shows a scene that was probably far from uncommon since alchemists worked with processes and materials whose explosive potential was only partially understood.

Chapter 9
The Principles of Alchemy

What is the connection between the great Greek philosopher Aristotle and the occult practice of alchemy? Why were so many of the ancient alchemists also astrologers? What are the differences between Chinese and Western alchemy? Alchemical theories, processes, and equipment go far back in time, and have been virtually unchanged through the years. Yet much of the apparatus of alchemy is as modern today as when it was developed, especially by the Arabs from the 7th to the 12th centuries. Is it possible that the principles and theories of this ancient science also have a modern application?

Prince Khalid ibn Yazid lived in Damascus in the 7th century A.D. Although he was the rightful caliph, he had been so sickened by political intrigue that he had retired from court and devoted his life to a study of alchemy. One day a manuscript that was supposed to contain the secrets of the Philosopher's Stone fell into his hands. Khalid studied it long and carefully, but was unable to understand it. He offered a magnificent reward to anyone who could solve the riddle of the manuscript and perform a successful transmutation.

Charlatans and rogues flocked to the Prince's house in Damascus. They ate his food and spent his money and not one of them made the least progress in interpreting the manuscript. At that time Morienus, a true alchemist, was living a simple life as a hermit in Jerusalem. When he heard how the Prince was being deceived he was determined to visit him. He hoped not only to enlighten Khalid about alchemy, but also to convert him to Christianity. The Prince received him warmly and gave him a house and equipment for his work. In a fairly short time Morienus succeeded in producing the magic substance. He presented it to the Prince in a vase inscribed with the words "He who possesses this has no need of others." Khalid was overjoyed and ordered the immediate execution of all the false alchemists. In the ensuing commotion Morienus disappeared, and Khalid found that although he had the Philosopher's Stone, he had no idea how to use it. His servants searched far and wide, and eventually traced Morienus to his hermitage in Jerusalem. He returned to the palace of the Prince and initiated him into the secrets of alchemy. Khalid preserved what he had learned in a series of alchemical poems known as *The Book of Amulets*, *The Great and Small Books of the Scroll*, and *The Paradise of Wisdom*.

Opposite: page from an 18th-century Arab alchemical manuscript. The two large figures represent the sun and the moon, and the small figures between them probably represent metals. The inscription below explains that substances in balance are stable; only those not in balance will undergo change.

Aristotle and "Prime Matter"

The story of Morienus is told in the first alchemy text that appeared in medieval Europe. This was the *Book of the Composition of Alchemy*, which was translated from Arabic into Latin in 1144 by an Englishman known as Robert of Chester.

It had been because of the Arab interest in learning that many Greek writings, including those on alchemy, were preserved. Within a century of the death of Muhammad, founder of Islam, the Arab empire reached from the Pyrenees to the Indus and incorporated hundreds of different tribes and races. Arabic had been made the official language, and all learned books were either translated into Arabic or written in Arabic. The city of Alexandria, an ancient Greek center of learning, had been conquered by the Arabs in A.D. 641. Its enormous library had already been partly destroyed. The Arabs eagerly seized what was left and later sent many of the books to Baghdad. In this way Arabic translations of Greek philosophers found their way all over the Arabic world, while for over 500 years the writings of the Greeks were almost unknown in Western Europe.

One of the most influential writers whose work was rediscovered in the library in Alexandria was Aristotle. His ideas had

Above: Jabir ibn Hayyan, most famous of the Arab alchemists. The Arabs, who preserved so much of the classical Western tradition while Europe was mired in the economic and social disasters of the Dark Ages, included alchemy among sciences that they studied.

Right: a learned discussion in an Arab library. It was in libraries like this that the knowledge of the Greek philosophers was preserved during the long years when learning in Europe languished. This manuscript illustration dates from 1237, when Western learning lived only in a few monasteries.

Above: soldiers of the Roman emperor Diocletian burning Egyptian alchemical books about A.D. 290. Apparently some alchemists who had mastered the art of preparing alloys that resembled gold and silver were passing off their good imitations as genuine metals. To end the nuisance, Diocletian ordered all the ancient books "which treated of the admirable art of making gold and silver" to be burned. As a result, we now have only a very few Egyptian technical manuscripts—those saved from the flames by chance. Two show clearly that the Egyptians were expert in metallurgy, which was a secret craft controlled by their powerful priesthood.

a particular influence on the development of alchemy. According to Aristotle, the basis of the entire material world was something that he called *prime* or *first matter*. This was not, as it may sound, some gray sludge from which the world gradually evolved. In fact, it was not a substance one could see or touch. It had no physical existence on its own account. However, it was the one unchangeable reality behind the ever-changing material world. To give this matter a physical identity and individual characteristics, various stages of *form* were needed.

The first stage of form, Aristotle believed, was found in the four elements of Earth, Air, Fire, and Water. The elements, while distinguished from each other, are also related by four qualities. These qualities are dry, moist, hot, and cold. Each element possesses two qualities, of which one predominates, and each element is linked to two other elements by the quality they possess in common. Here is how this system applies:

Fire is hot and dry with heat predominating.

Air is hot and moist with moistness predominating.

Water is moist and cold with cold predominating.

Earth is cold and dry with dryness predominating.

The diagram on page 160 shows the complex interrelationship of these qualities more clearly.

The main interest of Aristotle's theory of the elements from the point of view of alchemy is the idea of change. According to his theory each element can be transformed into another element through the quality they possess in common. In this way Fire can become Air through the action of heat; Air can become Water through the action of moistness; Water can become

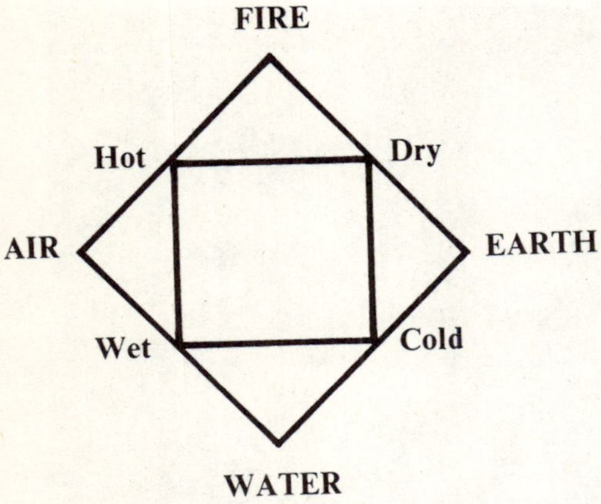

Above: the four elements and their qualities according to the theory of Aristotle, which formed the basis of the idea of transmutation—the changing of one element or material into another. The four elements were linked by the four qualities, each element possessing two qualities, both of which linked it to another element. This made it possible for it to change into either of them by the action of the quality that they shared between them.

Fire

Air

Water

Earth

Right: German medieval paintings of the four elements. These four elements also played a part in astrology, which was closely linked with alchemy at that time.

The Four Elements

Left: the four elements symbolized as an eagle (Earth), angel (Water), lion (Air), and bull (Fire), in a 17th-century German manuscript illustrating an alchemical poem. (Bodleian Library, Oxford, MS Add.A.287 f.23). In the multilayered fashion which was typical of alchemical writing and thought, these four symbols were also used to stand for the four evangelists. This connected the Aristotelian concepts into the fabric of the medieval Christian theology and provided yet another set of symbols for alchemists to use in their half-veiled explanations of the processes and materials they experimented with in their quest.

Earth through the action of coldness; and Earth can become Fire through the action of dryness. It is possible under this theory for an element gradually to complete the circle of change and go from Fire to Air, from Air to Water, from Water to Earth, and from Earth back to Fire, for example. It must be remembered that in all these changes the prime matter behind the form always remains the same.

The next stage of form in Aristotle's theory was that all physical manifestations in the world are composed of all four elements in different proportions. The varying amount of each element in the composition accounts for the infinite variety of things in the world. Because it was believed that elements could be transformed into other elements, it was only a small step to the assumption that all substances could be changed by altering the proportions of elements that constitute them. It is easy to see how alchemists took up this idea. If, as they believed, lead and gold both consisted of different proportions of the same four elements, what was there to prevent the one being transformed into the other?

Aristotle had another theory that influenced the ideas of alchemists. This was on the formation of metals and minerals. He believed that when the Sun's rays fell on water, they produced a vaporous exhalation that was moist and cold. This exhalation became imprisoned in the dry earth, was compressed, and finally was converted to metal. All metals that are fusible or malleable, such as iron, copper, or gold, were, according to Aristotle, formed in this way. The formation of minerals, on the other hand, occurred when the Sun's rays fell on dry land. They produced a smoky exhalation that was hot and dry, and the action of the heat produced the minerals. In this category Aristotle included substances that cannot be melted, as well as substances such as sulfur.

The alchemists not only inherited Aristotle's attempts to explain the nature of the Universe, but were also greatly influenced by the elaborate astrological beliefs of the Ancient World. In fact, astrology and alchemy were so closely linked

Complex Symbols of the Alchemists

Right: an alchemical process being carried out with the moon in Aries, from a woodcut illustrating a German text of 1519. Alchemists believed that the planets had the power of maturing metals in the earth, and so had an influence on alchemical operations that aimed at transmutation. Since the seven planets were believed to be associated with the seven metals, "favorable" times for experiments came to be when the right planet would be in exactly the right position.

Opposite: the mountain of the Adepts, an illustration of an alchemical book published in Germany in 1654. The complex symbolism of the picture relates the four elements shown by their Latin names, with the union of the King and Queen—under the signs of the sun and moon and the crowned eagle, which symbolizes Mercury—achieved in the heart of the mountain after the seven alchemical steps, or processes. Up the sides of the mountain stand the personifications of the seven planets (which also symbolize the seven metals) under the sun signs, which are given with their alchemical symbols. The two adepts at the bottom seem to symbolize the two paths of enlightenment in alchemy. One, blindfolded, is seeking divine inspiration, and the other, who is apparently observing two rabbits, has chosen the path of nature, presumably experimentation.

that many practicing alchemists were also astrologers.

From earliest times men have looked to the skies for explanations of their own lives, and the idea of the influence of the planets was widespread. Gradually, over centuries, in places such as Mesopotamia and Greece, a complex astrological system was built up. Its ideas permeated all aspects of daily life.

The basis of astrology can be summed up in the phrase so often quoted in occult literature, and in particular in alchemy: "as above, so below." This meant that everything in the Universe, or Macrocosm, had its parallel in the earthly world, or Microcosm. Everything worked in an ordered harmonious system, and everything was permeated by a Universal Spirit. It was this Spirit, which held the secret of the Universe, that the alchemists were trying to capture and compress into the Philosopher's Stone.

The system of correspondences, or connections, between the seven planets known to the Ancient World and all aspects of life was also extremely important. Tangible objects such as metals, animals, and plants, concepts such as colors, and abstract ideas such as love and wisdom were accorded to different planets, among which the ancients included the Sun and Moon. For example, some of the correspondences of Venus were copper, the color green, the dove and the sparrow, and the power of love. Alchemists made great use of this system of correspondences. Knowledge of the mysterious links between different things under the protection of the same planet was considered invaluable in many experiments. It also provided a ready-made symbolism or code in which one name could be substituted for another. Alchemists delighted in shrouding their writings with mystery and obscurity because they were always afraid the information would fall into the hands of the wrong people. Perhaps they also enjoyed the secrecy for its own sake.

Since astrology was an integral part of everyday life in much

IGNIS.
AERIS.
AQVÆ.
TERRÆ.
V.WIWV
TINCTVR.
COAGVLATION.
DISTILLATION.
PVTREFACTION.
SOLVTION.
SVBLIMATION.
CALTINATION.
FC. Sculpt.

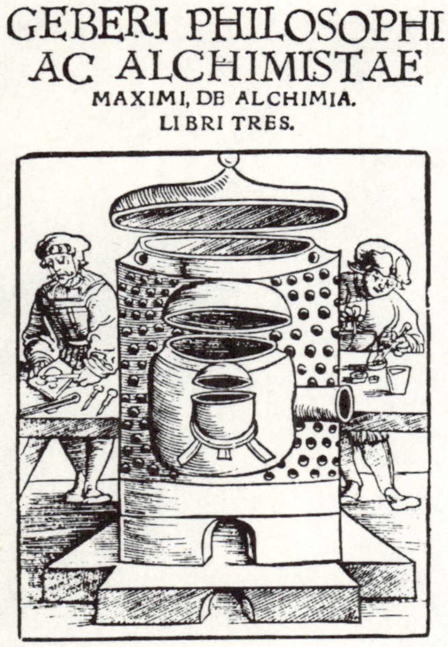

Above: the title page of a Latin work on alchemy attributed to Jabir, whose name is shown here in the Western form of Geber. He was recognized as the Father of Alchemy, and his reputation was so high that probably many books by other authors were attributed to him to give added authority. How many of them were actually written by Jabir is still vigorously debated by many scholars.

of the Ancient World, craftsmen incorporated many of its beliefs into their work. Horoscopes were frequently used to determine favorable conditions for preparing certain drugs or metal alloys. Calculations often involved the use of strange mystic numbers and magic squares. When alchemists took over the chemical skills and metalworking techniques of the ancient craftsmen, they also adopted their astrological practices and belief in the power of numbers.

When the Arabs conquered Egypt in the 7th century A.D. they came into contact with many practicing alchemists, and were able to learn their skills and ideas at first hand. One of the earliest Arab philosophers to benefit from the contact was Jabir ibn Hayyan, who lived in the 8th century A.D. He made his own significant contribution to the theory of alchemy—one which survived in one form or another until well into the 18th century. He observed that metals and minerals appeared to be comprised of an "earthy smoke" and a "watery vapor." The first consisted of "atoms" of earth on the way to becoming fire, the second of water on the way to becoming air. He thought that these two components were not immediately turned into metals and minerals when imprisoned in the bowels of the earth; one was converted into sulfur, and the other into mercury, both of which were then thought to be kinds of elemental building blocks. Different proportions gave birth to different metals, and only if the sulfur and mercury were completely pure did they produce gold. Since other metals were the result of the inclusion of impurities, the removal of these impurities must finally result in the production of gold.

Below: in a 14th-century work on alchemy an Arab is shown unlocking the gate to a town, probably symbolizing knowledge. The Arab contribution to alchemy was fully recognized by European alchemists.

Chinese Alchemy

Many thousands of miles away on the other side of the world, the Chinese were also experimenting in alchemy. From this distance in time it is impossible to decide whether alchemy originated in the West and spread to China, or sprang up in China and spread to the West. It may be, of course, that it developed in both places independently. There were certainly some similarities between Western and Eastern alchemy. The Chinese also wanted to discover the secret of immortality, even though they were not on the whole as concerned with transmuting base metals into gold.

One of the main differences was that, in place of the four elements defined by Aristotle, the Chinese designated five: water, fire, wood, metal, and earth. In addition, they recognized the principles of yang and yin instead of Jabir's theory of sulfur and mercury. According to the *Book of Tao*, written by the sage Lao-tzu about 550 B.C., all the energy of the Universe can be divided into the two forms of yang—which is active, masculine, fiery—and yin—which is passive, feminine, and watery. Immortality is a masculine quality, and gold and jade, which are almost pure yang, preserve bodies from corruption. "If there is gold and jade in the nine apertures of the corpse, it will preserve the body from putrefaction," wrote the alchemist Ko Hung in the 4th century A.D. Princes and lords were buried with boxes of jade for this reason.

The Chinese also related the Macrocosm of the Universe to the human body in the Microcosm of the world. For example, they identified the heart with the essence of fire, the liver with the essence of wood, the lungs with the essence of metal, the

Below: the jade funeral suit of a Chinese queen, the wife of a monarch who ruled in the late 2nd century B.C. It was believed that gold and jade, being almost purely yang, preserved the body.

The Arab Art of Distillation

Above: Arab symbolic figures and diagrams of stills (on the right) from a 12th-century Arab text on alchemy. In general the Arab alchemists were less secretive about their discoveries, and the Arab manuscripts are less shrouded in complicated symbolism than the later European alchemical works.

Below: the title page of a work written by Hieronymus Brunschwig in 1507 on the art of distillation. Although European alchemists spent much time and ingenuity on the arrangement of their stills, the art was developed, if not invented, by the Arabs, and it became an enormously important process.

stomach with the essence of earth, and the kidneys with the essence of water.

Like Western alchemy, Chinese alchemy is filled with symbols. The following details from the *Tsan-tung-chi*, written in about the 2nd or 3rd century A.D., read like a description of the embroidered pattern on a mandarin's robe: "Cooking and distillation takes place in the cauldron; below blazes the roaring flame. Before goes the White Tiger leading the way; following comes the Gray Dragon. The fluttering Scarlet Bird flies the five colours. Encountering ensnaring nets, it is helplessly and immovably pressed down, and cries with pathos like a child after its mother. Willy-nilly it is put into the cauldron of hot fluid to the detriment of its feathers. Before half the time has passed, Dragons appear with rapidity and in great number. The five dazzling colors change incessantly. Turbulently boils the fluid in the furnace. One after another they appear to form an array as irregular as dogs' teeth. Stalagmites which are like midwinter icicles are spat out horizontally and vertically. Rocky heights of no apparent regularity make their appearance, supporting one another. When yin and yang are properly matched, tranquility prevails."

In plain words, as the English writer E. J. Holmyard has pointed out, the solution is evaporated until it crystallizes.

Of course alchemy did not just consist of theories and symbols. Jabir, for example, was capable of providing explicit descriptions of alchemical processes and apparatus. He gave the earliest known formula for the manufacture of nitric acid, and noticed that copper compounds will color a flame blue-green. He knew the use of manganese dioxide in glassmaking, he described the making of steel, dyes, and varnishes, and he reported how to make acetic acid by distilling vinegar.

Al-Razi, another great figure who lived a little later than Jabir, goes into even greater detail about the contents of the alchemist's laboratory. Al-Razi was born in about A.D. 826. The apparatus he described hardly changed within the next thousand years. In fact, although modern chemical research apparatus is highly sophisticated, most teaching laboratories are still stocked with equipment that would not have been unfamiliar to Al-Razi.

The most important part of any laboratory were the furnaces. Until the invention of the thermometer in the 18th century, it was impossible to measure heat exactly. Alchemists usually recognized four "degrees" of heat. The first degree was that of a brooding hen, or a dungheap, or the Egyptian summer; the second that of a water bath just below boiling; the third that obtained by a bath of sand or ashes placed in the furnace; and the fourth degree that of "naked heat," when the furnace was hot enough to melt metals. The sand bath and water bath are known to this day. Both are effective methods of maintaining a steady temperature.

Alchemical processes depended on the maintenance of steady temperatures, and much experience was needed in the design of furnaces to provide them with all kinds of holes that could be covered or uncovered to regulate the heat and the draft.

The Arabs were the perfecters if not the inventors of the art of

Above: an Arab pharmacy from a manuscript of the 13th century. In the lower floor of the shop a pharmacist is preparing a medicine from honey. On the next level jars are stored and an assistant is checking the contents of one. The meditative figure at the upper left is the physician, who is the master of the entire pharmacy.

distillation, in which a liquid is converted into a vapor by boiling, and then condensed back into a liquid by cooling. The aim of distillation is purification. The alchemists developed different vessels for the distillation process. The lower part of a *still*, the apparatus used for distillation, is called a *cucurbit*; the liquid is heated in this container. The upper part, where the heated vapor condenses again, is the *alembic*. The receiver for the distilled liquid is the *aludel*.

Often the liquid was *refluxed* so that after condensation in the top of the still, it ran back to be reheated without being collected in an aludel. Flasks in which this process was performed were known as *pelicans* because the tube down which the refluxed liquid ran made them look something like pelicans with beaks tucked into their breasts. A special and important type of refluxing—one that is widely used in chemistry today—was employed to extract soluble material from a solid substance. The apparatus used was known as a *kerotakis*. At the bottom of the kerotakis is the furnace, which heats a liquid to boiling. The liquid vapor rises to the top of the still and condenses there, running down over the solid matter which is held in a sieve. If the solid contains anything that is even slightly soluble in the liquid, it will in the end be concentrated in the bottom of the still. Today, an apparatus of this kind is often used by analytical chemists. It is called a Soxhlet extractor.

So much for the heating of liquids. Frequently, however, it was necessary to heat substances to higher temperatures. For

The Laboratories of Early Alchemy

instance, in the calcination of metals—that is, the "burning" of them to form oxides—very strong heat is required. Similarly in the reverse process—the smelting, or "reduction" of ores to the metal—high temperatures are required. For these temperatures, a *crucible* was necessary.

The name of this apparatus, which means "little cross," describes its basic appearance. It was a small bowl, generally made of clay, with four lips extending in a cross shape so that it could be supported on the rim of a furnace. Similar was the *cupel*, a crucible made of bone ash. If gold or silver mixed with lead were heated in a cupel, the lead oxidized rapidly, the lead oxide was absorbed by the material of the cupel, and the gold or silver was left purified.

Al-Razi described much other equipment that would be familiar to any student of chemistry: beakers, flasks, crystallizing dishes, spatulas, funnels, filters made of cloth, and pestles and mortars. His shelves contained not only all the known metals, but also many other substances such as pyrites, mala-

Right: two of the ovens used by alchemists, from Hieronymus Brunschwig's 1519 work on equipment for distilling. The upper illustration shows the ordinary oven with the distilling apparatus in the flue. Below is a type of oven in which water is heated, with four distilling vessels embedded in sand in the top of it.

chite, lapis lazuli, gypsum, hematite, galena, turquoise, stibnite, alum, green vitriol, natron, borax, salt, lime, potash, cinnabar, white and red lead, iron oxide, copper oxide, vinegar, and probably caustic soda, glycerol, and sulfuric and nitric acids.

The Arabs had preserved the writings of Greek philosophers such as Aristotle, and had carried on the beliefs and practices of the early alchemists. They had also added a great deal of their own to alchemy, mainly in terms of chemical discoveries and improvements in apparatus. It was not until the 12th century, with the translations made by Robert of Chester and his followers, that medieval Europe learned of the mysterious science of alchemy.

Above: a German reconstruction of a 16th-century alchemical laboratory. The apparatus is neatly stored around the walls of the room, in which there are several furnaces. Judging from contemporary drawings and paintings, alchemists' workshops were seldom like this as far as tidiness is concerned.

Chapter 10
Two Mysterious Frenchmen

Have there been some alchemists who attained immortality? According to many stories, at least two Frenchmen have. One is Nicholas Flamel, who is believed to have discovered the Philosopher's Stone in the late 14th century and to have used it in successful transmutations of base metal into gold. Records of his many contributions to charity exist. Were they made from his alchemist's gold? Did he reappear alive in Paris both in the 18th and 19th centuries? What about the second famous French alchemist, Fulcanelli? This 20th-century practitioner was seen on the street long after he had mysteriously disappeared. Has he become immortal?

At least as late as the year 1742, there stood in the cemetery of the Holy Innocents in Paris an old arch with remarkable paintings on its walls. It had been built and decorated on the instructions of Nicholas Flamel, a man whose profession it was to copy out manuscripts and documents in the days before printing. The paintings showed the figure of Nicholas Flamel dressed as a pilgrim, strange symbolic scenes, and the various stages of a successful transmutation of ordinary metals into gold. Flamel explained the transmutation scenes as follows: "In the year of our Lord 1382, April 25, at five in the afternoon, this mercury I truly transmuted into almost as much gold, much better, indeed, than common gold, more soft also, and more pliable. I may speak it with truth, I have made it three times, with the help of Perrenelle [his wife] who understood it as well as I, because she helped me in my operations . . ."

Flamel wrote an account of his lengthy alchemical quest in 1413. His devoted wife and companion, Perrenelle, had died in 1399, and for a long time he had been inconsolable. They were a thrifty, industrious, and charitable couple, and Flamel's narrative, with its sober enthusiasm, has an authentic ring. His tale begins in the year 1357 when he purchased a very old and very large gilded book. "It was not of paper, nor parchment, as other books be, but was only made of delicate rinds (as it seemed unto me) of tender young trees; the cover of it was of brass, well bound, all engraven with letters or strange figures . . .

Opposite: the seekers after material gold in the garden, one of the drawings made following Nicholas Flamel's description of the illustrations in the *Book of Abraham the Jew*, which gave instructions for the transmutation. The figure at the bottom right of the picture is believed to be Flamel himself, who is thought to have lived from 1330–1416.

Right: an 18th-century print of the frescoes with the alchemic figures of Abraham the Jew which Flamel had erected in the cemetery of the Holy Innocents in Paris. The frescoe shows both Flamel and his wife Perrenelle kneeling.

Above: the alchemist Nicholas Flamel, who is said to have endowed churches, chapels, and hospitals with the alchemical gold he and his wife transmuted.

this I know that I could not read them nor were they either Latin or French letters, of which I understand something. As to the matter which was written within, it was engraved (as I suppose) with an iron pencil or graver upon the said bark leaves, done admirably well and in neat Latin letters, and curiously colored." The manuscript contained 21 leaves. The seventh, fourteenth, and twenty-first leaves were blank, apart from some strange illustrations. The seventh leaf showed "a Virgin and serpents swallowing her up," the fourteenth a cross with a serpent crucified on it, and the twenty-first "a desert with many springs out of which serpents writhed."

On the first page was written in capital letters in gold: "Abraham the Jew, Priest, Prince, Levite, Astrologer, and Philosopher, to the nation of the Jews dispersed by the wrath of God in France, wisheth health." Flamel afterward referred to the manuscript as the *Book of Abraham the Jew*. The dedication was followed by lengthy curses and execrations against anyone who might read the book who was neither a priest nor scribe. Flamel, who was a copyist or scribe, was exempt from these curses and felt emboldened to read further. On the third leaf and in all the following writings were instructions for the transmutation of metals to gold. The author wished to help the dispersed Jews pay their taxes to the Roman emperors. The instructions were clear and easy to follow. The only problem was that they referred to the later stages of the transmutation. There were no written instructions given as to what the *prima materia*, or first matter, consisted of, and so it seemed impossible to carry out the essential first stages of the transmutation.

The only clue the author gave to the identity of the first matter was that he had depicted it in the illustrations on the fourth and fifth leaves of the book. Flamel found to his disappointment that, although these pictures were clear and singularly well painted, "yet by that could no man ever have been able to understand it without being well skilled in their [the Hebrews'] Cabala, which is a series of old traditions, and also to have been well studied in their books." Flamel had the pictures copied and showed them to various people in the hope that someone would be able to interpret them. One one side of the fourth page was a painting of a young man with wings at his ankles. In his hand he held the *caduceus*, the snake entwined rod of Mercury, messenger of the gods. Running and flying at him with open wings came an old man with an hourglass on his head and a scythe in his hands, as if he were about to cut off the young man's feet. On the other side of the page was a picture of a high mountain. On its summit was a blue plant with gold leaves and white and red flowers, shaking in the strong north wind, "and round about it the dragons and griffins of the north made their nest and abode."

On the first side of the fifth leaf was a rose tree in flower against the side of a hollow oak. A pure spring bubbled up at the foot of the oak and ran down through a garden to disappear into the depths. It ran through the hands of many blind people who were digging for it, but who could not recognize it except

Flamel's Find

Left: *The Last Coin*, by Steen. The alchemist's wife sees their last coin disappear as her husband tries once again to produce gold. Perrenelle Flamel was fortunate—most alchemists' wives are shown in contemporary prints and paintings as desperately poor, surrounded by hungry children.

Deciphering the Manuscript

for a few who could feel its weight. On the other side of this leaf the painting showed a king with a broad sword ordering his soldiers to slaughter hundreds of babies, while their mothers flung themselves weeping at his feet. The soldiers collected the infants' blood into a bath, where the Sun and Moon came to bathe themselves.

No one who saw the pictures could understand them. At last, a man named Anselm, who was deeply interested in alchemy, claimed to be able to interpret them. Unfortunately, he started Flamel off on the wrong track. "This strange and foreign discourse to the matter was the cause of my erring, and made me wander for the space of one and twenty years in a perfect meander from the verity; in which space of time I went through a thousand labyrinths or processes, but all in vain."

Finally, Flamel's wife Perrenelle suggested that, since the manuscript came from a Jewish source, he should seek the advice of a learned Jew in interpreting it. Many Jews had at that time settled in Spain. Flamel decided to go on a pilgrimage to Saint James of Compostella, and at the same time seek help in the synagogues. Attired as a pilgrim, and carrying careful copies of the mystifying illustrations, he set off for his journey to Spain.

After he had made his devotions at the Shrine of Saint James of Compostella, Flamel tried without success to find someone who could enlighten him as to the true meaning of the pictures. He traveled on to León, where quite by chance he was introduced to a certain Master Canches, who was well-versed in the secrets of the Cabala and other Jewish mysteries. When he saw

Right: Flamel's instruments, in a miniature illustrating *Alchimie de Flamel*, a 16th-century French manuscript. The strip at the top shows the seven colors of the process, in the proper order.

Far right: the mercurial serpent is crucified, a version of one of the illustrations Flamel described. It was taken to symbolize the transformation of mercury.

Left: the planets around the piller of life, from the 16th-century French manuscript. Each stage of the process had its own prescribed planetary situation, a typical linking of astrology with the alchemical tradition.

Flamel's copies of the illustrations he was "ravished with great astonishment and joy." He recognized them as part of a book which it was believed had been completely lost. Master Canches immediately resolved to return with Flamel to France to find out more about the manuscript. On the journey he interpreted Flamel's illustrations with such accuracy, even to the smallest detail, that Flamel was able to find out what he needed to know about the nature of the first matter. Unfortunately, Master Canches fell sick and died when they reached Orléans. Flamel buried him as well as he could afford, and sadly returned to Paris. But nothing could stifle his joy when at last he came in sight of his small house and was reunited with his wife Perrenelle. He put up a painting on the door of the chapel next to his home. It showed him kneeling with his wife and giving thanks to God for granting him the desired knowledge.

However, Flamel's troubles were not yet over. "Well, I had now the *prima materia*, the first principles, yet not their first preparation, which is a thing most difficult, above all the things in the world; but in the end I had that also, after long errors of

Flamel's First Transmutation

three years, or thereabouts . . . Finally, I found that which I desired, which I also soon knew by the strong scent and odor thereof. Having this, I easily accomplished the Mastery, for knowing the preparation of the first Agents, and after following my Book according to the letter, I could not have missed it though I would. Then the first time that I made projection was upon Mercury, whereof I turned half a pound, or thereabouts, into pure silver, better than that of the Mine, as I myself assayed [tested], and made others assay many times. This was upon a Monday, the 17 of January about noon, in my home, Perrenelle only being present, in the year of the restoring of mankind 1382."

Three months later, Flamel made his first transmutation into gold. For a long time he was worried that Perrenelle, who was overjoyed at the final outcome of so many years of experiments, would let some word slip among her family and reveal the secret of their sudden wealth. "But the goodness of the most great God

Below: Flamel's tombstone, one of the few indisputable relics left of his historical reality. The upper portion shows carved representations of Christ, Saint Peter, and Saint Paul, and between them the symbols of gold (or the sun) and silver (or the moon), but the inscription makes no mention of his alchemical achievements.

Right: a reconstruction of Flamel's house in Paris. Across the front was a frieze that showed Flamel and his wife in prayer, surrounded by various alchemical figures. It was probably to this house that King Charles VI of France sent his minister to investigate rumors that Flamel was a successful alchemist. The minister visited the pair, but observing that they ate off earthenware platters, decided that the tales of Flamel's alchemy were obviously pure invention, and reported so to his king.

had not only given and filled me with this blessing, to give me a chaste and sober wife, but she was also a wise and prudent woman, not only capable of reason but also to do what was reasonable, and was more discreet and secret than ordinarily other women are."

Because she was now well past the age for bearing children, Perrenelle suggested that their riches should be devoted to charity. She and Flamel founded and endowed "fourteen hospitals, three chapels, and seven churches, in the city of Paris, all which we had new built from the ground, and enriched with great gifts and revenues, with many reparations in their churchyards. We also have done at Boulogne about as much as we have done at Paris, not to speak of the charitable acts which we both did to particular poor people, principally to widows and orphans . . ."

The arch built by Flamel in the cemetery of the Holy Innocents, with its strange alchemical paintings, disappeared some time in the 18th century. The painting of Flamel and his wife giving thanks to God on the door of the chapel next to their home has also vanished. But one day in the mid-19th century, a herbalist in one of the streets near where Flamel used to live turned over the finely polished marble slab on which he had for years been chopping his dried herbs, and found it to be Flamel's tombstone. It is now preserved in the Museum of Cluny in Paris, and the inscription reads: "Nicholas Flamel, formerly a scrivener, left in his will for the administration of this church certain rents and houses which he acquired and bought during his lifetime to provide for masses and distribution of alms each year, in particular the Quinze-Vingts [a hospital in Paris for blind men] cathedral and other churches and hospitals of

Above: the church of Saint-Jacques-la-Boucherie where Flamel was buried. The church was demolished in the late 18th century, with only the tower, now used as a meteorological station, remaining.

Below: Flamel's house as it looked in 1900.

Paris." The will of Perrenelle, dated 1399, survives, and so does Flamel's, which he signed on November 22, 1416. Three years later he died.

After Flamel's death, many people thought that some of the Philosopher's Stone must still be hidden in one of his houses. His property was searched over and over again, and so thoroughly that one house was reduced to a pile of rubble with only the cellars remaining. By about 1560 the local magistrate, in the name of the king, took possession of all property that had once belonged to Flamel, so that a final thorough search could be made. But nobody ever admitted to having found anything.

There were those, of course, who insisted that Flamel, having

Above: this figure described by Flamel has been interpreted as signifying the fixing of mercury. The old man with the scythe, symbolizing lead, cuts off the feet of Mercury and renders ordinary quicksilver, regarded as a baser, immobile form of silver.

Right: another of the figures is called The Three Colors of the Work. The first rider, mounted on a black lion, symbolizes gold in maceration; the second, on the red lion, shows the inner ferment; and the crowned rider on the white lion symbolizes final success.

Did Flamel Die?

discovered the secret of the Philosopher's Stone, had also discovered the secret of immortality. The 17th-century traveler Paul Lucas, during a discussion on alchemy and magic with a Turkish philosopher from Asia Minor, was told "that true philosophers had the secret of prolonging life for anything up to a thousand years."

"At last I took the liberty of naming the celebrated Flamel, who, it was said, possessed the Philosopher's Stone, yet was certainly dead. He smiled at my simplicity, and asked with an air of mirth: 'Do you really believe this? No, no, my friend, Flamel is still living; neither he nor his wife has yet tasted death. It is not above three years since I left both the one and the other

Left: another of the figures of Abraham described by Flamel has come to be called The Fair Flower on the Mountain. The red and white flowers stand for the red and white stages of the Great Work; the dragons for sophic mercury, which the adepts identified with the "essence" of silver; and the griffins, which were a combination of lion and eagle, were interpreted as both the fixed and the volatile.

Symbols in Stone?

in India; he is one of my best friends.' "

According to the Turk, Flamel had realized the danger he was in if ever the news got out that he possessed the Philosopher's Stone. Perrenelle had therefore feigned illness and had gone to Switzerland, leaving Nicholas to announce her death. He buried a log in her grave. After several years he in his turn carried out the same deception. Nearly a century later, in 1761, Flamel and his wife were reported to have attended a performance of the opera in Paris, and there were many other stories of a similar nature.

One of the most detailed and most fantastic of such tales appears in the little-known work of *Le Corbeau Menteur* (The Lying Raven) by the 19th-century French writer Ninian Bres. He wrote: "He was a little less than middle height, stooping somewhat with the weight of years, but still with a firm step and a clear eye, and with a complexion strangely smooth and almost transparent, like fine alabaster. Both he and the woman with him—clearly his wife, although she appeared almost imperceptibly the older and more decisive of the two—were dressed in a style that seemed only a few years out of fashion and yet had an indefinable air of antiquity about it. I stood, half concealed in a little archway toward the end of the boulevard du Temple: my hands were stained with acid, and my topcoat stank of the furnace. As the couple came abreast of the spot where I stood, Flamel turned toward me and seemed about to speak, but Perrenelle drew him quickly on, and they were almost at once lost in the crowd. You ask how I am so confident that this was Nicholas Flamel? I tell you that I have spent many hours in the Bibliothèque Nationale, poring over the *Figures d'Abraham Juif* [*Pictures of Abraham the Jew*]: look carefully at the first side of the fifth leaf and there, in the lower right-hand corner of the representation of those who seek for gold in the garden, you will see the face that searched mine that evening on the boulevard du Temple, and that has haunted my dreams ever since."

The illustration to which Bres refers is from a manuscript previously thought to be of Flamel's day but now considered to be of the 17th century. It is only one of many different attempts to reproduce the book that Flamel described so carefully. In different but obviously similar forms these pictures have appeared over and over again in alchemical works through the centuries. The manuscript also attempts an explanation of the meaning of the illustrations that puzzled Flamel for so long, and this interpretation has been expanded by numerous later writers. For example, take the illustration of the young man with wings on his ankles being attacked by an old man with a scythe. The first stage in the explanation was that these two figures stood for Mercury and Saturn. The second stage was that Mercury, in alchemical terms, represented an impure form of silver, and Saturn meant lead. When imperfect silver and lead are heated together in a cupel, the inpurities of the silver are absorbed into the material of the crucible, and the resulting silver is said to be "fixed" in the sense of stable or permanent. This illustration, represented in symbolic terms, is the alchemical process necessary for the fixing of silver.

Opposite: Nôtre-Dame Cathedral. It has long been claimed that the Gothic cathedrals in France were secret textbooks of hidden wisdom; using complicated linguistic arguments, Fulcanelli declared that the secrets were those of alchemy, awaiting a student capable of understanding them.

Below: Louis Pauwels, the French writer, photographed in 1974. Twenty-one years earlier Pauwels had a strange encounter with a mysterious alchemist in a Parisian café. The alchemist, who seemed to belong to another age, implied that Fulcanelli was not dead, as his student, Eugene Canseliet, apparently suggested in his preface to Fulcanelli's *The Mystery of the Cathedrals*. Pauwels came to believe that the alchemist he had met was Fulcanelli himself.

From the time of Flamel on, alchemy became increasingly symbolical. The mysterious 20th-century alchemist Fulcanelli, in fact, suggested that the whole of Flamel's story was pure symbolism. He wrote: "We are prepared to certify—if our sincerity is to be trusted—that Flamel never quitted the cellar where his furnaces roared. Anyone who knows the significance of the pilgrim's staff, the begging bowl and the cockleshell in Saint James' hat will also know that we are speaking the truth. By substituting himself for the material and modeling himself upon other secret workers, the great Adept was obeying the rules of philosophic discipline and following the example of his predecessors."

The true identity of Fulcanelli himself is uncertain. He is best known as the alleged author of a book in French, *The Mystery of the Cathedrals*. In this he claims to show that all the secrets of alchemy are concealed in the carvings of the central porch of Notre Dame and various of the porches of the cathedral in Amiens. Fulcanelli proposes that gothic art, *l'art goth*, of which the French cathedrals are outstanding examples, is really *argot*, the language of the common people. They in turn are descendants of those intrepid adventurers who sought the Golden Fleece, the sailors aboard the *Argo*. In all this he claims to discover what he has called "the phonetic Cabala."

One example must suffice. In writing of the labyrinth, Fulcanelli refers to the thread of Ariadne in the Greek myth. Ariadne is Ariane in French. "Ariane is a forme of *airagne* (*araignée*, the spider) by metathesis [transposition] of the i," he said. ". . . Is not our soul the spider, which weaves our own body? But this word appears in other forms. The verb *airo* (Greek) means to take, to seize, to draw, to attract; whence *airen*, that which takes, seizes, attracts. Thus *airen* is the lodestone, that virtue shut up in the body, which the wise call their Magnesia . . . In Provençal iron is called aran and iran, according to the different dialects. This is the masonic Hiram, the divine ram, the architect of the Temple of Solomon . . . Compare all that with the Greek *Sideros*, which may mean either iron or lodestone. Nor is this all. The verb *aruo* means the rising star from out of the sea, whence *aryan*, the star which rises out of the sea; our *ariane* is thus the Orient, by the permutation of vowels. Further *arua* has also the sense to attract; thus *aryan* is also the lodestone. If we now compare *Sideros*, which has given the Latin *sidus*, *sideris*, a star, we shall recognize our Provençal aran, iran, airan—the Greek *aryan*, the rising sun."

Is this genuine, or is it some heavy-handed hoax? Scholars have argued for and against the existence of Fulcanelli ever since the publication of his book in 1925. In his preface to the first edition, Eugene Canseliet, a well-known writer on alchemy, wrote: "For a long time now the author of this book has not been among us . . . My Master . . . disappeared when the fatal hour struck, when the Sign was accomplished . . . Fulcanelli is no more." Then in March 1953 the French writer Louis Pauwels met an alchemist in the Café Procope in Paris. "How old can he be? He says 35. That seems surprising. He has white curly hair, trimmed so as to look like a wig. Lots of deep wrinkles in a pink skin and full features. Few gestures, but slow, calculated and effective when he does make them. A calm, keen smile; eyes that laugh, but in a detached sort of way. Everything about him suggests another age . . . I asked him about Fulcanelli, and he gave me to understand that Fulcanelli is not dead . . ."

A few weeks later Pauwels met Jacques Bergier, a scientist, with whom he later collaborated in writing on the occult. Bergier told Pauwels of his own meeting with a man whom he guessed to be Fulcanelli. It happened one afternoon in June 1937. Bergier said that he met the alchemist by appointment in a laboratory of the Gas Board in Paris. Bergier at that time was working as research assistant to André Helbronner, the French atomic physicist. Fulcanelli (if it was he) told Bergier: "You are on the brink of success, as indeed are several other of our scientists today. May I be allowed to warn you to be careful? . . . The liberation of atomic energy is easier than you think, and the radioactivity artificially produced can poison the atmosphere of our planet in the space of a few years. Moreover, atomic explosives can be produced from a few grains of metal powerful enough to destroy whole cities. I am telling you this for a fact: the alchemists have known it for a very long time . . .

"I shall not attempt to prove to you what I am now going to say, but I ask you to repeat it to M. Helbronner: certain geometrical arrangements of highly purified materials are enough to release atomic forces without having recourse to either electricity or vacuum techniques . . . The secret of alchemy is this: there is a way of manipulating matter and energy so as to produce what modern scientists call a *field of force*. This field acts on the observer and puts him in a privileged position vis-à-vis the Universe. From this position he has access to the realities which are ordinarily hidden from us by time and space, matter and energy. This is what we call the Great Work."

In an introduction to the English edition of *The Mystery of the Cathedrals* Walter Lang carries the Fulcanelli legend further, reporting that "after a lapse of many years, Canseliet received a message from the alchemist and met him at a prearranged rendezvous. The reunion was brief, for Fulcanelli once again severed contact and once again disappeared without leaving a trace of his whereabouts." But, says Lang, Fulcanelli had grown younger, for whereas he had been an old man of 80 when Canseliet had first met him, 30 years later he appeared to be a man of 50.

Says Louis Pauwels: "All that we know of him is that he survived the war and disappeared completely after the Liberation. Every attempt to find him failed." It is difficult to decide how deliberate these attempts to find Fulcanelli were. In August 1945 the American intelligence services asked Bergier to contact urgently a certain anonymous major who worked for an organization searching out German research reports on atomic energy. This major desperately wanted to know the whereabouts of Fulcanelli—but he appears to have been satisfied when Bergier assured him that the veteran alchemist had once more disappeared. After 50 years, we know no more of Fulcanelli now than we knew in 1925. Perhaps, with Nicholas Flamel, he lives the life of an Indian Mahatma in the distant hills. Perhaps, who knows, he *is* Nicholas Flamel.

The Alchemist's Warning Words

Below: André Helbronner, noted French atomic physicist. His research assistant, Jacques Bergier, was approached by a mysterious stranger in 1937, who warned him that science was on the brink of manipulating nuclear energy, and that in the past this same abyss had been crossed with disastrous consequences. The stranger asked Bergier to convey the warning to Helbronner. Bergier was convinced that the stranger was Fulcanelli. Helbronner was later killed by the Nazis during World War II.

Eamus
Quesitum Quatuor
Elemementorum
naturas

Chapter 11
The Medieval Masters

The fullest blossoming of alchemy can be said to have come in the 16th century with such great exponents as Paracelsus, Agrippa, and Trismosin. Famous for his miracle cures, Paracelsus oddly enough influenced the course of alchemy in two almost opposing directions: into its use strictly for making medical compounds and into deeper mysticism away from hopes of gold-making. Trismosin left a formula for producing the Philosopher's Stone, but in that symbolic and mystical vein that obscures so much of the alchemical literature. In fact, by the end of the Middle Ages, alchemists themselves were caught in their own web of mystification.

Maybe the newly appointed city physician had been drinking too much. He usually had. "Always drunk and always lucid," someone has described him. He stood in the city square of Basel, Switzerland, with a large brass pan in which charcoal was burning. In one hand he held a book of the works of Avicenna, and in the other works of Galen. Then he thrust them into the flames and sprinkled them with sulfur and saltpeter so that they burned with an unearthly light. "If your physicians," he said "only knew that their prince Galen—they call none like him—was sticking in hell, from whence he has sent letters to me, they would make the sign of the cross upon themselves with a fox's tail. In the same way your Avicenna sits in the vestibule of the infernal portal . . ."

At that time, in the 16th century, medical knowledge was based almost exclusively on the writings of Galen, a Greek physician of the 2nd century A.D., and Avicenna, the Arab philosopher who died in 1037. It was unheard of to question their authority, let alone to claim to know better. Yet here was someone not only insulting these masters, but also all the doctors who followed their teachings. "Come then, and listen, impostors who prevail only by the authority of your high positions!" the scoffer continued. "After my death, my disciples will burst forth and drag you to the light, and shall expose your dirty drugs . . ." and so on. The speech of this overwhelmingly self-confident man could truly be called *bombastic*—and that was

Opposite: an alchemist from *Splendor Solis*, a manuscript reputedly written by the most mysterious medieval alchemist, who is known to us now only by his pseudonym, Solomon Trismosin. Nothing but what he wrote of himself has survived—but if he wrote the truth, he succeeded in finding both the Philosopher's Stone and the coveted Elixir of Life.

Above: the title page of Hieronymus Brunschwig's 1519 work on distillation. The techniques of distillation were used not only for alchemical work, but also for the widely used herbal medicines.

Below: this drawing, a *Young Man with a Broad-brimmed Hat*, is frequently assumed to be a portrait of the young Paracelsus.

his name—Philippus Aureolus Theophrastus Bombastus von Hohenheim. But he is known to generations of alchemists as Paracelsus, the name he gave himself to indicate that he was greater (*para* is Greek for beyond) than Celsus, the Roman medical authority of the beginning of the Christian era.

Paracelsus was born on December 17, 1493 near Zurich, the son of a local physician. His father taught him the rudiments of alchemy, astrology, and medicine as soon as he was old enough to understand. At 16 Paracelsus entered the university in Basel, and later he probably went to Würzburg to study under Hans von Trittenheim, a celebrated expert on magic. When he was 22 he worked for a year at the mining school of Sigismund Fugger, who was renowned as an alchemist. But this was far from being the completion of Paracelsus' education. He next set out on an odyssey that probably went through Germany, Italy, France, the Netherlands, England, Scandinavia, and Russia. In Italy he served as an army surgeon, and took a degree in medicine at the University of Ferrara. At the age of 33 he was invited to Basel in his native Switzerland to take up the post of town physician and professor of medicine.

Although Paracelsus performed some marvelous cures in Basel, he soon made enemies. One day, for example, he invited all the doctors to a lecture in which he proposed to teach them some of his greatest secrets. When he began by uncovering a dish full of dung, they left the hall in a hurry. Paracelsus boomed after them: "If you will not learn the mysteries of putrefactive fermentation, you are unworthy of the name of physicians."

It was not long before Paracelsus had quarreled bitterly with the city authorities, and was on the road again. For most of the rest of his life he wandered around, writing as he traveled in a strange mixture of German, Latin, and words that he made up himself. Capriciously, he took the Arabic word for black eye-paint, *al-kohl*, and gave it to spirits of wine, which has borne the name alcohol ever since. He invented the name zinc. From the German *all-geist* he derived the word *alkahest*, the imaginary universal solvent with the power to convert all bodies into their liquid primary matter. For his own kind of alchemy, which was concerned with healing, he coined the word "spagyric."

Paracelsus' main aim in alchemy was to use its methods to prepare medicines. Although he did not deny the possibility of making gold, it was of little importance to him. "Men have said of alchemy," he wrote, "that it is for the making of gold and silver. For me such is not the aim, but to consider only that virtue and power may lie in medicines." At that time doctors used herbal remedies almost exclusively. Paracelsus' introduction of medicines based on chemical substances was revolutionary, and its effects were far-reaching. Inspired by his work in alchemy, a whole new school of medical chemistry sprang up. This school united the discoveries of medicine with those of alchemy.

Paracelsus heaped abuse on most of the doctors of his time. He was warm in his praise, however, for those few physicians who had studied alchemy and knew how to apply their knowledge. "They are sooty and dirty like the smiths and charcoal-burners," he said, "and hence make little show, make not

Paracelsus, the Father of Chemistry

Left: *The Apothecary, late 16th Century*, by H. Stacey Marks. Apothecaries relied on herbs for their medicines, and persecuted Paracelsus when he began to develop medicines based on chemical substances. Their enmity helped drive Paracelsus on his wanderings in other countries, where he spread medical alchemy.

Above: *Paracelsus Lecturing on the Elixir Vitae*, by David Scott. One of the ways that Paracelsus infuriated his colleagues and critics was his insistence on giving his lectures in German rather than in the accepted Latin language, as befitted a scholar. His style of argument, as well, gave full scope to his remarkable gift for heaping invective on those who disagreed with him.

many words and gossip with their patients, do not highly praise their own remedies, for they well know that the work must praise the master, not the master his work. . . . Therefore they let such things alone and busy themselves with working with their fires and learning the steps of alchemy."

The bombastic doctor seems to have been responsible for diverting the course of alchemy away from transmutation of metals. Some practitioners, under his guidance, used alchemical

The Three Prime Substances

Left: the 24th Figure of the 32 allegorical prophecies of Paracelsus, first published in 1530. The text accompanying this one said in part, "Ye should not be as beasts but as men, but as ye are not so, he will rule you that is above you, of whome stands written; give unto him what to him belongs." Paracelsus' "elucidation" says, "Therefore also alliances must be dissolved that were only made to cause discord and to accomplish the heart's desire."

processes to find medical cures. Others turned to mystic contemplation. Paracelsus believed that the gold that could be made by transmutation was poor and unproductive in comparison with the "gold" that could be produced by exercising the secret powers existing in the soul. Many alchemists, influenced by Paracelsus, abandoned the physical search for gold, and began to look within themselves for secret strength.

Paracelsus believed that the material world was ultimately composed of the four Aristotelian elements of Earth, Air, Fire, and Water, but that more immediately it was made up of three substances. These were known as mercury, sulfur, and salt, and were sometimes referred to as the *tria prima*. They were not the actual substances that we know by these names today, but stood for certain principles. Mercury, also known as the spirit, stood for the principles of fusibility and volatility. Sulfur, which represented the soul, stood for inflammability, and salt, the body, stood for incombustibility and nonvolatility. In this theory Paracelsus had revived an old Arabic idea that metals were formed from a combination of sulfur and mercury. He added the third principle of salt, and extended the definition to include all material substances.

"As many as there are kinds of fruit, so many kinds there are of sulfur, salt, and so many of mercury. A different sulfur is in gold, another in silver, another in lead, another in iron, tin, etc. Also a different one in sapphire, another in the emerald, another in the ruby, chrysolite, amethyst, magnets, etc. Also another in stones, flint, salts, springwaters, etc. And not only so many kinds of sulfur but also as many kinds of salt, different ones in metals, different ones in gems, stones, others in salts, in vitriol, in alum. Similarly with mercuries, a different one in the metals, another in gems, and as often as there is a species there is a different mercury. . . . And further they are still more divided, as there is not merely one kind of gold but many kinds of gold. . . . Therefore there are just as many kinds of sulfurs of gold, salts of gold, mercuries of gold."

Mystic Aspects of Alchemy

This kind of philosophy, emanating from someone with as strong a personality as Paracelsus, had an immeasurable influence on the theories of the alchemists. In the sense that it made all practical work much more difficult to conceive, it is certainly true that Paracelsus' doctrine encouraged a more mystic approach to alchemy. So, on the one hand, he was claimed by those looking to alchemy for medical cures as the father of medical chemistry. On the other hand, he was regarded by those turning from practical experiments in transmutation to contemplation as the founder of mystic alchemy.

Paracelsus was not the only physician of this time to be subsequently claimed by both scientists and magicians as a major influence. Cornelius Heinrich Agrippa of Nettesheim was another. His whole career, in fact, was very like that of his contemporary Paracelsus, who was only seven years older than he. Agrippa served as a soldier in Germany, traveled through France, Spain, Italy, England, and Switzerland, and during his short life was a professor, courtier, theologian, lawyer, doctor, and alchemist. He died at the age of 49.

Agrippa's philosophy was expressed at length in his famous work on magic, *The Occult Philosophy*, which he probably wrote in 1510 during a visit to England. It is based on the idea that "man is made in the image of God." God is seen as consisting of the whole Universe, and therefore man is the miniature replica of the Universe. Just as man's body contains his spirit, so all material substances are permeated by a Universal Spirit. This spirit was especially abundant in the various celestial bodies, and fell to earth in the rays of the stars. It was widely held at the time that various substances such as gems, metals, plants, and animals were under the influence of a particular planet or star. Agrippa believed that they were also particularly imbued with the spirit from that star. He strongly advocated charms of all kinds, which could be "worn on the body bound to any part of it or hung round the neck, changing sickness into health or health into sickness. . . . When any star ascends fortunately take a herb and stone that are under that star, make a ring of the metal that is congruous therewith, and in that fix the stone with the herb under it."

It was only a short step from this belief to the belief that it was possible to extract this spirit from the metal that was under a particular star, and project it upon another metal—if possible, under the influence of that same star. In this way the quintessence of gold might be removed from gold and projected upon lead to turn the lead into gold. But Agrippa realized that this method was unlikely to result in the multiplication of gold. In 1526 he wrote cynically to a friend: "Blessed be the Lord, I am a rich man, if there be truth in fable. A man of considerations . . . has brought me seeds of gold and planted them over my furnace within long-necked flasks, putting underneath a little fire as of the Sun's heat, and as hens brood over eggs we keep the warmth up night and day, expecting forthwith to produce enormous golden chicks. If all be hatched we shall exceed Midas in wealth, or at least in length of ears . . . ."—that is, in stupidity.

Agrippa continued his alchemical studies for many years, but final disillusionment led him to attack not only the physicians

Below: Cornelius Heinrich Agrippa, after a drawing by Theodore de Bry. Agrippa was a flamboyant character, not unlike Paracelsus in personality. Both men were interested in the mysticism behind alchemy, both men were fatally incapable of keeping their mouths shut—and consequently both were continually in trouble with those they had insulted or offended.

and apothecaries of his time, but the alchemists as well. In *The Vanity of Sciences and Arts*, published in 1531, he said:

"The alchemist may earn a scanty livelihood by the production of medicaments or cosmetics, or he may use his art, as very many do, to carry on the business of a coiner. But the true searcher after the Stone which is to metamorphose all base metals into gold, converts only farms, goods and patrimonies into ashes and smoke." He added somewhat grudgingly, "Nevertheless, I do not deny that to this art many excellent inventions owe their origin. Hence we have the discovery of azure, cinnabar, minium, purple, that which is called musical gold, and other colors. Hence we derive the knowledge of brass and mixed metals, solders, tests and precipitants."

Contemporary with Paracelsus and Agrippa there lived a third alchemist who, if the story is to be believed, succeeded in preparing a tincture that was the Philosopher's Stone. When one part of this tincture was added to 1500 parts of silver, it turned it all to gold. We do not know this alchemist's real name, but he wrote under the pseudonym of Solomon Trismosin. One of his works, *Aureum Vellus*, sometimes translated as *The Golden*

Below: an alchemist at work, an engraving taken from the 1558 painting by Pieter Brueghel the Elder. Agrippa became sufficiently disillusioned with alchemy and alchemists to write bleakly of alchemists very much like the one Brueghel pictured: stubbornly pursuing his research while his wife and children starved, and eventually being led off to the poorhouse, all his money spent.

Symbolism Explained

Opposite: Introduction of the Great Work, from the manuscript *Splendor Solis* by Solomon Trismosin. The picture is symbolic of the first stages of the process. The man on the left is the alchemist, being introduced by the philosopher to the living tree. Mercury is the man in black taking a branch. The tree emerges from the *materia confusa*, the ordinary stuff that the alchemist will have to work into gold. The crown around it signifies that it will be transformed. The birds represent the results of the first calcination, in which material is burned black and then turns into white, which in actuality is the ash.

Fleece, was published in 1598.

According to the preface to *Aureum Vellus*, Trismosin set out on his wanderings in 1473. The first alchemist he came across was a miner named Flocker, but he was extremely secretive and Trismosin learned nothing from him. "He used a process with common lead," Trismosin recounts, "adding to it a peculiar Sulfur, or Brimstone, he fixed the lead until it became hard, then fluid, and later on soft like Wax. Of this prepared lead he took 20 loth [10 ounces], and 1 mark [about 8 ounces] pure unalloyed silver, cast it in an ingot, when half of it was gold. . . . Shortly thereafter he tumbled down a mine and no one could tell what was the artifice he had used."

In the course of the next 18 months' travel, Trismosin observed all kinds of alchemical operations "of no great importance," although he claimed that he had seen "the reality of some of the *particular* processes," and spent a good sum of his own money. In Italy he worked with a tradesman who made English tin look like the best silver, and sold it as such. Trismosin took some of this silvered tin to Venice to have it professionally analyzed, but though it looked convincing, it did not stand up to the test.

One of the assistants who had helped test the metal was curious to know how Trismosin had come by it. Trismosin offered to show him the secret, and they struck up an acquaintance. When the assistant found that Trismosin was traveling in order to gain experience of working in alchemical laboratories, he told him of an Italian nobleman who had just such a laboratory, and who was in need of some help. He introduced Trismosin to the nobleman's chief chemist, who took him to a large mansion some miles outside Venice. "I never saw such laboratory work, in all kinds of Particular Processes, and medicines, as in that place," said Trismosin. "There everything one could think of was provided and ready for use. Each workman has his own private room, and there was a special cook for the whole staff of laboratory assistants."

As a test the chief chemist gave him some metal to work on. It was cinnabar, which he had covered with all kinds of dirt in order to find out how much Trismosin knew. He had two days in which to turn it to gold. "I was kept busy, but succeeded with the Particular Process, and on testing the ingot of the fixed Mercury, the whole weighed nine loth, the test gave three loth of fine Gold. That was my first work and stroke of luck. The Chief Chemist reported it to the nobleman, who came out unexpectedly, spoke to me in Latin, called me his Fortunatum, tapped me on the shoulder and gave me 29 crowns."

Trismosin reported that this nobleman had spent some 30,000 crowns on his experiments. "I myself witnessed that he paid 6000 crowns for the manuscript *Sarlamethon*, a process for a Tincture in the Greek language. . . . I brought that process to a finish in 15 weeks. Therewith I tinged three metals into fine Gold."

Unhappily, the nobleman was drowned in a storm in the Adriatic, and the laboratory was shut up and the men paid off. Trismosin describes how he then moved on "to a still better place for my purpose, where Cabalistic and Magical books in

Three Stages in the Great Work

Three stages of the Great Work—the creation of the Philosopher's Stone—from *Splendor Solis*.
Right: the boy, probably Mercurius as the midget, is pouring liquid on the dragon and puffing as this earthy matter is inflamed and heated during the process of calcination, during which it is burned down into ashes.
Below: the three birds, red, white, and black, within the alembic symbolize the matter that is heated up into elements which are separate. They separate only to reunite, and the three birds recombine in the next stage into a superior single bird created from the materials of the three.

Egyptian language were entrusted to my care, these I had carefully translated into Greek, and then again retranslated into Latin. There I found and captured the Treasure of the Egyptians. I also saw what was the great Subject they worked with . . . After a while I saw the fundamental principles of this art, then I began working out the Best Tincture (but they all proceed, in the most indescribable manner, from the same root)."

Alchemists could judge whether or not their work was progressing successfully by certain color changes that occurred at the end of each stage. The first stage led to a process of rotting or putrefaction in which the material was reduced to first matter. This was known as the *nigredo* or black stage. Following this the material was reborn, the color gradually lightened, and at a certain point there would be a multitude of colors. The next color change was to white, the *albedo* stage. Then the material would pass through a yellow stage to the final one, the *rubedo* or red stage. This red tincture was the miraculous Philosopher's Stone that could turn metals to gold. Trismosin describes this stage as follows: "When I came to the end of the work I found such a beautiful red color as no scarlet can compare with, and such treasure as words cannot tell, and which can be infinitely augmented."

This translation of Solomon Trismosin's life story was made in 1921 by a certain J.K., whose true identity remains unknown. J.K. also added a summary in his own words of how he interpreted Trismosin's description of "the alchemical process called the 'Red Lion.'" The following, in which J.K. makes comments in parentheses, is his summary:

"1. Take 4 ounces calcined alum, 4 ounces calcined saltpeter, and 2 ounces calcined sublimate, and sublimate [refine] in a proper subliming vessel.

2. Carefully take out the sublimate, and resublimate it with 10 ounces fresh salts. During this operation it will be wholesome, on account of the poisonous fumes, to eat bread thickly spread with butter.

3. Put the sublimate in a glass retort, and cover it with alcohol, and distill it over in water bath until half the fluid remains as an oil behind.

4. The alcohol distilled over is poured back (cohobated) on the residue in the retort, until it is covered about a finger's breadth.

5. This distillation repeat three times, and the whole of the sublimate will pass over into the recipient. This is the Mercury of the Philosophers, the Mercurial Water, as it were "the Hellish fire in water." This Mercurial Water fumes always, and must be kept in a closed phial, or glass-stoppered bottle.

6. Take fine gold, in leaf or thin beaten, put it in a glass retort, just cover it with the Mercurial Water, and put the retort on gentle heat, when the Water will begin to act upon the gold, and dissolve it, but it will not be reduced to a liquid entirely, and only remain at the bottom like a greasy substance, then pour off the Mercurial Water, which can be used again.

7. The gold sediment divide into two parts. Take one half and pour thereon alcohol, and let the mixture putrefy on gentle heat fifteen days, and it will become blood red; this is the *Lion's Blood.*

8. This Lion's Blood pour into another glass retort, or phial, which seal hermetically, and give it the heat of the Dog Days, and it will at first turn black, then variegated, then light gray; when heat is increased it will turn yellow and at last deep red. This is the first Tincture. (Provided it does not explode!)

9. The Red Tincture triturate (How will a fulminate triturate?) in a glass mortar. Take one grain thereof, wrap it in paper and project it on 1000 grains of gold in fusion. When it has remained in fusion for $\frac{3}{4}$ hour, the gold will turn to the second Tincture.

10. Take one part of this Tincture, project it on one thousand parts fine silver, and it will transmute it into fine gold.

11. Project one part of the first Tincture, wrapped in paper, upon 1000 parts of pure quicksilver, which has been heated until

Below: a late stage in the Great Work. The peacock symbolizes the rainbow colors that would appear to reassure the adept that he was on the right path. Alchemists believed that there was a definite sequence of colors during the progress of the Work, and if the wrong color occurred at the wrong time, it indicated sure failure. It was often recorded that as the colors of the peacock's tail appeared in the Philosopher's Egg, a wonderful scent also came forth.

Right: a section of the first *Ripley Scrowle*, produced in Lübeck in 1589, part of the papers of the English alchemist George Ripley. At the top are shown the seven processes of the alchemist, who is portrayed as a monk. Each is linked to the whole Work, shown as a red essence of the Stone. At the bottom a woman embraces a man, symbolizing the union of the male and female (in alchemical terms, opposites). The man is rising out of the fountain where the Tree of Life grows inside the Fortress. The figures on the Fortress walls are alchemists. Beneath them, a dragon threatens a toad, which was Ripley's symbol for the important *materia prima*.

the fumes arise, and the quicksilver will be changed into the third Tincture.
12. Take one part of this Tincture, wrapped in paper, project the same on 1000 parts heated quicksilver, and it will become transmuted into fine gold.
13. Take one part of the second Tincture, and project it on copper in fusion, and it will be transmuted into gold of a very red color.
14. Project some of the second Tincture on red hot iron, insert the iron again into the blaze, and it will be transmuted into brittle gold.
15. Melt the gold that has been transmuted of the iron, with equal gold that has been transmuted from quicksilver, and it will become good malleable gold.
16. Dissolve some of the second Tincture in strong alcoholic wine, and take a spoonful in the morning. It will strengthen and renew your constitution. It rejuvenates the aged and makes women prolific."

These instructions may be impossible to follow, especially since the unstable substance formed at one stage is, J.K. suggests, the mercury fulminate used in percussion caps. But they are at least clear and couched in ordinary language. Most alchemical writings concealed their true meanings in a wealth of obscure symbols and doubletalk, as in the *Vision* of George Ripley. Ripley was born early in the 15th century in Yorkshire, England, and died at a Carmelite monastery in Lincolnshire in 1490. He was reportedly an accomplished alchemist and wrote a number of works. His *Compound of Alchimie* was written in 1471, and was dedicated to King Edward IV. But his most famous composition was his *Vision*, a poem that was copied in many different manuscripts, and was reprinted several times.

Ripley describes how, when he was reading late one night, he had a strange vision of a toad who drank the juice of grapes so quickly that its body became bloated and poisoned.

"A toade full rudde I saw did drink the juice of grapes so fast,
Till over charged with the broth, his bowels all to brast;
And after that from poysoned bulke he cast his venom fell."

The toad returned to his "secret den," exuding venom.

"His cave with blasts of fumous ayre he all be-whyted then;
And from the which in space a golden humor did ensue,
Whose falling drops from high did stain the soile with ruddy hew;"

As the toad began to die it turned coal black in color. Decaying in its own poison, it stood rotting for 84 days. Then Ripley put the carcass over a gentle heat in order to expel the remainder of the venom. When this had been done, a wonderful transformation took place.

"The toade with Colors rare through every side was pearst,
And White appeared when all the sundry hewes were past,
Which after being tincted Rudde, for evermore did last.
Then of the venome handled thus a medicine I did make,
Which venome kills and saveth such as venome chance to take.
Glory be to Him the graunter of such secret wayes,
Dominion, and Honor, both with Worship and with Prayes."

If we look carefully at the poem it gradually becomes clear

More Symbolism Interpreted

Below: a 16th-century engraving of the green lion devouring the sun. In the complicated alchemical symbolism, this can be translated as meaning that *aqua regia* (royal water)—a mixture of nitric and hydrochloric acids—dissolved gold, represented by the sun. The gold often contained some copper, which would color the acid bluish-green, and this explains the color of the lion. The engraving can therefore be seen as a vivid description of a straightforward chemical process.

The Obscurity of Alchemical Books

that Ripley is not describing the death and decay of a drunken toad, but is using complex symbolism to describe the alchemical process. The color changes of alchemy are set down clearly in the correct order. First there is the black stage of rotting or putrefaction when the substance has been reduced to first matter. Then, having gone through many colors, the white stage is reached, and finally, at the end of the process the substance turns red. Several commentaries were published on these verses. Some 200 years after they were written, they were reprinted with a particularly detailed interpretation by someone calling himself Eiranaeus Philalethes. His true identity is not certain. Like so many alchemists, he is a shadowy figure, but he is thought to have been an *adept*—that is, an alchemist who has attained the secret of the Philosopher's Stone. He is also supposed to have been the only person to have successfully performed a transmutation in North America.

In Philalethes' interpretation of Ripley's poem, the toad represents gold. Its black and stinking decay stands for the stage of putrefaction, necessary to attain first matter. The juice of grapes that the toad drinks is philosopher's mercury, a strange substance, perhaps only understood by alchemists. The "secret den" to which the bloated toad retreats is really the hermetically sealed, egg-shaped glass vessel in which the various stages of the alchemical process take place. In his own strange language Philalethes described the amount of time needed for the various essential color changes to occur: "In six and forty or fifty days expect the beginning of intire Blackness; and after six and fifty days more, or sixty, expect the Peacocks Tayl, and Colors of the Rainbow; and after two and twenty days more, or four and twenty, expect *Luna* perfect, the Whitest White, which will grow more and more glorious for the space of twenty days, or two and twenty at the most: After which, in a little more increased Fire, expect the Rule of *Venus* for the space of forty days more; and after him the Rule of *Sol flavus* forty days, or two and forty: And then in a moment comes the Tyrian Color, the sparkling Red, the fiery Vermilion, and Red Poppy of the Rock . . ."

For all its deliberately obscure symbolism, this is obviously a report on the observation of a real experiment, and it is not difficult to compare it with the process described by J.K. At the same time, the magic nature of the process, the attempt to imitate nature, is also apparent. The total time required adds up to the nine months that is the period of human gestation, and each stage takes place under the influence of an appropriate planet according to the principles expressed by Agrippa. As for the symbols, they also contributed an extra dimension to the meaning of the writing: they were influenced by medieval philosophy which believed that things which were superficially alike possessed some underlying similarity of nature. Therefore the lion, which was proud and tawny-colored and walked in the Sun, was not only a suitable symbol for gold, but could be thought to be an actual aspect of the nature of gold. With animals and mythic beasts, with incidents from the legends of antiquity, with acrostics and anagrams, secret alphabets and ciphers, these early alchemists gradually wove a net of mystification which in the end even they themselves could not penetrate.

Opposite: woodcuts from one of the early printed works on alchemy, *The New Pearl of Great Price* by Petrus Bonus. It was printed by the Aldine press, Venice, in 1546. One scholar remarks that the rare existing copies almost always are in a dilapidated condition because they were so subject to accidents near the furnaces of the adepts, among whom the book was a great favorite. In this sequence of illustrations a crowned king (symbolizing gold) is petitioned by his son (mercury) and five servants (silver, copper, iron, tin, and lead) for some of his power. He says nothing, and is slain by mercury. After a series of dramatic happenings, each of which represents an alchemical operation, the king is restored to life, and finally is able to crown his son and servants, although one—possibly lead, which was viewed with some suspicion by alchemists—is missing in the last scene of the resurrected king.

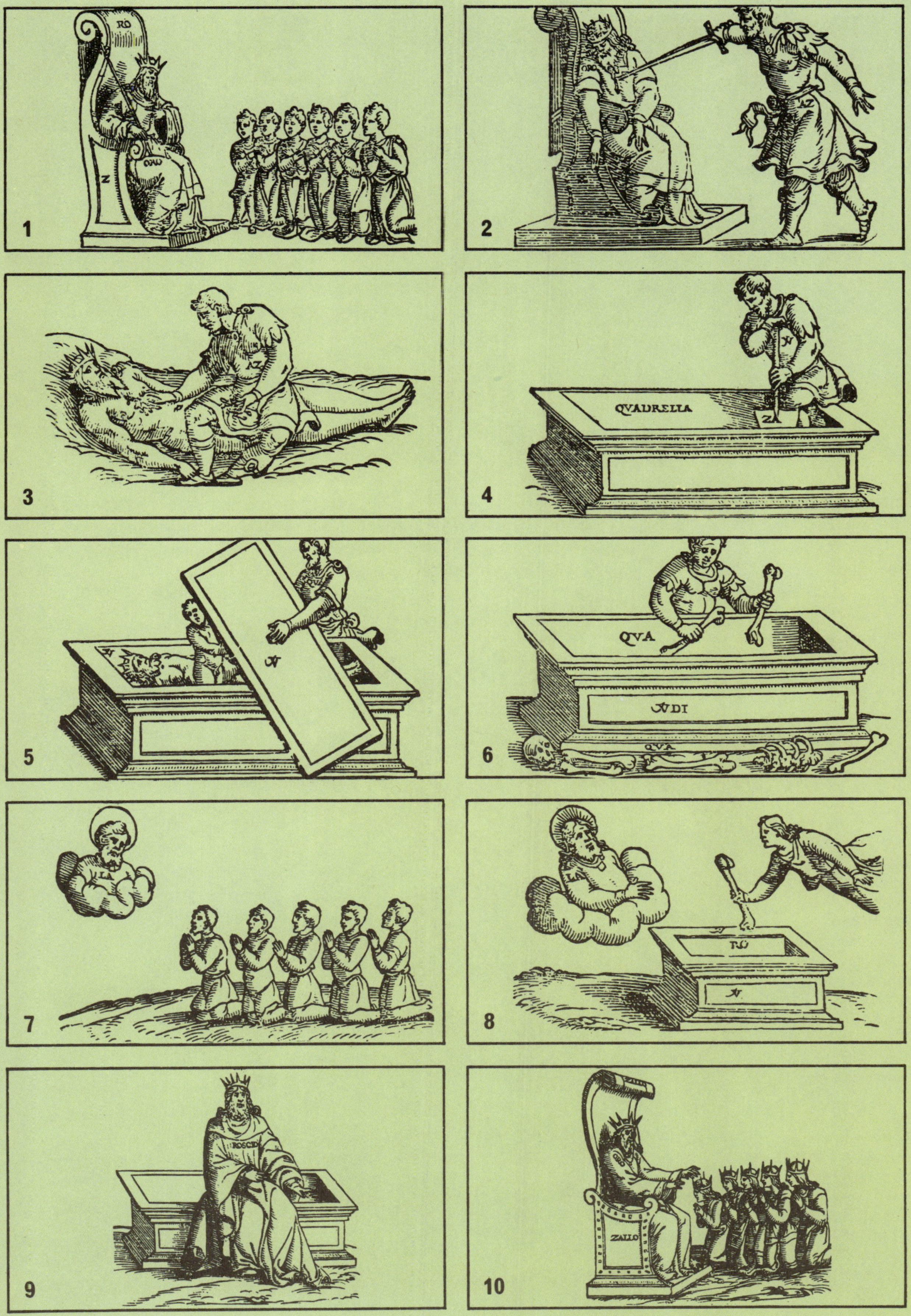
1
2
3
4
QVADRELLA
ZA
5
6
QVA
QVA
7
8
9
10
ZALLO

OPVS·MECHANICE

Chapter 12
The Wandering Alchemists

Why did the 17th-century alchemists wander from one European court to another? What did they hope to do? Was it all for personal gain? Dr. John Dee, the respected Elizabethan scholar, and Edward Kelley, his disreputable assistant, spent years in the employ of Emperor Rudolf II of Bohemia. Setonius and Sendivogius were virtually kept prisoner by Christian II of Saxony after they claimed to be able to produce the all-important Philosopher's Stone. But they and their contemporaries were the last of a dying breed as alchemy began to give way to the age of science.

Of all the monarchs of Europe who dabbled in alchemy, the Emperor Rudolf II was by far the most enthusiastic. His laboratory in Prague, in the country then called Bohemia, occupied two rooms of an old one-story building having three great furnaces and their flues along one wall. One furnace was designed to produce great heat for the smelting of ores, the second heated a large *bain-marie* or water bath, and the third was kept at low heat for the distillation of volatile liquids. On this third furnace stood a huge cucurbit surmounted by five *helms* (caps or covers) one above the other, with their long necks fitting into phials to collect the distillates. The shelves along the other walls were crammed with alembics, descensories, pelicans, aludels, and other pieces of apparatus, and there were glass jars, bottles, and gallipots, or glazed earthenware pots, packed with solids and liquids. A great wooden block in the center of one room held a vast mortar, with its pestle suspended from a rocking beam hanging from the rafters. On a ledge near one of the smoke-grimed windows lay well-thumbed books and old manuscripts, and a nearby table was piled with glass phials, pewter funnels, hourglasses of different sizes, spoons, spatulas, and knives. In the corridor between the two rooms were stocks of charcoal, nests of crucibles, clay, and other materials for sealing the necks of flasks, and all kinds of pots and pans.

The alchemists who were encouraged to work in this laboratory lived nearby in a narrow street that wound steeply upward

Opposite: a 16th-century miniature of an alchemist approaching a lady, probably representing an earth spirit, who gives life to plants and has a kind of darker magic. Thus the alchemist draws on the powers of earth for his work, indicated by the furnace.

Above: a medal that was struck from alchemical gold transmuted before His Highness Charles Philip, Count Palatine of the Rhineland on December 31, 1716.

Below: Emperor Rudolf II, who died in 1612. He was greatly interested in all aspects of the science of his time, being a patron of the astronomers Tycho Brahe and Johannes Kepler, but alchemy came to obsess his mind and near the end of his life he neglected the affairs of state. Haughty and suspicious, he was not popular.

from the cloisters of Saint George's church toward Saint Vitus' cathedral. To this day it is known as Golden Lane. Close by lived Dr. Thaddeus Hajek, the court physician and director of the laboratory. On September 3, 1584, he received two visitors from England: Dr. John Dee and his assistant Edward Kelley.

Exactly what Dee was doing in Bohemia has been the subject of speculation for the past 400 years. He was a famous scientist, England's leading mathematician and navigational expert, the owner of the largest library in the land, court astrologer to Queen Elizabeth I, and almost certainly an important spy for his country. The previous September he had left England secretly with Kelley, their two wives, and a certain Polish count named Albert Laski, who had hopes of becoming the king of Poland. They had spent an unhappy winter in Cracow, Poland, and when Laski had run short of funds without seeing any improvement in his hopes of gaining the throne, he had suggested that the two Englishmen present themselves to the Emperor Rudolf II. Perhaps he thought they would be able to raise more money by demonstrating their skills at alchemy, because Kelley claimed to possess the Philosopher's Stone.

Kelley's story was plausible. According to him he was born Edward Talbot in Worcester in 1555, and he later studied for a time at Oxford without taking a degree. His father may have been an apothecary, which would account for the skill he possessed in chemistry, and he appears to have set himself up as a notary—that is, someone who witnessed legal documents. He was found to have forged some title deeds for one of his clients, and it is said that his ears were clipped for the offense. Certainly he always wore a close-fitting skull cap that concealed the tops of his ears. After his sentence he could no longer practice, and for some time he led a wandering existence in Wales. It was at this time that he seems to have changed his name to Kelley.

Staying in an inn outside Bristol one night, Kelley was shown an old manuscript by the innkeeper. This manuscript, it appeared, had been stolen from a monastery some years before, and it was said that it had been taken from the broken tomb of Saint Dunstan, the Abbot of Glastonbury. Kelley had some knowledge of Welsh and could make some sense of the old Celtic language. Moreover his experience as a notary had given him skill in deciphering old documents. He soon discovered that the manuscript was a treatise on alchemy. He concealed his excitement, and asked the innkeeper whether anything else had been taken from the tomb. Only two small ivory bottles that had contained a red and a white powder, said the publican. He had given them to his children as playthings, but he thought the one containing the red powder was still intact. For the sum of one guinea, Kelley could keep the manuscript and the bottle.

Early in 1582 Kelley turned up at Dr. John Dee's house just outside London. At that time Dee had just begun his experiments in scrying or crystal-gazing. He had a glass sphere, and a disk of polished black obsidian that had been brought from Mexico by one of the early American explorers—both of which are now in the British Museum. He called these two objects his "shewstones," but he himself did not have the gift of "sight" and he had to employ a medium to see and describe the visions

American Gold?

that appeared in them. Kelley proved to be a skillful scryer, and soon he and Dee were spending every available moment in conjuring up visions of spirits and angels. We do not know whether he attempted to use his red powder at that time, although some 80 years later Elias Ashmole, a well-known archeologist and antiquarian, wrote that "Mr. Lilly [the famous 17th-century astrologer] told me that John Evans informed him that he was acquainted with Kelley's sister in Worcester, that she showed him some of the gold her brother had transmuted . . ."

There is no doubt, however, that Dee took his shewstones to Cracow and to Prague, and that Kelley took his powder. When they visited Dr. Hajek, the director of Emperor Rudolf's laboratory in Prague, Kelley demonstrated a transmutation in Hajek's cellar. Hajek then arranged an audience with the Emperor, during which Kelley scryed with the shewstone. He revealed through the medium of the spirit Zadkiel a formula for

Below: the Golden Lane in Prague, which was also called the Street of the Alchemists, after the many men who worked for Rudolf II.

Above: Edward Kelley, in a print made about 1600, a few years after his death. Medium, alchemist, and convicted criminal, his role in both magical and alchemical transactions with John Dee has always been disputed. Certainly Dee believed Kelley was absolutely essential to his work, and would go to great lengths to please him.

the Philosopher's Stone, which the Emperor carefully copied down. When Dee sought a second audience, he was told that the Emperor was away hunting, and that he should make all his communications in future through Dr. Kurtz, a member of the council.

Dee and Kelley were very short of money by then: they had been a year out of England, and Mrs. Dee had recently given birth to a fourth child. Among Dee's papers in the British Museum is a petition written for Jane Dee by Edward Kelley:

"We desire God, of his greate and infinite mercies to grant us the helpe of His hevenly mynisters, that we may by them be directed how or by whom to be ayded and released in this necessitie for meate and drinke for us and for our familie, wherewith we stand at this instant much opressed . . ."

Dee spent some time in trying to interest Dr. Kurtz in his experiments, and even turned down an offer of a salary of a thousand marks from the Czar of Russia because he hoped for more encouragement from the Emperor Rudolf. During his time abroad Dee had been successfully spreading his own religious and scientific beliefs. He was one of the foremost thinkers of his age, and his ideas carried great weight. However, they did not at all accord with those of the Catholic Church, and in the spring of 1586 it became apparent that the Church was about to take action against both him and Kelley. They left Prague hurriedly, and learned not long after that it was just in time. The Pope's representative had accused them of conjuring and black magic, and had ordered Rudolf to arrest them and send them to Rome for interrogation.

For several months they wandered, until in September 1586 Count Wilhelm Rosenberg of Bohemia invited them to stay in his castle at Trebona. Kelley immersed himself in his alchemical experiments, and even Dee began to take a necessary interest in the subject. There are many stories that they succeeded in making gold. John Aubrey, the 17th-century writer and antiquarian, wrote that "Arthur Dee, his sonne, a physician at Norwich, and intimate friend of Sir Thomas Browne, told Mr. Bathurst that (being but a boy) he was used to play at quoits with the plates of gold made by projection in the garret of Dr. Dee's lodgings. . . ." There is also a report in the manuscripts of Elias Ashmole that Queen Elizabeth was impressed by some of this gold. "On the continent Kelley anointed a warming pan belonging to a Mr. Willoughby with a certain oil which changed a portion of the lid to gold. This piece was cut out and, with the pan, sent to Elizabeth who, observing the perfect fit of the gold plate into the hole in the lid, was thus convinced of Kelley's powers."

The Emperor Rudolf, it seems, also became convinced of Kelley's powers. Kelley managed to make several visits to Prague without being arrested, and brought back large sums of money for Dee. He was even made "a Baron of the Kingdom of Bohemia," and insisted thereafter in calling himself Sir Edward Kelley. Poor Dee, with his shewstones, was pushed into the background, and in the autumn of 1589 he decided at last to return to England. But Kelley would not go with him. He was sure that, although his stock of red powder was almost ex-

Below: one of the alchemical symbols from Edward Kelley's book *Theater of Terrestrial Alchemy*, showing the Philosopher's Egg. It was titled "Of the Exaltation of Mercurial Water" which was an essential element of his process.

Edward Kelley and Dr John Dee

Left: Dr. John Dee. He was a recognized scholar, astrologer to Queen Elizabeth I, and a dedicated and pious seeker into the mysteries of magic and the occult. Having no mediumistic gift himself, he was always dependent upon an assistant scryer. Thus he came into association with Kelley, who was said to have remarkable gifts.

hausted, he could renew it by carefully following the instructions in one of his books. These included the *Book of Zacharias* with, as Dee had noted, "the Alkanor that I translated out of French . . . Rowlaschy his Third boke of Waters Philosophicall; the Boke called *Angellicum Opus*, all in pictures of the work from the beginning to the end; the copy of the man of Budwise Conclusions for the Transmutation of Metalls and 40 leaves in 4°, entitled *Extractiones Dunstani*, which he himself extracted and noted out of Dunstan's his boke and the very boke of Dunstan was cast on the bed hard by the table."

Was this "very boke of Dunstan" the manuscript that Kelley had bought from the innkeeper? There are many who believe that it was, and that Kelley incorporated the teachings of this manuscript in his own book *The Stone of the Philosophers*. Dee's son Arthur, who later took the post in Russia that his father had refused, often referred to the *Book of Dunstan* in his writings.

Despite his extensive collection of reference material, Kelley appears to have had problems in duplicating the essential red powder. He continued his experiments, but both Count Rosenberg and the Emperor Rudolf became increasingly impatient. In England, impressed by the gold lid of the warming pan she had seen, Queen Elizabeth asked her Lord Treasurer to see

The Failed Alchemist

If the golden rewards of success often dangled temptingly before alchemists and persuaded some of the weaker practitioners into fraud, the penalties for failure were often drastic. One who discovered this to his cost was Georg Honauer, who called himself Lord of Brunnhof and Grobschütz. He came to the court of Duke Frederick of Württemberg, who sought in the alchemist's art an answer to his own financial problems.

Honauer at first was successful, but to make sure of this, he had secretly thrown charcoal mixed with gold into the bubbling quicksilver in the crucible. Not content with this, he managed to satisfy another of the duke's tests by bringing a large chest with a secret compartment into his laboratory. After the duke had formally sealed up the room during the transmutation, the hidden accomplice emerged from the chest, and put the needed gold into the crucible.

Honauer was defeated when the duke presented him with iron weighing 52 hundredweight, and demanded that it be made into the finest gold. The duke had the iron covered with gold-leaf and made into gallows. On a fine spring day in 1597 he hanged his unsuccessful alchemist on the gleaming golden iron he had failed to transmute.

whether he could persuade Kelley "to come over to his native countrie and honour her Majestie with the fruites of such knowledge as God has given him." Still Kelley would not come, and the Lord Treasurer finally wrote: "Many say that if you come not, it is because you cannot perform what has been reported of you. . . . I am expressly commanded by Her Majestie to require you to have regard to her honour . . . be assured of worldly reward, you can make your Queen so happie . . . surely as no subject she hath can do the like. Good Knight, let me end my letter, conjuring you in God's holy name not to keep God's gift from your natural countrie, but rather helpe make Her Majestie a glorious and victorious power against the mallyce of hers and God's enemies."

Then came news that Kelley was imprisoned by the Emperor on charges of sorcery and heresy. It was probably intended more as a warning than a punishment, because Kelley was allowed his books, and devoted the time to writing his treatise on the Philosopher's Stone. In 1593 he was once more at liberty, and even persuaded the Emperor to extend an invitation to Dee to revisit Prague—an invitation that Dee, then 66 and as always short of money, did not accept. In December of that year a certain Philip Gawdy wrote home: "Kelley is delivered out of prison and restored to his former estate and maketh gold as fast as a hen will cracke nuttes"—a most ambiguous remark when one considers the normal diet of the hen.

Shortly after this, Kelley was once more imprisoned, and his end remains a mystery. It was reported that he had twisted his bedclothes into a rope to escape from his prison, fell to the ground, broke both legs and a couple of ribs, and died some days later. There is some doubtful evidence that Dee had spoken to Elizabeth on his behalf, and that the escape had been engineered from England. Other reports stated that he had been killed in prison, and even that he had killed himself.

Dee, for the remaining 15 years of his life, gave up the practice of magic. Without Kelley as his link with the world of spirits he could only "dream after midnight of my working of the Philosopher's Stone with others." He died in December 1608 "firmly believing that the secrets of the Universe were still within his grasp and that, though he had proved unworthy to receive them in his lifetime, beyond the grave they would be vouchsafed to him."

Dee had many other reasons for his journey to Europe beside the desire to spread the knowledge of alchemy. But by the 17th century, many alchemists began to travel with that purpose chiefly in mind. Wandering emissaries appeared at various places on the continent. They would arrive unannounced in some town, make contact with the local alchemists, instruct them in the secrets of transmutation, and disappear again. The first of these was Alexander Seton, a Scot.

In 1601 Seton had given shelter to a Dutch sea captain, Jacob Haussen, whose ship had been driven ashore near Seton's house in Scotland. The following year, Seton turned up at Haussen's home in Enkhuisen, and confided to him that he was an adept. He said he had a mission to teach the art of transmutation. Before he left, he prepared for the skeptical sailor a bar of gold, and cut a time and date into it with a steel point. It was 4 p.m. on the afternoon of March 13, 1602.

From Enkhuisen Seton traveled to Amsterdam and Rotterdam, giving demonstrations of his skill in both cities. He took a ship from Rotterdam, disappearing for over a year. We next pick up his trail in Zurich, Switzerland, where he obtained a letter of introduction to the scientist Dr. Jacob Zwinger of Basel. He traveled to Basel in the company of Professor Wolfgang Dienheim of Freiburg, who wrote a detailed record of everything that took place. Part of this report follows:

"I . . . found myself traveling in company with a gentleman of remarkable intellectual gifts. He was short of stature and rather stout, with a high color, and sanguine temperament, and wore his brown beard trimmed in the French style. He was dressed in a suit of black satin, and was accompanied by one servant only,

Alchemical Gold?

Left: a watercolor painting of some Eskimoes in Baffin Bay, Canada, seen by explorer Martin Frobisher and his crews during their search for the Northwest Passage. A little known side of Frobisher's second and third voyages had to do with a search for gold that ended in failure. It started when a sailor brought a black stone back to England after the first voyage in 1576, and though two assayers found it worthless, an Italian assayer said it contained gold. When questioned about this assessment, the Italian remarked in a way worthy of the alchemists' mysteriousness that ". . . nature needs to be flattered." Frobisher brought back 200 tons of supposed gold ore on his second journey, and 1000 tons on his third. Then the crushing truth came out: there was no gold in the stones. The speculators—which included Dee among them—lost heavily. The serious search for a Northwest Passage was set back. And Martin Frobisher never got another opportunity for exploration.

who was distinguishable from everyone else by his red hair and beard." Throughout the journey the two men disputed about alchemy and the possibility of transmutation, and in Basel they persuaded Dr. Zwinger to provide some slabs of lead, a crucible borrowed from a local goldsmith, and some ordinary sulfur.

"Setonius did not touch any of these things. He asked for a fire to be lit, ordered the lead and sulfur to be put in the crucible over the fire, the mass to be stirred, and the lid to be put on . . . At the end of a quarter of an hour he said: 'Throw this paper into the molten lead, but make sure that it goes right into the middle, and that none falls into the fire.' In the paper was a heavy sort of lemon-yellow powder—but you needed good eyesight to see it. Although we were as doubting as Saint Thomas himself, we did everything he told us. After the mass had been heated for another quarter of an hour and stirred continuously with little iron rods, the goldsmith was told to extinguish the fire by pouring water over it. We found not a vestige of lead remaining, only the finest gold which, in the opinion of the goldsmith, was of a quality better even than the excellent Hungarian or Arabian gold. It weighed exactly the same as the lead we had put in originally."

Zwinger confirmed this account in a letter to another professor in Basel, Emmanuel König, who later published it. The second letter also states that Seton performed a further trans-

Below: Emperor Rudolf II in the laboratory of his alchemist, after a painting by Vaczlar Brozik. In fact he had many alchemists, and often visited them to watch their operations. Their failures were on occasion tolerated, but at other times punished by torture or death.

The Alchemists' Emperor Patron

Left: Rudolf as the Roman god Vertumnus, an extraordinary portrait by Giuseppe Arcimboldo. Vertumnus was the god of changing seasons, and hence of flower and fruit. Rudolf, who was apparently eccentric to the point of madness, was immensely pleased by this portrait and ennobled the artist.

Alchemist at Risk

Opposite: an alchemist being tortured by an avaricious ruler. Christian II, who had Seton put through similar ordeals, found himself at length in an unfortunate dilemma. Seton, still stubborn about not revealing how he produced red powder, was clearly near to death, and if he died the secret would be lost forever. Christian then reluctantly gave up on his attempt to extract the information and put him in solitary confinement. Sendivogius, who was a stranger to Seton, rescued him from jail—mainly in the hope of discovering the gold-making secret himself.

Below: Christian II of Saxony, before whom Alexander Seton made a successful transmutation. The Elector was determined to discover his secret, and when Seton refused to tell him, had him tortured.

mutation before he left the city.

Seton seems next to have appeared in Strasbourg under the alias of Hirschberger. In that city he performed a transmutation in the shop of the goldsmith Gustenhöfer, and presented him with a small sample of his red powder before leaving. However, his visit eventually brought misfortune to the goldsmith. The Emperor Rudolf heard of his success, but only after he had used up the supply of powder. The Emperor summoned him to Prague and insisted that he perform a transmutation. The unfortunate Gustenhöfer confessed that the powder had been given him by a stranger, and he had no idea how to make any more. The Emperor refused to believe him and had him imprisoned for life.

Meanwhile Seton had traveled on to Frankfurt, where he represented himself as a French count. He made friends with a merchant named Koch, who later wrote to the historian Theobald de Hogelande: "He did not put a hand to the work himself, but allowed me to do everything. He gave me a reddish-gray powder, weighing about three grains. I dropped it into two half-ounces of quicksilver in a crucible. Then I filled the crucible about halfway up with potash, and we put it over a gentle heat. After this I filled the furnace with charcoal, so that the crucible was entirely embedded in a very hot fire; I left it there for about half an hour. When the crucible was red hot, he told me to throw a little piece of yellow wax into it. A few minutes later, I cooled the crucible and broke it open. At the bottom I found a small piece of gold that weighed 54 ounces three grains. It was melted in my presence and submitted to an assay; 23 carats 15 grains of gold resulted, together with six of silver—both of an exceptionally brilliant color. I had a stud made for my shirt with part of the gold."

Seton next went to Cologne, where he demonstrated the art before the skeptical city surgeon Meister Georg and completely convinced him. He then traveled on to Hamburg. News of his exploits had spread all over the Rhineland, but because he constantly changed his alias, and because he went from city to city, he was nicknamed the Cosmopolite from the Greek meaning a citizen of the world. His destination after Hamburg was Munich, where he fell in love with a pretty girl and eloped with her. In the autumn of 1603 he reached Crossen, and Christian II of Saxony invited him to come to his court and demonstrate a transmutation.

Seton was deeply in love with his new wife and, rather foolishly, sent his servant Hamilton to court in his place. Hamilton successfully carried out a transmutation but, probably realizing the intentions of the Saxony ruler, hastily disappeared. Christian's greed, coupled with his feeling that he had been insulted by Seton's indifference and his fear that Seton would run away, caused him to make an immediate arrest of Seton.

Christian II wanted no less than full details of how to prepare the red powder for himself, but Seton had sworn never to reveal the secret. He was thrown into prison and tortured over and over again, but nothing would persuade him to tell the ruler what he wanted to know.

At this point in the story a certain Michael Sendivogius, who

Transmutation – or Trickery?

Right: Michael Sendivogius in a stylized portrait published in 1624. His early career is obscure. It has been reported that he was the natural son of a Polish nobleman, but certainly he had no success in alchemy until he encountered Alexander Seton.

lived near Cracow, appeared on the scene. He heard of Seton's imprisonment and decided, with ulterior motives, to help him escape. He sold his house in Cracow and used the money to ingratiate himself with Seton's jailers. One night, having got them drunk, he unlocked the prisoner's cell and carried out the weak and broken man. Stopping only to pick up Seton's wife and her supply of the Philosopher's Stone, he drove his carriage at breakneck speed through the night until the party was safely out of Saxony.

But, even out of gratitude for his rescue, Seton would not reveal his secret. Shortly afterwards he died from the effects of his terrible tortures. Sendivogius married Seton's widow, and inherited the supply of red powder; but although he spent years experimenting he could find no way to make more. He went to Prague and showed the Emperor Rudolf how to carry out a transmutation. The Emperor had a marble plaque carved,

Right: a piece of alchemical gold now in the British Museum, shown here magnified about four times. The accompanying label—in 19th-century handwriting—states that it was made in Bapora in October 1814, in the presence of Colonel Macdonald and Doctor Colquhoun.

which may be seen to this day, with the Latin words *Faciat hoc quispiam alius quod fecit Sendivogius Polonus*—"Whoever else could do what Sendivogius the Pole has done?"

On his way back from Prague to Cracow, Sendivogius was taken prisoner by a nobleman who hoped to have more success with him than Christian II had had with Seton. Sendivogius kept a little of his wonderful powder in a gold box, which he hung around his neck, but most of it was hidden in a hole cut in the step of his carriage, and the nobleman did not find it. The prisoner managed to get hold of a file and cut through one of the bars of his cell window. Then, tying his clothes into a rope, he escaped naked into the night and fled back to Prague. There he told his story to the Emperor, who confiscated the nobleman's estate and presented it to Sendivogius.

But the red powder did not last forever, and soon Sendivogius had spent everything he had in trying to manufacture more. In the end he was reduced to borrowing money from various acquaintances, and borrowing more when he was forced to repay his first loans. He earned a little by writing alchemical treatises, for which he took the name of the Cosmopolite to give them greater authority. He died, a near pauper, in 1646.

There were other wandering adepts, all of whom were vouched for by distinguished scholars, and dozens of learned books published throughout Europe in the first half of the 17th century with detailed descriptions of transmutations. But alchemy's flourishing days were numbered. The scientific revolution had begun.

Below: Sendivogius making gold—presumably using Seton's red powder because he failed once it was used up—in the royal castle in Cracow before King Sigismund III and a Jesuit priest. The fireplace shown here was still to be seen in the castle as late as 1950.

Chapter 13
What Happened to Alchemy?

Alchemy could not stand as a house divided. With some adherents concentrating almost solely on using its processes to make medicines, and others concerning themselves almost entirely with the mystical inner search, alchemy was dealt a death blow. As scientific thought and experiment advanced in the 17th century, alchemical methods and equipment became less mysterious. In addition, charlatans took over with promises of get-rich-quick schemes, and the influence of the mystical society of Rosicrucians made it ever more obscure. By the late 18th century respectable scientists would have nothing to do with the ancient lore of alchemy.

Since its beginnings in the early centuries after Christ, Western alchemy had been a strange tightly woven network of varied beliefs and practices. No two ideas were more closely linked than the belief that the quest to transmute ordinary metals into gold went hand in hand with a quest for spiritual perfection. For the true alchemist, the struggles in the laboratory reflected the struggles in his soul. As he seemed to approach nearer his physical aim of making gold, so he came nearer to his spiritual aim of a perfect soul. This explains the fact that in true alchemy, the desire for gold had nothing whatever to do with the desire for riches. Indeed, alchemists were not interested in amassing fortunes. The ability to make gold was a sign that they had reached a state of inward perfection and discovered the secret workings of the Universe. Of course there were always alchemists who became so involved in the spiritual quest that they neglected the practical aims of the laboratory, and those who became so absorbed in the practical side that they neglected their spiritual development. But ideally, until the decline of alchemy, the practical search for the perfect metal and the spiritual search for the perfect soul were inseparable.

Like almost every Western scientist and philosopher up to the 17th century, alchemists unquestioningly accepted Aristotle's theory of the Universe. According to him, all material things in the world were composed of varying proportions of the four elements of Earth, Air, Fire, and Water. But substances could

Opposite: in this painting of *The Discovery of Phosphorus*, the dazzled alchemist kneels awestruck before the luminous spectacle of phosphorus within his receiver.

From Alchemy to Chemistry

be altered into other substances by the appropriate application of one of the four qualities of wetness, dryness, cold, or heat. This idea of change was fundamental to the alchemist's belief that base metals could be transmuted into gold.

Another important contribution to alchemy was made by the mystical and hermetic beliefs that arose in the early years of the Christian era, and were revived, with the ideas of Aristotle, in the Middle Ages and early Renaissance. Man, the Microcosm, was thought to be a reflection on a small scale of the Universe or Macrocosm. All things in the Universe were linked in harmony with each other. Man could discover and use this harmony for his own benefit, primarily through the system of correspondences that outlined a special relationship between certain planets, feelings, and objects, and ultimately by discovering the universal spirit that permeated the Universe. It was this spirit that the alchemists were attempting to identify and possess in the Philosopher's Stone.

When alchemy first developed in the early centuries after Christ, it was able to draw on the technical achievements of the ancient world. In the previous 3000 years many crafts had become highly developed, and a vast amount of knowledge and expertise had been accumulated in many fields. Craftsmen had become expert in metalwork and glassmaking. The preparation of dyes, perfumes, and cosmetics, not to mention drugs and poisons, was highly skilled and had led to a detailed knowledge of many chemical compounds. In Egypt, one of the earliest and most influential civilizations, craftsmen produced the most beautiful objects for the rich in gold, silver, and precious stones. With equal skill, and for their poorer customers, they produced excellent imitations in colored alloys that could pass for gold, and colored glass that looked deceptively like real gems.

The early alchemists therefore had at their disposal a great deal of useful information about substances, highly skilled techniques, and the basic equipment. However, they were also innovators. They adapted and invented apparatus in order to carry out the endless processes of heating and cooling, separating and combining, vaporizing and solidifying that they deemed so essential to their task. In their ceaseless search for the Philosopher's Stone, they discovered many new substances and methods of treatment. By the 16th century the alchemist's laboratory was an extremely sophisticated place, in many ways resembling a modern chemical laboratory. But the alchemist was far from being a chemist in our sense of the term.

Chemistry, as we know it today, deals with the structure, composition, and properties of substances, and the way they react under different conditions. Before coming to any general conclusion, a chemist will repeat an experiment many times under identical conditions, and will keep careful records of the results. The alchemist's only interest in substances until the 16th century was as the possible ingredients of the Philosopher's Stone. Alchemists were not concerned to examine them further because they had a ready-made answer as to the nature of substances—first in the theory of the four elements of Aristotle, and then in the additional division of substances into sulfur and mercury or sulfur, mercury, and salt of later alchemists. Their

Below: opening of a course of Lectures in Transmutative Chemistry, from a book by Annibal Barlet. With such lectures given in public—a world away from the secretive private instruction expressed in illusions and wary symbolism—some alchemists moved toward the science of chemistry.

belief in a mystical, hermetic philosophy, with its ideas of occult sympathies between objects, encouraged them to wild flights of fancy and speculation, often on the basis of a single observation. Many single chemical facts were established by the alchemists, but each existed in isolation and was of little general use.

Left: Francis Bacon, Viscount St. Albans, after the marble tomb effigy in the church in St. Albans. He once wrote that alchemists were like the sons of the man who told them he had left gold buried in the vineyard. By their vigorous digging they found no gold, but by turning up the mold around the roots of the vines, produced a plentiful vintage. So, said Bacon, did the attempts to make gold bring to light many useful inventions and instructive experiments for others to make use of.

The Royal Society and the Alchemists

It was Paracelsus, the great 16th-century physician, who perhaps unwittingly started the decline in alchemy and the progress toward true chemistry. A more than life-size figure himself, he embraced the mystical and the practical aspects of alchemy in revolutionary ways. Brushing aside the question of transmuting metals to gold, he insisted that the true purpose of mystical alchemy was to develop secret powers within one's soul, and the true goal of practical alchemy was to find medical cures. His followers found both these ideas too much to contend with. Some retreated from the laboratory to concentrate on their spiritual development. Others, joyfully released from the rigidity of searching for the Philosopher's Stone, began to experiment

Right: King Charles II, who gave the Royal Society its first charter in 1660, and so helped chemistry establish itself as a nonmystical field of study.

more constructively. In so doing they made many important new discoveries. The foundations were laid first for *iatro*, or medical chemistry, and then for chemistry itself.

Gradually hermetic beliefs in the unity of the cosmos fell out of fashion, and scientists began to look for new theories to supplement or replace Aristotle's ideas. Many throughout the 17th and early 18th centuries continued to believe in the possibility of transmuting metals to gold, but they were too busy either with their own souls or with their laboratory experiments to look closely into the question. Creating gold from base metals fell into the hands of those who hoped to amass riches or to dupe others, which was a far cry from the spiritual aims of the early alchemists.

Scientific ideas from other sources also gradually began to erode the position of alchemy in the 16th and 17th centuries. Francis Bacon, the great English essayist and scientific philosopher who died in 1626, had insisted on the need for properly organizing experiments and recording results so that they could be repeated and verified. He believed that experiments should lead to generalizations, which in turn would lead to new experiments. These ideas were revolutionary to the alchemist, whose experiments were largely haphazard, rarely repeated and certainly never led toward any scientific conclusion. Bacon also suggested that scientists from different fields should meet together to discuss their work and exchange ideas. Alchemists were used to working in secret, jealously guarding their ideas and only communicating by means of obscure and almost incomprehensible symbolism. The open discussions between groups of eminent scientists and thinkers that began to take place in Europe from the mid-16th century onward dealt yet another blow to the mysterious image of the alchemist.

In England in 1660 Charles II helped inaugurate just such a scientific group by founding the Royal Society of London. One of its first members, Robert Boyle, was instrumental in setting chemistry on its feet as a science in its own right, freeing it both from the aims of transmuting metals and from preparing medicines. In the *Sceptical Chymist*, published in 1661, he attacked both the Aristotelian idea of four elements, and the alchemist's notion of the three principles of salt, sulfur, and mercury. He gave a totally new definition of an element as a substance that could not be broken down into component parts. Boyle was extremely interested in a new element that, according to tradition, had been discovered by a German alchemist named Brandt in the city of Hamburg. Boyle obtained a sample of this substance, which we know as phosphorus today, and with the help of an assistant, began to manufacture it. The product soon sold widely throughout Europe. Although Boyle's influence was strong, some scientists continued to accept Aristotle's ideas until late in the 18th century. In the controversy, it is not surprising that many alchemists retreated from the scientific fray into the comparative safety of mysticism.

One of the strangest manifestations of alchemical mysticism is the story of the Rosicrucian fraternity, an order that claimed to possess immense power and to count as members the great alchemists of two centuries. All that is known of it is contained

Above: a meeting of the Royal Society, the national academy of science for Great Britain and Northern Ireland. The Society began about 1645 as a weekly gathering of a group of thinkers who had been influenced by "the New or Experimental Philosophy" that Francis Bacon advocated.

Below: Robert Boyle. Although he did his utmost to establish chemistry as an independent branch of natural philosophy, separate from both the gold-seeking alchemists and the medically minded followers of Paracelsus, he did believe in the possibility of transmutation.

Above: Heinrich Khunrath at prayer in his laboratory. Khunrath, who died in 1605, was one of the alchemists who moved toward a deeply mystical approach to the art. His working place, as shown here, is half church and half laboratory, adorned with many inscriptions. Among them are these: "When we attend strictly to our work, God himself will help us" and "That which is wisely tried again will succeed sometime"—no doubt a comfort in moments of alchemical melancholia.

in three anonymous pamphlets published in Germany between 1614 and 1616. They are full of the strange symbolism that is so beloved of mystical alchemists, and are extremely difficult to understand. They gave no information on who the leaders of the fraternity were or where they were to be found. No one to this day has been able to determine whether the brotherhood actually existed, whether it had been invented to convey certain ideas in symbolic terms, or whether it was a hoax designed to discredit eager dabblers in alchemy and the occult. The publication of the pamphlets aroused intense excitement and eager speculation in Europe. Many believers tried to get in touch with the authors, some by publishing their own pam-

Mystical Alchemy

Left: the tomb of Christian Rosenkreuz, who is shown as the man at the bottom of the picture. The tomb symbolizes the Hill of the philosophers, covered with alchemical symbols. If the spiral path were followed, it would lead through all the processes to the crowning work at the top. By this time, mystical alchemy—of which Rosicrucianism is one of the most elaborate forms—had moved far beyond the original goal of transmuting metal to gold.

phlets in reply. The interest lasted throughout the 17th century. Even famous scientists and philosophers such as Descartes and Leibniz tried hard to get at the truth, but without success.

The first of the pamphlets, *Fama Fraternitatis*, tells of the travels of Brother C.R.C. in search of scientific skills and true wisdom. C.R.C. was thought to stand for Christian Rosenkreuz, the last name meaning "Rosy Cross." Rosenkreuz settled in Germany and founded the Rosicrucian Order, or Fraternity of the Rosy Cross, with three other monks. They assisted him in writing down everything he had learned in science, magic, and healing. Gradually the order was increased to eight members. They later dispersed, having pledged to keep the identity of

Above: Johann Valentin Andreae, a respected German theologian. Late in his life he wrote an autobiography in which he admitted that he wrote *The Chemical Wedding*, the third of the pamphlets introducing Rosicrucianism, as a joke. He did not claim authorship of the other two pamphlets, however.

Below: Frederick V, Elector Palatine of the Rhine, with his bride the Princess Elizabeth, daughter of James I of England. It has been suggested that Andreae's *Chemical Wedding* could have been purely a satire on the elaborate festivities of the royal wedding in 1613. Others say that no matter what Andreae said later, it was written in complete seriousness at the time, using the theme of the royal wedding as the basis for allegory.

the fraternity secret for 100 years. Long after his death the tomb of Christian Rosenkreuz was said to have been opened, and his body found in a perfect state of preservation. The *Fama* aroused such excitement and interest that it had to be reprinted many times.

In 1615 the *Confessio* appeared. It was written in the same vague language, and though it invited readers to join the Brotherhood, it did not say how this could be done. The third pamphlet, *The Chemical Wedding*, was published in 1616. Even apart from its title, there was no doubt that *The Chemical Wedding* was inspired by alchemy. It was full of familiar alchemical symbols as well as much else that would appeal to the Renaissance magician, such as mathematical puzzles, descriptions of wonderful mechanical toys, and "most strange Figures, and dark Sentences and Speeches." In it, a Christian Rosenkreuz who may or may not be the same one as in the first pamphlet, is invited to a royal wedding. After encountering various hazards, he reaches the castle, and there submits to certain tests. Finally he witnesses the marriage, and afterward is made a Knight.

Many years later a well-known German theologian, Johann Valentin Andreae of Würtemberg, confessed that he had written *The Chemical Wedding* as a schoolboy joke. Whether he was also the author of the other two pamphlets, and whether they were also intended as jokes, was unclear. However, even after this confession, many continued to take all the pamphlets seriously. At one level they were interpreted by occultists as describing various alchemical and hermetic secrets. Others read into them a deeper social purpose in which a reformation in science, similar to the Lutheran reformation in religion, was advocated. They argued that if greed and fraud were eliminated from science, and proper methods of research and experiment established, it would be of great benefit to humanity. Since it was not clear how anyone could join the Rosicrucians, some less scrupulous, or more excitable, people claimed that they were already members, or founded orders of their own.

One such person was Michael Maier, a successful physician who was born in Rendsberg, Germany in about 1568. He had been ennobled for his medical skill by the Emperor Rudolf II, but he seems to have become infected by that ruler's passion for alchemy. He abandoned medicine and devoted his later life to the pursuit of the Philosopher's Stone, losing both his health and his fortune in the process. When the Rosicrucian controversy broke he played a prominent role, defending the fraternity's claims in several tracts. He claimed both to be a member of the Rosicrucian Order, and to have founded a similar order himself. He visited the alchemical writer, Robert Fludd, in England, and converted him to Rosicrucian ideas. Fludd later published his own defense of Rosicrucianism.

Jacob Boehme was another supporter of the Rosicrucians. He was born in Germany in 1575 and started work as an itinerant shoemaker. When he finally settled down, he began to study alchemy. He soon abandoned the practical work, but he used the symbolic language of alchemy to describe his mystical visions. The Philosopher's Stone became the Spirit of Christ which must tincture the individual soul.

It was the mysterious nature of alchemical symbolism that enabled alchemists to make such differing interpretations. Some symbols could be interpreted as parts of the laboratory process, or as stages in the progress of the soul, or as both. Alchemy used an extraordinarily rich variety of symbolism, drawing on astrology, religion, and magic. Alchemists had always been concerned to preserve secrecy about their work, and symbols served a dual purpose. They were a convenient way of remembering things without writing them down, and they were an equally convenient way of confusing others when written down. There was no consistency in alchemical language, which often had hundreds of different symbolic terms for each

"The Chemical Wedding"

Below: a 17th-century drawing of the ship of the argonauts, a float in the wedding pageant of Princess Elizabeth in 1613. In Greek myth the argonauts were a group of sailors who searched for the Golden Fleece—an obvious tie-in with the Chemical Wedding, in which another kind of search for gold goes on. This royal wedding was also seen as an important political event.

Alchemists Among the New Scientists

of the various substances and processes. An outsider would be totally baffled by an alchemical manuscript, and even an experienced alchemist might spend years in trial and error attempting to decipher it. A few symbols were generally understood, but they rarely amounted to a set of instructions. The black crow, for example, represented the stage of putrefied matter, and the dove the pure white substance obtained by sublimation. The red king stood for gold, or philosopher's sulfur, and the white queen for silver, or philosopher's mercury. The toad stood for earthy matter, the winged lion was mercury, and the wingless lion was sulfur. The gray wolf stood for antimony, and the newborn baby with a crown for the Philosopher's Stone.

The 17th century was a time of great progress in both scientific thought and discovery, but strangely enough, many pioneering experimenters and philosophers were also staunch believers in alchemy. One of the most famous of these was Sir Isaac Newton, who propounded the law of gravity. He spent much time speculating on alchemy and the magical nature of things, and his mathematical investigations confirmed his belief in the mystical harmonies of the Universe. For example, although there were only six distinct colors in the spectrum, Newton felt obliged to identify seven because of the magical significance of this number. His description of gravity was at first viewed with great suspicion by fellow members of the Royal Society. Gravity, or *gravitas*, was a quality associated with the planet Saturn and the metal lead. The whole thing smacked too much of alchemy and magic. Only Newton's faultless mathematics preserved his reputation.

Newton was not the only important thinker to believe in alchemy. Descartes, who is regarded by many as being the father of modern philosophy, was deeply interested in the subject. Leibniz, another great philosopher, spent several formative years as secretary to an alchemical society in Nürnberg. He retained a life-long preoccupation with the nature of the Philosopher's Stone. A rather more eccentric figure was Johann Rudolf Glauber. Born in Germany in 1604, he became a physician and chemist, and was an ardent believer in alchemy. He made many important discoveries, especially in the chemistry of wines and the distillation of spirits. On examining the waters of a mineral spring where he had gone to take a cure, he found them to contain what we now know as sodium sulfate. Overjoyed, he believed that at last he had found one of the vital constituents of the Philosopher's Stone. Crystallized sodium is known as Glauber's Salt to this day. It is used not as an elixir of life, however, but as a laxative.

One important scientist who claimed to have carried out a successful transmutation was John Baptist van Helmont. He lived near Brussels and devoted his life to chemical investigation. He was the first man to identify gases as a distinct group of substances, and to distinguish between them in terms of their chemical and physical properties. His reputation for integrity was unquestioned. He was also a firm believer in alchemy. He tells how in 1618 he received a visit from a stranger who gave him a minute particle of the Philosopher's Stone, which he

Below: Michael Maier, 16th-century physician and Rosicrucian with a keen interest in alchemy. He assembled a collection of alchemical writings he called *The Golden Tripod*, which consisted of translations of three books, one of them being Valentine's *12 Keys*.

Above: Sir Isaac Newton, famed as the man who first stated the Law of Gravitation. In spite of his present-day reputation as a strictly scientific thinker, he was much interested in alchemy.

described as "of color such as saffron in its powder, yet weighty and shining like unto powdered glass." Van Helmont heated about eight ounces of mercury in a crucible and added the powder. "Straightway all the Quicksilver with a certain degree of noise stood still from flowing and being congealed settled like unto a yellow lump; but after poring it out, the bellows blowing, there were found eight ounces and a little less than eleven grains of gold." Van Helmont was convinced he had turned mercury into gold, and called his new son Mercurius in celebration of the event.

However, not all those interested in alchemy were sincere in their beliefs. As it began to decline, alchemy attracted many rogues and charlatans who saw it as a means to easy riches—though not through transmutation. By means of tricks such as hollow stirring rods, or crucibles with false bottoms, they were able to convince many gullible onlookers that they possessed the secret of making gold. Borrowing money on the pretext of financing further transmutations, they would disappear before anyone had time to realize that he or she had been duped.

In one celebrated case in the 18th century the motive for deception appears to have been fame rather than money, but the trickster was cornered by investigators and the whole episode ended in tragedy. James Price was born as James Higginbotham in London in 1722. He studied at Oxford, took

Right: a caricature called *Marquis of Outrage-Nature in his Laboratory Dress*, published in 1716. By then the public was more geared to the rationalist thought of Newton and the scientists, and found the trappings of the traditional alchemists comical.

Below: J. B. van Helmont and his son F. M. van Helmont. Both he and his sons were doctors. The father claimed to have performed transmutations, using a saffron-colored powder that had been given him by a mysterious stranger.

a series of degrees, and soon established a reputation as a chemist. In 1781, in accordance with the wishes of a relative who had left him a large sum of money, he changed his name to Price. In the same year he was elected to the Royal Society, and in 1782 he moved to a country house in the southeast of England. He soon announced to his astonished friends that he had succeeded in performing a transmutation in his private laboratory.

Various highly distinguished men were invited to his home to witness his experiments. First he added a small quantity of white powder to some mercury. This was mixed with a flux of borax and niter and then heated in a crucible. When the crucible had cooled it was found to contain an ingot of silver equal in weight to the amount of mercury used. The same kind of procedure was followed again, this time using a red powder, and the crucible was found to contain an ingot of gold. The metals were tested and found to be genuine. They were exhibited to King George III, and caused an enormous sensation.

Price published a pamphlet describing these experiments

which created great interest in the scientific world. In a second edition of the pamphlet he stated that his supply of the powders necessary for the transmutations was exhausted, and that the cost of preparing new powders in terms of time and his own health would be too great. However, the controversy aroused by his claims was so great that the Royal Society felt bound to investigate them officially. Unwillingly Price agreed to prepare new stocks of the powders. He was given six weeks to do so. On the appointed day the representatives arrived. Price showed them into his laboratory, excused himself for a moment, and on leaving the room, drank a concoction of prussic acid. He returned and died before their eyes. A verdict of death while of unsound mind was recorded. It was the last occasion on which a learned scientific association was prepared to officially investigate the claims of alchemy.

Investigation – and Ridicule!

Left: Sir Joseph Banks. At the time that the Royal Society was investigating the alchemical claims of James Price, Sir Joseph was president of the Society.

Chapter 14
Sex and Symbolism

In the 18th and 19th centuries alchemy still had its advocates, but mostly among occultists and in a far different form. No more apparatus or laboratories. Far fewer mystical manuscripts and dusty tomes. The new infusion of life came from the East, from Taoism and Tantra with their stress on ritual sex as the means of reaching spiritual immortality. According to Eastern alchemists, the sex act brought into harmony the two elements of yang and yin—male and female. Was sexual intercourse an external symbol of the inner quest for the key to understanding the Universe?

In six centuries of manuscripts and books on the Western European alchemical tradition, there seems to be no obvious reference to sex. True, phrases such as "the chemical wedding" and "the faire Whyte Woman married to the Ruddy Man" keep recurring, but these are symbolic of stages in the alchemical process. Although for 600 years all kinds of accusations were leveled at "false Alchymists, who use all manner of filthy things," it was never suggested that alchemy involved anything of a sexual nature. The alchemical tradition was one of hard work and modest ascetism. It was only in the 18th and 19th centuries, when ideas from the East began to reach Europe, that it became apparent that a different sort of alchemy had for a long time been practiced in China and India. This was a sexual alchemy. The transmutation took place entirely within the alchemist who sought through various sexual, respiratory, and mental practices to achieve immortality through union with the Universe.

The Chinese alchemists were usually followers of Taoism, one of the great religions of China. Its founding is traditionally ascribed to Lao-tzu in the 6th century B.C., although its roots probably go back much further. Lao-tzu is said to have inscribed his teachings on a bamboo parchment, and these precepts form the basis of Taoist belief. Over the centuries, however, scholars have interpreted and reinterpreted these original sayings, and have built up whole schools of thought and custom on a single phrase, often straying far from early Taoist

Opposite: an Indian painting of about 1800. In eastern alchemy—as here, in Tantra—sexual intercourse became the method by which the adept moved toward the spiritual goal.

Right: Shou-lao, Tao god of longevity. Taoist alchemists believed that their work could bring immortality.

simplicity. The use of the words "long life" in Lao-tzu's writings led to a quest for elixirs of longevity, and the mention of sexual organs to the development of sexual mysticism. The phrase "breath retention" encouraged the elaboration of techniques of respiratory control akin to yoga and, strangest of all, the words "harmonious infant" led to the idea that one could produce within one's body, and by oneself, an embryonic seed that would be immortal.

Taoism, as we have seen, embraced the idea that there are two basic principles that underlie the Universe: the active force of yang and the equally important passive force of yin. All things were said to be composed of varying proportions of yang and yin. It was believed that men had a greater proportion of yang and women of yin, and that sexual intercourse was a way of achieving harmony between the two principles.

Many magic and occult ideas were gradually absorbed by certain branches of Taoism, and alchemy found a home among these strange and varied beliefs. Unlike their Western counterparts however, Taoist alchemists were less concerned with transmuting base metals to gold. Their prime quest was the secret of immortality. At first they tried mixing various substances in the hope of finding a formula for a magic elixir, but by the 6th century A.D. most alchemists had abandoned the search for an actual elixir. Instead they had begun to concentrate on perfecting certain techniques of sexual control and various breathing exercises. They believed that if an individual was able to attain a true harmony of yang and yin within himself, he would be able to achieve immortality. In order to do this, sexual energies should not be dissipated but should be carefully conserved and converted into higher forms of energy. They thought that man had the power to produce within himself a "harmonious infant," that is, a being on another plane

The Inner Alchemy of the Taoists

Below left: adepts, shown as children, symbolize immortality.

Below: the Taoist subtle body, as seen in the inner alchemy, showing the circulation system. Alchemists start with breathing exercises designed to exert pressure on *ching*, or sexual energy. They then try to activate the second, higher energy *ch'i*. Finally they hope to reach the highest energy, *shen*, in the head.

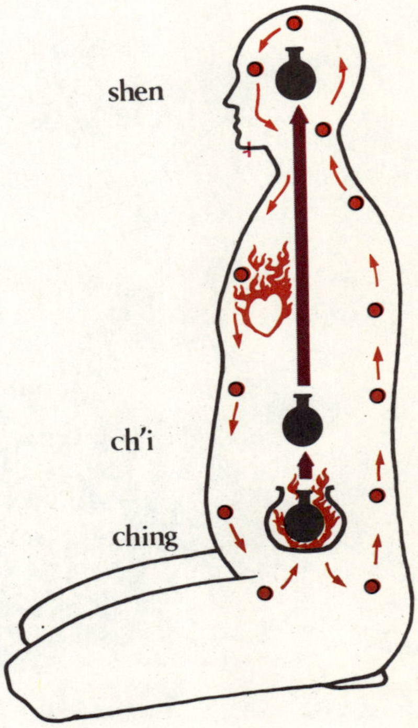

Sexual Union of Irreconcilables

Opposite: a 16th-century Tibetan statue showing the condition of enlightenment, in which the male and female principles unite in perfect combination. The gods here are Krishna and his consort Radna.

Below: a 19th-century German drawing after an Indian original, showing the union of the irreconcilables, fire and water. This idea of the union of the opposites was a powerful one in both Western and Eastern alchemy, although in the East it was expressed far more directly in overt sexual terms.

who was somehow attuned to the mysterious workings of the Universe. Taoist alchemists who could produce this divine embryo considered that they had achieved immortality.

The Taoist alchemist visualized the body as having three important psychic centers, which he termed "crucibles." These crucibles were used to store the three main forms of energy. In the lowest crucible at the base of the spine, sexual energy known as *ching* was stored. The second crucible was in the solar plexus behind the stomach. It housed a higher form of energy known as *ch'i*. The top crucible in the head contained the highest form of all, spiritual energy or *shen*.

This inner alchemy was achieved entirely by meditation and breathing. The first stage was known as "lighting the inner fire." The alchemist began deep breathing, which exerted pressure on the lowest crucible containing *ching*, the sexual energy. Heat was generated by breathing and the *ching* rose through the spinal column to the top of the head. It then descended down to the spine again. After this process had been repeated many times, the alchemist might consider the force pure enough to be transformed into a higher form of energy. It would then be driven up into the second crucible where it would mingle with the higher energy *ch'i*. These two combined forces then traveled up to the head and back again, until they in their turn reached a sufficient state of purity to mingle with *shen*, the spiritual force in the top crucible.

These three combined forces rose and fell in the body, gradually becoming purer and purer, until they finally reached a state of oneness with the energies of the Universe. It was then that the divine embryo was conceived. A special ambrosia flowed like saliva into the mouth, and was impregnated by a gold and a silver light. Gradually, nurtured by special concentration and breathing techniques on the part of the alchemist, the embryo grew until it reached maturity. It then ascended into the crown of the head, and the alchemist, turning his attention totally inward, perceived the psychic light that emanated from it. He then believed that he had achieved immortality. The embryo was sent down to the abdomen. The alchemist had completed his task.

This brief description of Taoist inner alchemy bears a striking resemblance to the alchemy developed by the followers of Tantra. Tantra is the name given to a strange set of beliefs practiced for centuries in India and other neighboring countries. Its disciples claim that it is the oldest religion in India, and that all systems of yoga derive from it. Its critics dispute whether it is a religion at all because its ideas are so entwined with strange sexual activity, magic, and the occult.

Tantra is based on the premise that the Universe is composed of a male and a female force. The female force is represented by the goddess Shakti who has an all-important and active role. The passive male force is personified by the god Shiva. He is helpless without Shakti, and man in turn is considered helpless without woman. Women are the key to salvation and it is through women, by ritual sexual intercourse, that the goddess Shakti can be approached. Ritual sexual intercourse may be physical, or may be merely symbolic. Those who choose the

Tantric Alchemy

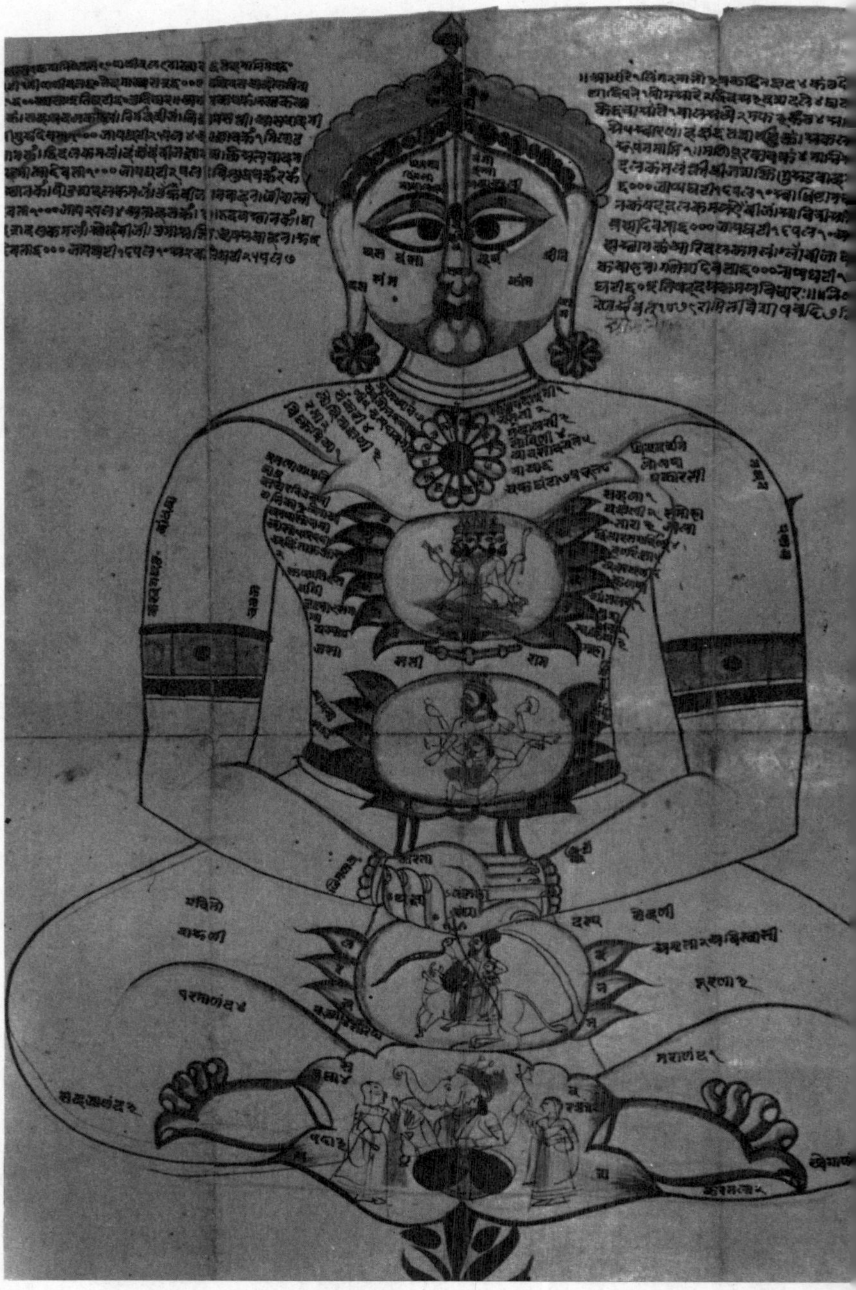

Right: the subtle body, shown as a plant growing from the ground of the beyond, in an Indian 18th-century drawing. The chakras, through which the awakened kundalini would rise, are shown here within the body, with symbolic drawings. Tantric alchemy was emphatic about the great power of the forces aroused through their exercises, and would-be alchemists spent years learning to direct the energies properly toward union with the Infinite.

physical way are known as followers of the left hand way because the female sexual partner is seated on the left of the male at the start of the ritual. Those who choose the symbolic method are known as followers of the right hand way because the woman sits on the right of the man.

The Tantrist obtains energy through sexual intercourse, in which the woman is regarded as the possessor of important power. Because it is the intercourse itself that is important, and because its ritual character should be entirely free of any emotional or social connotations, it may be performed with a woman of the lowest caste, and preferably in the most degrading and defiling of conditions. The most powerful rite of all is performed with a woman while she is menstruating, and takes place among the smoldering bodies in a crematory.

Tantra opposes all social conventions and ordinary morality. Many of its sexual rites include group sex, adultery, and incest, which are intended to jolt its followers into a new level of awareness beyond the limitations of family or society. Rather than control or conquer physical desire, the Tantrist believes in releasing sexual energy and then reabsorbing it back into the system in order to gain greater power. The emphasis on various sexual practices and the link with magic and the occult have brought Tantra into disrepute with more orthodox religions. But it is far from merely being a disguised method of obtaining sexual pleasure. To perform the sexual rites successfully requires years of training in difficult physical techniques. Apart from complex breathing exercises, the Tantrist will aim to control certain seemingly involuntary functions such as the pulse rate and the body temperature. Above all, Tantrists concentrate on alchemy.

Tantric, like Taoist, alchemy is mainly internal. It aims to effect a transmutation in the body by producing certain bodily fluids that will enable the Tantrist to be at one with the Universe, and to acquire supernatural powers. According to the Tantrist, the body has seven main centers of supernormal psychic energy. They have no physical existence, but can be identified by the Tantrist as being situated along a line between the bottom of the spine and the crown of the head. These centers are known as *chakras* or wheels. The lowest chakra is inhabited by the *kundalini*, which in the normal person lies curled up, asleep, like a small serpent, its head blocking the path of ascent to the next *chakra*. If awakened by an inexperienced person, the kundalini will cause havoc and destruction. All kinds of physical energies will be stirred up, and the novice will be unable to control them. The Tantrist takes years of training and discipline before being able to control the aroused kundalini. Once properly awakened, often by various sexual postures, the kundalini is ready to begin its gradual ascent through the chakras, and the process of inner alchemy begins. To aid the ascent the Tantrist will often visualize an ideal woman, since woman holds the key to vital energy. When the kundalini reaches the uppermost chakra in the crown of the head, the alchemist has achieved the goal. Shakti and Shiva, the two principles of the Universe, are fused in a transcendental sexual union, and supreme ecstasy is attained. Transmutation has taken place in the desired spiritual way. The self is at one with the Infinite.

While Eastern alchemists were concerned with internal or sexual alchemy, their Western counterparts, as we already know, were pursuing different aims. They were searching for the Philosopher's Stone, which they believed could turn base metals to gold, and for spiritual perfection. Neither of these aims had any clear sexual element. But in the 18th and 19th centuries ideas from the East began to trickle through, and Western writers began to look at sex in a new light. They began to consider that perhaps a sexual motivation lay behind many aspects of human behavior, previously accepted at face value, and they began to see sexual symbolism in many ordinary objects of use.

These ideas gradually affected alchemy which, in the face of

Below: a Tantric yogi seated in his meditation band, a 17th-century stone statuette from South India. Of course, all the exercises of the Tantrist were not sexual; a great deal of solitary meditation and physical and breathing exercises were a vital part of the philosophy.

Tantric Sexual Alchemy Revived

O.T.O.

Gross-Orient

des Alten und Angenommenen Schottischen Ritus der Freimaurer

Deus Meumque Jus

Souveränes Sanktuarium des Alten u. Primitif Ritus von Memphis u. Misraim in und für das Deutsche Reich.

Friede – Toleranz – Wahrheit

An alle erleuchteten und erhabenen Freimaurer der Welt!

Unsern Gruss zuvor!

Hiermit wird beurkundet, dass unser erleuchteter und erhabener Bruder Eugen John Wieland of London dessen Unterschrift nebenan steht

Ehrenmitglied der St. Johannis-Freimaurerloge zum „Heiligen Gral" im Or.: von München zum Chevalier Rose Croix und Inhaber des 18° A. A. Ritus proklamirt worden ist.

Wir befehlen allen Prinzen-Rittern und Meistern unserer Jurisdiction, und wir bitten alle Brüder Freimaurer der ganzen Welt ihn als Prinz Maurer und Chevalier Rose Croix (18°) A. A. Ritus anzuerkennen, und wir versprechen allen Brüdern ausserhalb unserer Jurisdiction, deren regelmässig beglaubigten Patente in unsern Logen, Kapiteln und Grossräten etc. gleichfalls anzuerkennen.

Urkundlich dessen ist gegenwärtiges Patent ausgefertigt, unterschrieben und gesiegelt worden im Gross Orient und Souveränen Sanktuarium in und für das Deutsche Reich im Thale von Berlin und London am 18 Tage des Monats Mechir, 000,000,000, d.i. 18. August 1912, E.V.

Theodor Reuss, 33°. 90°. 96°

Souv. General Grossmeister ad Vitam

Henry Klein 33° 95°

General Gross Registrar

Right: a certificate of membership in the Ordo Templis Orientis, usually known simply as OTO. The society, which attempted to incorporate sexual alchemy within the magical tradition, was first established by Karl Kellner, a German who went to India to study Tantric sexual alchemy. He was one of the first to bring its teachings back to western Europe.

growing materialism and the achievements of scientific chemistry, was fast becoming a mystical rite. Just as astronomy had grown out of astrology and left the older system of thought to the occultists, so had the scientists deserted alchemy and left it to those more attuned to the supernatural.

So it was that Dr. W. R. Woodman and Dr. Wynn Westcott, two English physicians who were interested in alchemy, joined forces with Samuel Liddell Macgregor Mathers, a strange figure who became well known in occult circles, to found the Hermetic Order of the Golden Dawn in 1888. The Golden Dawn was a secret society whose members studied the Cabala, divination, ritual magic, and other occult subjects including alchemy.

Westcott had been influenced by the writings of Ethan Allen Hitchcock, an American who, he believed, "furnishes us the key to the understanding of the hermetic masters. The subject is man . . . The work of the alchemists was one of contemplation and not a work of the hands. Their alembic, furnace, cucurbit, retort, philosophical Egg . . . in which the work of fermentation, distillation, extraction of essences and spirits, and the preparation of salts is said to have taken place was Man . . ." This idea was one that proved immensely attractive to late 19th- and early 20th-century occultists. Discoveries by scientists about the nature of matter appeared to have demolished the idea of a Philosopher's Stone, but if the true aim of alchemy could be seen as a change within a person, then the way was wide open to new spiritual, sexual, or psychological interpretations of alchemy.

Ithell Colquhoun, a member of a group much influenced by the Golden Dawn, unequivocally identified the objects of alchemy with those of sex. She maintained that the alembic was the uterus and the bath of Venus was the vagina. "Moderate fire" referred to the sexual heat of the body, and aqua vitae to female secretions.

A sexual alchemy even more directly related to Eastern mysticism was developed by Karl Kellner. He was a wealthy German who had spent many years in India at the end of the 19th century studying the secrets of Tantric sexual alchemy. On his return to Germany he suggested to various friends who were already interested in the occult that they form a secret society to incorporate Tantric beliefs and practices. In 1902 he and others formed the *Ordo Templis Orientis*, or Order of the Templars of the East. It was devoted to sexual magic. There were nine degrees of sexual ritual to be mastered, the highest being the sexual union of the Tantric alchemist. Members claimed that sexual magic was the key to all the secrets of the Universe and to all the symbolism ever used by secret societies and religions. In the ritual of the Order of the Templars of the East, traditional Western alchemy was given a sexual interpretation. The athanor, the alchemist's most important furnace, symbolized the phallus. The serpent, or blood of the Red Lion, was the semen. The cucurbit stood for the vagina, and the mysterious first matter of the alchemists was composed of vaginal secretions mixed with semen. Franz Hartmann, one of the founder members of the Order, saw the base metals used in alchemy as the animal driving forces in human nature which were capable of being transformed into pure spirituality—or the true gold of the alchemist.

Other interpretations of alchemy have been made by 20th-century psychologists. One of the greatest of these, Carl Jung, devoted many years of his life to a study of alchemy. He noticed that many alchemical symbols occurred in the dreams of his patients, and in mythologies and religions throughout the world. He came to the conclusion that these symbols stemmed from a common source that he termed "the collective unconscious." This level of the mind is made up not of personal experiences, but of archetypes, which are the distilled memories, in some way inherited, of human experience many thousands of years ago. These archetypes are too far out of reach of the conscious mind to be expressed in words. In certain universal situations such as danger, conflict, or desire, however, they will struggle to find expression by means of symbols. These symbols

Above: an illustration from a book by Franz Hartmann, one of the founding members of the OTO, which shows the traditional Philosopher's Egg with the symbols of the zodiac inside it.

Alchemy and Psychology

Below: Carl Jung (left), the great psychologist, was particularly attracted by the symbolism of alchemy, finding within its images many of the archetypes he believed were embedded deep within mankind's collective unconscious, beyond conscious memory.

are common to peoples who have had no contact with each other and who, one might think, have had no particular experience that might lead to the choice of such a specific image. Jung's belief was that if we could learn to recognize what the symbols stood for, we might become more in tune with our own unconscious and hence lead a fuller and more integrated life. The alchemical symbols can therefore be interpreted as providing a clue to our truer nature. The image of the hermaphrodite so commonly used in alchemy, for example, indicates the female side of man's nature, and the male side of woman's, which must be recognized rather than suppressed.

Jung's idea of a "complete self" was one in which all the opposing forces in human nature, conscious and unconscious, had become reconciled so that the person was at one with himself. In alchemy, in the idea of the Philosopher's Stone, he found the same ideal of a reconciliation of opposites that would result in something of far greater power than the mere addition of the two separate forces. Symbolic descriptions of the Philosopher's Stone suggest this union. It has been described as being made of fire and water, as the masculine-feminine, and as a stone and not a stone. It has been symbolized as the marriage of the king and queen, the sun and moon, and the fair white woman and the ruddy man. It has also been seen in terms of incest between such close relations as brother and

sister and between mother and son.

Herbert Silberer, a German psychologist, has taken this interpretation of incest even more literally. In his book *The Hidden Symbolism of Alchemy*, published in 1917, he examines a vision recorded by the earliest known alchemical writer, Zosimos of Egypt. This dream describes a ritual involving a priest and resulting in much blood and sacrifice. It has generally been taken to symbolize the various alchemical stages in the transmutation of base metals to gold. Silberer, however, sees the dream of Zosimos in terms of sexual symbolism. He comes to the conclusion that the alchemical quest represented no more or less than the lifelong penance of the son for his childhood urge to castrate his father and replace him in his mother's bed.

All these varying interpretations of alchemy may seem confusing, but one thing is clear. Alchemy represents a long and difficult search for a key to understand the mysterious workings of the Universe. The route chosen is often that most suited to the society in which the alchemist is living. The East, with its tradition of yoga and meditation, developed a system of internal sexual alchemy. To the medieval Western alchemist the idea of a Philosopher's Stone that would transmute base metals to gold was in accordance with many of the beliefs of the time. The 20th-century Westerner interested in alchemy will probably find a psychological or sexual interpretation more relevant.

Above: a hermaphrodite, from an alchemical book published in 1572. The symbol, which Jung recognized as an archetype, was used to represent the union of opposites.

Left: another example of the hermaphrodite, used here as the symbol for the process in the Work when a substance combined of opposites is placed in the fire.

Chapter 15
Alchemy Lives On

Can there be more to alchemical theories than orthodox science has been willing to accept? Has the Philosopher's Stone actually been produced in the 20th century? Does the successful transmutation of elements in 1919 point to the possibility of transmutation of metals? This century has seen one alchemist employed by the Nazis to make gold, another signed up by an international syndicate, and at least two reputed to treat illness successfully with gold cures they claimed to have created through alchemical processes. Can the ancient alchemical concern for spiritual perfection also have meaning in the modern world?

After the physical and chemical discoveries of the 18th and 19th centuries, it would have seemed natural for alchemy in the 20th century to have advanced ever farther into the realms of symbolism and mysticism, and away from anything to do with physical transmutation. But in 1919 the eminent English physicist Lord Rutherford succeeded in transmuting nitrogen into oxygen in the laboratory, and every aspiring alchemist took new heart. Admittedly, the quantity of oxygen produced was hardly impressive, and the experiment involved the use of high-energy radioactivity. But at least it refuted the continual insistence by scientists that transmutation was an impossibility. One of the first to take inspiration and renewed hope from this experiment was Franz Tausend, a 36-year-old chemical assistant in Munich. He had developed his own theories about the structure of chemical elements. These were a strange mixture of the beliefs of the Greek philosopher Pythagoras about the structure of the Universe, and the findings of the Russian chemist Mendeleev in 1863. Mendeleev devised a way of classifying chemical elements by arranging them in order of their atomic weights, and discovered that chemically similar elements recurred at approximately equal intervals or periods. This became known as the *Periodic System*. Tausend wrote a pamphlet, *180 Elements, the Atomic Weight, and their incorporation in the System of Harmonic Periods*, on his theories. His belief was that every atom of an element had a characteristic frequency of vibration, which was

Opposite: a modern Iranian alchemist at work on the age-old goal of transmuting base metals to gold.

Pre-War Alchemy

Above: Franz Tausend, the modern German alchemist who claimed in the 1920s that he had been totally successful in changing iron oxide and quartz to gold. Although there were many who claimed that he was entirely fraudulent, the evidence is ambiguous, and there were certainly some who were convinced that he had done what he said.

Opposite above: the extensive laboratory and factory in which Tausend worked on his gold-making project, during the period in which General Erich von Ludendorff was involved with the enterprise.

Opposite below: General von Ludendorff, the World War I military leader. His interest in Tausend was strictly to raise money for the Nazi cause to which he had become completely converted.

related to the atomic weight of the nucleus and the various orbital rings of electrons around it. Later research was to show that this part of Tausend's theory was true. He went on, however, to suggested that matter could be as it were "orchestrated." By this he meant adding a carefully selected substance to one element to change its vibration frequency into that of another.

At about this time in 1924 Adolf Hitler was sent to jail for organizing an armed rising in Munich. His fellow conspirator, General Erich von Ludendorff, was acquitted. In the following year Ludendorff ran for election as president of the German republic, but he was heavily defeated in the polls by General Hindenburg. He then turned his attention to fund-raising for the Nazis. He heard the rumors that a certain Tausend in Munich had succeeded in making gold, and got together a party of associates to visit Tausend. The group consisted of Kummer, a chemical engineer, Alfred Mannesmann, a business magnate, Osthoff, a banker, Stremmel, a merchant, and a fifth man known as Franz von Rebay. Stremmel had bought the necessary substances, largely iron oxide and quartz, on Tausend's instructions. He had them melted down by Kummer and von Rebay, and took the crucible to his hotel bedroom in Munich for the night so that no one could tamper with it. In the morning, Tausend heated the crucible again in the electric furnace, added a small quantity of a white powder to the molten mass, and allowed it to cool. When the crucible was broken, a nugget of gold weighing seven grams was found inside.

Ludendorff than formed a company called Company 164 with himself at its head. He was to receive 75 percent of the profits, and Tausend five percent. Investments poured in, of which Ludendorff succeeded in diverting some 400,000 marks "to patriotic ends"—the financing of the Nazi party. This affected the company adversely. In December 1926 he resigned as the company head and restored all rights to Tausend, but left him to shoulder all the debts. Tausend continued to raise money, however; and on June 16, 1928 is said to have made 723 grams of gold in a single large-scale operation. No doubt it was this success that encouraged him to issue a series of share certificates, each to the value of 10 kilograms of gold.

But time was running out for Tausend. A year later, when no more gold had been produced, he was arrested for fraud. After a long wait in prison and a sensational trial, he was found guilty on February 5, 1931, and sentenced to nearly four years' imprisonment. While awaiting trial, he had allegedly made gold under supervision at the Munich Mint—but experts disagreed so violently on what had happened that the evidence was of no value in court.

In the same year, a Polish engineer named Dunikovski announced in Paris that he had discovered a new kind of radiation that he named "Z rays." He said these rays would transmute sand or quartz into gold. The mineral was ground up, spread on copper plates, and melted by application of 110,000 volts. Then it was irradiated by Dunikovski's Z rays.

The engineer succeeded in raising an investment of some two million francs. When after a few months he had not produced any gold, he, like Tausend, was brought to trial for fraud. In

due course he was found guilty and sent to jail for four years. After two years his lawyer succeeded in obtaining his release, and in 1934 Dunikovski took his family to San Remo, a seaside town in Italy, where he renewed his experiments.

Soon rumors began to reach Paris that the engineer was supporting his wife and children by the occasional sale of lumps of gold. His lawyer, accompanied by the well-known French chemist Albert Bonn, traveled to San Remo to see for himself. They discovered that the sand that Dunikovski was using in his experiments contained a small proportion of gold, but whereas normal methods of extraction yielded only some 10 grams of gold per ton, Dunikovski's method produced nearly 100 times as much. This sounds impressive, but it must be remembered that, since each experiment involved only a few hundred grams of sand, the quantity of gold being extracted was extremely small.

Nevertheless, the two Frenchmen were sufficiently impressed to ask the French government to reopen the Dunikovski case. On March 26, 1935, Dunikovski himself addressed an open letter to the prime minister, offering the French government a first option on his invention. The French newspapers, however, opposed the idea vociferously.

In October 1936 Dunikovski gave a demonstration to an audience of invited scientists. He was naturally secretive about the details of his apparatus, but the theoretical explanation he gave is interesting in that it went right back to the primitive

"Gold Therapy"

Below: Dunikovski, the Polish engineer. While he was living in Italy in the 1930s rumors began that he was successfully extracting gold from sand, using what he called "embryonic atoms," which he believed exist in all minerals.

beginnings of alchemy. He believed that all minerals contained atoms in the course of transformation, a process that takes thousands of years in nature. He called these atoms "embryonic atoms," and claimed that his process accelerated the growth of the embryonic gold in quartz.

The demonstration attracted a great deal of attention. Mussolini instructed an Italian professor to look into the process. Paris financiers retained the chemist Coupie. An Anglo-French syndicate was formed. Sand was to be brought from Africa and treated in a big new laboratory in England.

Then came World War II. There were stories that a factory for transmuting base metals into gold had been established in Saint Blaise on the French-Swiss border. Rumor further insisted that the Germans had found some way to bolster their sinking economy by the manufacture of gold. But no proof has ever been found. Meanwhile in England, in a crammed laboratory in the center of London, a modern alchemist claimed to have made the Philosopher's Stone.

His name was Archibald Cockren. He had qualified as an osteopath in London in 1904. During World War I he had been in charge of the department of electrical massage and remedial treatment, first at the Russian Hospital in London, and then at the Prisoners of War Hospital. Later he had been attached to the Australian Army, and served on the staff of the Australian prime minister at the peace conference. He was clearly a respected and responsible practitioner.

He spent the next 20 years in private practice. During this period it became fairly common to inject gold salts as a cure for rheumatism and arthritis, and Cockren became very interested in such gold therapy. He also experimented with homeopathic methods of healing by making use of microscopic doses of gold. Looking for new ways to make solutions of compounds of gold, he decided to try to prepare the "oil of gold" of which so many alchemists had written.

Cockren had read *The Triumphal Chariot of Antimony* by Basil Valentine, a strange figure whose true identity lies hidden in the alchemical legends of the 15th and 16th centuries. Valentine is credited with the discovery of the element antimony. He was supposed to have given it the name *antimoine*, which in French would mean "against a monk," because he had used it successfully to poison several monks. Whatever the truth of the legend, Cockren decided to begin his experiments with antimony. He managed to produce a "fragrant golden liquid." Then he went on to work with iron and copper. "The oil of these metals was obtained, a few drops of which used singly, or in conjunction, proved very efficacious in cases of anemia and debility." He related how, on one occasion, he took a few drops of the oil himself after a particularly laborious day, and found himself reinvigorated. The prospect of a "bout of fairly strenuous mental effort held no terrors at all."

After continuing his experiments with silver and mercury, Cockren finally turned his attention to gold; but he found that his watery mixture would not retain gold in solution. He realized that what he lacked was the "alkahest of the philosophers," the universal solvent that alchemists believed would dissolve all matter. Only with this, thought Cockren, could he achieve the real oil of gold. He plunged into a study of alchemical writings, anxious to find a clue to the identity of this strange solvent. The experiments he had already made helped considerably. One day, while sitting quietly in a state of deep concentration, the solution to the problem was revealed to him in a flash, and he suddenly understood many of the puzzling statements of the alchemists.

"Here, then, I entered upon a new course of experiment with a metal for experimental purposes with which I had no previous experience. The metal, after being reduced to its salts and undergoing special preparation and distillation, delivered up the Mercury of the Philosophers."

The first intimation Cockren had that he had been successful was a violent hissing. Jets of vapor poured from the retort and into the receiver "like sharp bursts from a machine gun." Then there was a violent explosion and "a very potent and subtle odor filled the laboratory and its surroundings." A friend of Cockren's described this odor as resembling "the dry earth on a June morning, with the hint of growing flowers in the air, the breath of wind over heather and hill, and the sweet smell of rain on the parched earth."

Cockren's next problem was to find a way of storing this "subtle gas" without endangering anything. He achieved this by an arrangement of coils of glass piping in water joined up with the receiver, and a carefully regulated system of heating. The result was that the gas gradually condensed into a clear golden "water" that was extremely inflammable and volatile. The water then had to be separated by distillation, "the outcome being the white mercurial water." This mercurial water, added Cockren, was absolutely essential to the production of the oil of gold. It was added to the salts of gold after the salts had been washed several times with distilled water to remove the acidity of the Aqua Regia, a mixture of nitric and hydrochloric acid that had been used to dissolve the gold. He found that when the mercurial water was added to the salts of gold, there was a slight hissing sound and in increase in temperature, after which the gold became a deep red liquid. When this was distilled the oil of gold, a deep amber liquid of an oily consistency, was produced. "From the golden water I have described can be obtained this white water, and a deep red tincture which deepens in color the longer it is kept; these two are the mercury and the sulfur described by the alchemists."

To make the Philosopher's Stone, Cockren took the black dregs of the metal left after the extraction of the golden water, heated it to red hot, and then treated it until it became a white salt. He then took a certain quantity of this "salt" and of the "mercury" and "sulfur" that he had already produced and put them in a hermetically sealed flask over a moderate heat. The mixture looked at first like leaden mud, which slowly rose like dough until it produced a crystalline formation "rather like a coral plant in growth." Edward Garstin, a writer and friend of Cockren's, visited him at this time and saw "a glass vessel of oval shape containing layer upon layer of basic matter in the traditional colors of black, white, gray, and yellow. At the top

The Fragrant Explosion

Archibald Cockren believed fully that behind alchemy's transmutation of metals lay the transmutation of the baser elements in the human. But he also believed that the work in the laboratory could be accomplished. Using the texts of the alchemists and putting aside his own knowledge of more orthodox chemistry, Cockren set about the Great Work in his 20th-century London laboratory.

Following the 12 Keys of Basil Valentine, he began experimenting with antimony, but realized that he had still not grasped what was meant by the First Matter. The answer came to him suddenly, full-blown—although he does not say what it was. He started work again with a metal he had not used before.

Cockren went through the old series of stages—the reduction to its salts, heating, distillation—and then suddenly he knew he had achieved success. There was a violent hissing, and jets of vapor poured out of the retort and into the receiver with a series of loud noises like machine gun shots. The whole apparatus exploded, and a strange fragrance filled the laboratory: the fresh smell of the earth on a June morning, with dew, flowers, and gentle wind. He had made the Mercury of the Philosophers.

Alchemists of Modern France

Right: Eugene Canseliet, the well-known French alchemist and writer on alchemy. Like many of the contemporary alchemists, he has returned to work in the laboratory.

these had blossomed into a flower-like form, a pattern arranged like petals around a center, all of a glowing orange-scarlet."

The heat was gradually raised until this formation melted into an amber-colored liquid, which then thickened and sank into a black earth on the bottom of the glass. "When more mercury was added, the black powder dissolved and from this conjunction it seems that a new substance is born . . . As the black color abates, color after color comes and goes until the mixture becomes white and shining; the White Elixir. The heat is gradually raised yet more, and from white the color changes to citrine and finally to red—the Elixir Vitae, the Philosopher's Stone, the medicine of men and metals."

Soon after this, Cockren was killed in the blitz of London, and his secret perished with him. He left many who believed in the curative powers of his oil of gold. Mrs. Maiya Tranchell Hayes, who headed a surviving temple of the Golden Dawn, swore by it, as did Mrs. Meyer Sassoon, widow of a well-known financier. As late as 1965 there were elderly people in London who still took small doses of Cockren's elixir.

Since the war, most alchemical speculation seems to have taken place in France. Eugene Canseliet, who has written many books on alchemy, has been seen on television at work in his laboratory. Others, like the author Roger Caro and the painter Louis Cattiaux, have also established laboratories. But the most famous French alchemist is probably Armand Barbault, author of *Gold of a Thousand Mornings*. He carries out his work only at times that he has determined by detailed astrological calculation.

Perhaps Barbault gained his initial inspiration from a well-known theory that the name of the Rosicrucians is derived not from *rosa*, the Latin word for rose, but from *ros*, the Latin word for dew. An essential part of his process, for example, is the gathering of dew in canvas sheets every morning from March 21 to June 24. The idea of gathering dew was first put forward at the end of the 17th century in a mysterious book of engravings without captions entitled *Mutus Liber*, the *Wordless Book*. The author of another book of about the same date, the *Polygraphice*, writes: "Gather Dew in the Month of May, with a clean white Linnen Cloth spread upon the Grass." When this filtered dew has been left for 14 days in horse dung, and then distilled to a quarter of its bulk four times running, it yields a potent Spirit of Dew. "And if you are indeed an Artist, you may by this turn all Metals into their first matter."

Barbault describes his first matter as a germ, growing a few centimeters below the surface in black earth in a woodland clearing. This substance, whatever it is, is placed in a closed flask, kept at a steady temperature of 40°C (104°F). Dew, in which the tips of young plants have been fermented for 40 days, is added through a faucet. As far as it is possible to make out from Barbault's erratic account, the final ingredient is a "mother plant." There are detailed instructions on how to draw this plant whole from the ground by tying one end of a string to it, and the other end of the string to a nearby bush that has been bent over. The bush is then released, and as it springs back to place, it pulls the plant out.

The flask is kept at the temperature of 40°C (104°F) for 40 days, extra dew being added as necessary. Later, the temperature is raised until a dry ash is obtained. This is then put into long test tubes, together with about 2.5 grams of powdered gold and some dew, and the tubes are sealed with a rubber stopper. Barbault has a thermostatically controlled oven maintained at a temperature between 150° and 200°C (302° and 392°F)—that is, substantially above the boiling point of water—and 12 test tubes are inserted partway into this oven so that the contents boil. The steam condenses in the upper part of the tubes, which are outside the oven, and liquid returns to solid matter below. After four hours of boiling, and four hours of standing, repeated seven times, the liquor in the tubes is a clear golden color—but, says Barbault, spectrum analysis does not reveal the presence of any gold in solution.

Armand Barbault regards this liquor as the alchemists' elixir, and calls it vegetable gold. It seems, in fact, to be a typical homeopathic remedy effective in microscopic doses. Dr. Ruth Jensen-Hillringhaus of Freiburg, Germany claimed to have used it to cure a woman paralyzed by multiple sclerosis. Another doctor tried several drops of the elixir each morning and reported a marked reduction in tiredness, increase in initiative, and improved urination. Others reported miracle cures of uremia and syphilis. Barbault, who found it too expensive to continue adding gold to his liquors, was last reported to be em-

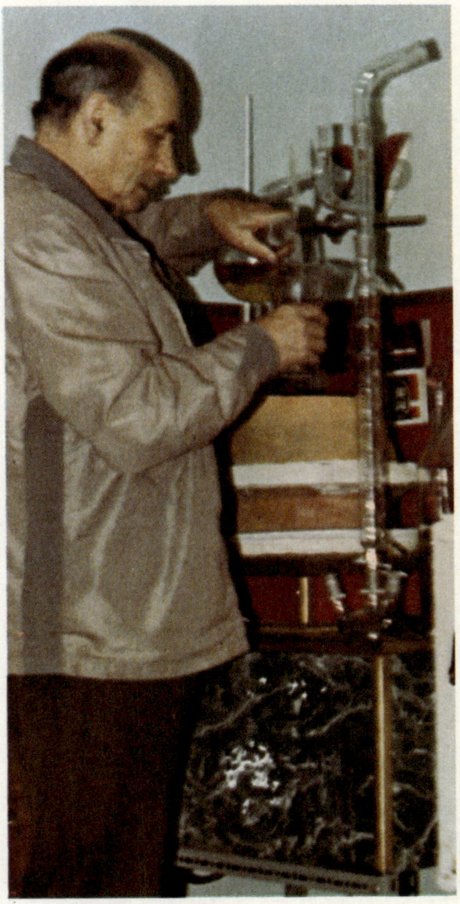

Above: Armand Barbault at work. He began as an engineer, but through his interest in astrology was drawn—encouraged by his wife—into an exploration of the practical possibilities of alchemy.

Barbault Follows the Wordless Book

Right: wringing the morning dew out of the canvas spread to collect it, from *The Wordless Book*. Barbault followed this example in his own alchemical work, collecting dew every day before sunrise for three months, as instructed.

Above: Barbault collecting dew. *The Wordless Book* showed the collection from canvas spread on the grass, but Barbault found much more dew could be gathered by dragging the sheet along the ground, over the tops of plants.

Above right: wringing out the heavily dew-laden canvasses. According to Barbault, the quality of the dew depends on the kind of plant from which it has been collected.

ploying the "Blood of the Green Lion"—extracted vegetable sap.

The story of alchemy is like a detective novel. But, although in this last chapter it is possible to unravel some of the tangled threads and make some deductions, there can be no dramatic last-minute revelation. We can only guess at the possible nature of first matter and the Philosopher's Stone.

We do not know whether seemingly objective scientific witnesses ever saw a real transmutation in an alchemist's laboratory, but we do know that transmutation is possible. It goes on naturally all the time as radioactive elements decay and give off radiation—and the end-product of this "putrefaction" is lead.

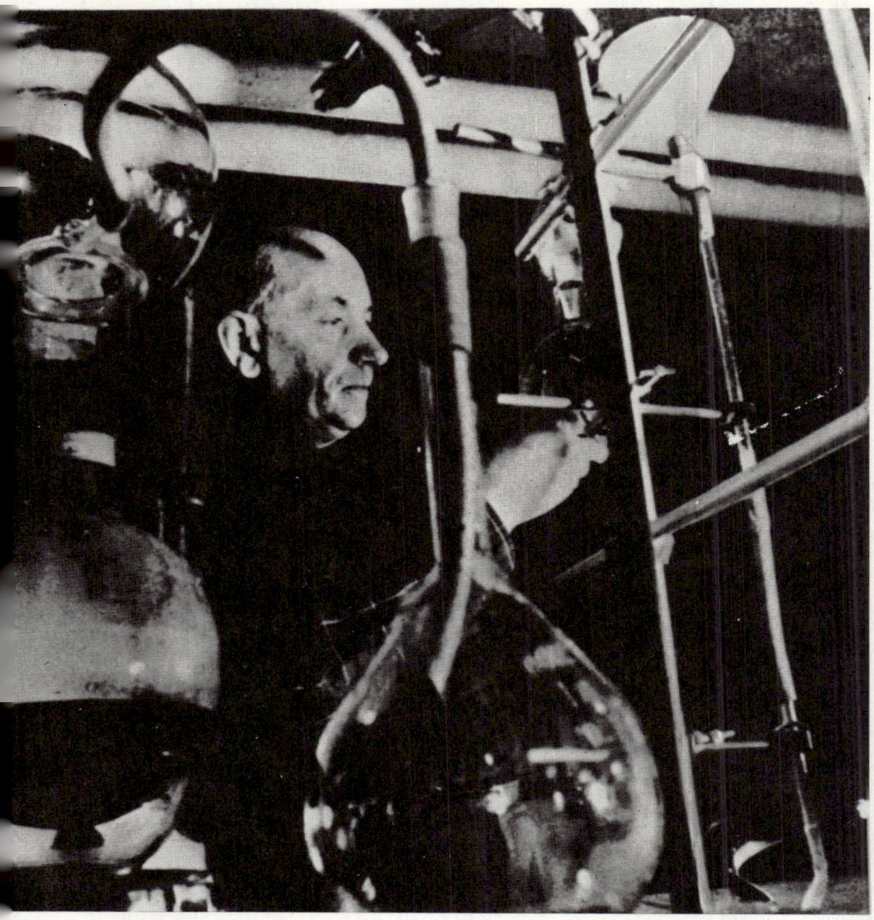

Left: Armand Barbault in his modern laboratory. As a 20th-century alchemist, he uses the conveniences developed since the times of the medieval workers. All the heating is controlled by thermostats, and many of the operations are fully automatic.

Below: Barbault's starting point is a mixture of earth and plants. It is moistened with the dew, baked in the alembic, remoistened, and the process is repeated until this black substance is produced.

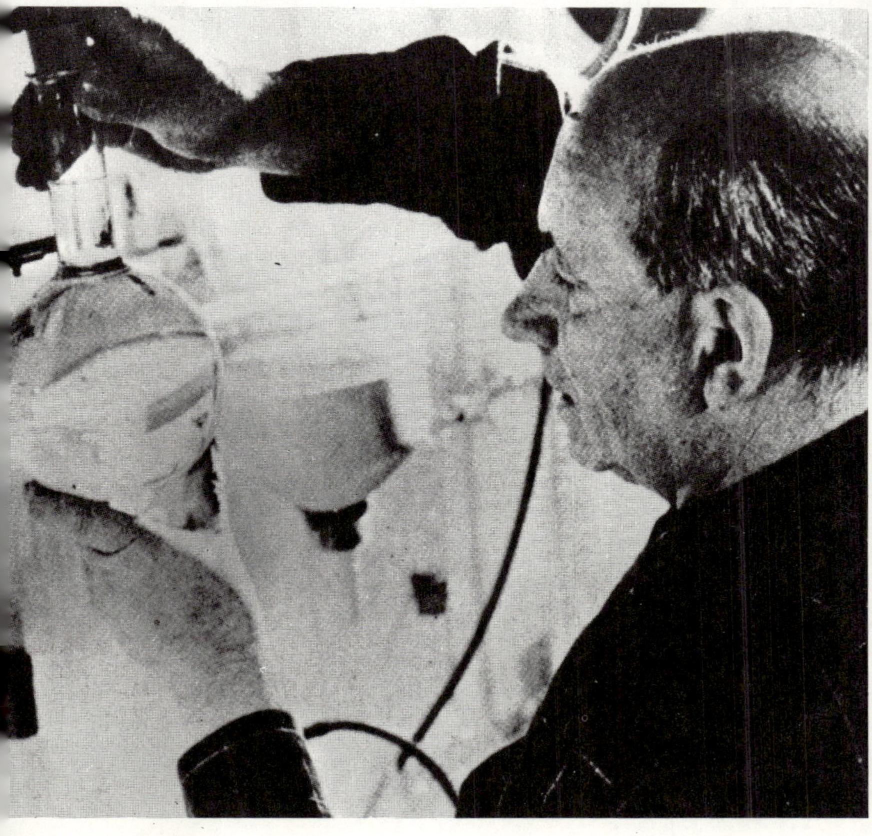

Left: the liquor of gold. After it has been produced, it is carefully checked over a week to be sure it is free of impurities. Only then can it be used as the alchemists' elixir. A few drops are claimed to work wonders in curing a variety of diseases.

From Imagery to the Metalloids–Alchemy Lives On!

Transmutation is also possible in a modern laboratory. Apart from the changes from one known element to another, as in Rutherford's experiment, there are more than a dozen new elements known to science which do not occur naturally at all, but which have been made in the course of experiments in nuclear energy. The only limitation to laboratory transmutation at the moment is that subatomic particles that travel at high speeds and with immense energies are needed.

Alchemical tests are full of tantalizing information about the nature of first matter. This desirable substance is, apparently, to be found everywhere, is walked on by everybody, prized by nobody. Quartz and sand, the essential ingredients of both Tausend's and Dunikovski's process, answer well to this description. These minerals are almost pure silicon dioxide, and it is possible that when Cockren spoke of using "a metal . . . with which I had had no previous experience," he was referring to silicon. This element is not in fact a metal. However it is known as a metalloid because in its physical nature and chemical properties it belongs to a group of elements including germanium, tin, and lead, and of which the first member is carbon. Silicon is of particular interest in that it can take the place of carbon in a great number of chemical compounds, producing silicones. It has even been suggested that life, which on Earth is sustained by compounds of carbon, may be sustained by silicones on some other planet in another galaxy.

This is as far as the clues in our detective story lead us. It is disappointing not to be able to conclude by unmasking an alchemical "butler," but our present-day knowledge of the nature of matter is still too sketchy. It may be naive to suppose that any alchemist ever succeeded in preparing gold by transmutation, although the possibility exists; but there seems every reason to believe that, by some means that we still call magic, men were able to perceive a vision of what we are only just beginning to discover by experiment. They told their vision in a succession of charming allegorical stories. The birth of metals and their progression through seven stages to the perfection of gold paralleled the seven ages of man, or the passing of the soul through the seven planetary spheres to heaven. The quest for the Philosopher's Stone and the Elixir of Life obsessed and impoverished many alchemists—but it is possible that they knew something that our modern scientists are only just beginning to discover.

Opposite: Saturn, symbolizing lead, is cooked in a bath until the white dove, or spirit, ascends. By the bath the earnest alchemist puffs away at the bellows. Behind the elegant imagery, and the carefully obscure texts, still lies the tantalizing mystery of alchemy. After all these centuries it still fascinates, still obsesses people by the ancient promise of untold riches and the hope of spiritual fulfillment.

Index

References to illustrations are shown in italics.

Picture Credits

Key to picture positions: (T) top (C) center (B) bottom; and in combinations, e.g. (TR) top right (BL) bottom left.

Photo AGIP 182; Aerofilms 124, 134; Aldus Archives 17(T), 22(B), 26, 30(R), 42, 47, 50, 52, 70(B)–71, 85(T), 90(R)–91, 105, 108–109, 112(L), 114(T), 115–117, 145(TL), 147(R)–148, 153(B)–154, 155(B), 163–164(T), 166, 172(T), 177(T), 186(T), 189, 199, 204(B), 216, 220, 222(T), 224, 226, 237, 239, 248(T); © Aldus Books (Mike Busselle) 12–13, 67(B), 80–81, (Gianetto Coppola) 34–35, 106–107, Gino d'Achille 132–133, (Geoffrey Drury) 75, (Ann Dunn) 53–54(T), 56, 113(T), 114(B), 127, 160(L), 231(R), (Bruno Elletori) 14–15, (Mark Parry-Maddocks) 57, (Eileen Tweedy) 21(TC); Archiv für Kunst und Geschichte, Berlin 76; Ashmolean Museum, Oxford 205, 222(B); John Reed, *Through Alchemy to Chemistry*, G. Bell & Son Ltd., London 213; Biblioteca Estense, Moderna 32; Biblioteca Medicea Laurenziana, Florence 158(L); Biblioteca Nazionale Centrale, Firenze 140; Bibliothèque Nationale, Paris 158(R), 170, 174–175, 178–179, (Giraudon) 89, (Photo Thames and Hudson Ltd.) 55; Reproduced by permission of the artist, Peter Birkhauser 24; Reproduced by permission of the British Library Board 153(T), 156, 162, 168, 184, 193–196, 251, (Photo Peter J. Davey © Aldus Books) 19(T); Reproduced by permission of the Trustees of the British Museum 27, 38, 54(B), 66, 74, 104, 197, 212(B), 232, (Photos © Aldus Books) (R. B. Fleming) 207, (David Swann) 28, 31(T), 92, (Eileen Tweedy) 191, 204(T); British Tourist Authority 122, 129; Karsh of Ottawa/Camera Press Ltd. 16; From *A Book of Automatic Drawing*, Catalpa Press, London, 1972 111; Photos J.-L. Charmet, Paris 72, 93, (Académie des Beaux-Arts) 200, (Bibliothèque de l'Arsenal) 146, (Famille Barbault) 247, (Musée Carnavalet) 172(B), 176(R), 177(B), (Musée de Cluny) 176(L); Jean-Claude Ciancimino 233; Paul Christian, *The History and the Practice of Magic*, Citadel Press 33, (after Citadel Press © Aldus Books) 36–37; K. E. Maltwood, *A Guide to Glastonbury's Temple of the Stars*, James Clarke and Co. Ltd., London, 1964 126; Terence Spencer/Colorific 135; John Cutten and Richard Szumski, San Jose University 43–45; Percival David Foundation of Chinese Art 231(L); Derby Art Gallery 214; Equinox Bookshop/Photos Eileen Tweedy © Aldus Books 59, (painting by Godfrey Dowson) 48, (painting by Mark Parry-Maddocks) 60; Mary Evans Picture Library 78(T), 147(L), 211; Courtesy of Fisher Collection, Fishing Scientific Company, Pittsburgh 138, 155(T), 208; Sven Gahlin, London/Photo A. C. Cooper 228; John Michell, *City of Revelation* and *The Old Straight Track*, Garnstone Press Ltd., London 130–131; Photos Leif Geiges 8, 10–11; Adam Woolfitt/Susan Griggs 181; Gulbenkian Museum of Oriental Art, University of Durham 230; Roland Michaud/John Hillelson Agency 240; Michael Holford Library photo (Corpus Christi College Library) 51(T), (The Wellcome Museum) 17(B); Francis King/Photos Thames and Hudson Ltd. 119; Kunsthistorisches Museum, Wien 112–113(CB), 202(T); Kupferstichkabinett Basel 186(B); The Mansell Collection, London 62, 102(T), 141, 159, 202(B), 219(T), (Photo Alinari) 145(B); © Marshall Cavendish Ltd. 137, (Boleskine Collection) 110; The Metropolitan Museum of Art, New York 18, (The Cora Timken Burnett Collection of Persian Miniatures and Other Persian Art Objects. Bequest of Cora Timken Burnett, 1957) 167; Mount Wilson and Palomar Observatories 20; Musée du Louvre, Paris/Photo Chuzeville 23; Museo del Prado, Madrid/Photo Manso 51(B); Museum der Bildenden Künste, Leipzig/Photo Gerhard Reinhold 77; National Galleries of Scotland, Edinburgh/Photo Tom Scott © Aldus Books 188; National Gallery, London 2; National Portrait Gallery, London 96(L), 217–218, 219(B), 225, 227; Osterreichischen Nationalbibliothek Wien 190; J. J. Pauvert, Paris 246; Picturepoint, London 19(B), 78(B), 125, 203, 236; Photo Rosmarie Pierer, Hamburg 87(B); Popperfoto 97, 238; *The I Ching: or Book of Changes*, translated by Richard Wilhelm, rendered into English by Cary F. Baynes, Bollingen Series XIX (© 1950 and 1967 by Bollingen Foundation). Reproduced by permission of Princeton University Press, Routledge & Kegan Paul Ltd., London, Eugen Diederichs Verlag, Düsseldorf 22(T); Mauro Pucciarelli, Rome 87(T), (Rijksmuseum, Amsterdam) 88; *Radio Times* Hulton Picture Library 58, 68(R), 82, 96(R), 118(R), 120–121, 143, 169, 183, 187, 212(T); From *The Encyclopaedia of the Unexplained*, George Rainbird Ltd., and Ellic Howe 118(L); From the Waite Tarot Pack published by Rider & Co. 63; Roger-Viollet 244; St. Mark's, Venice/Foto Fiorentini © Aldus Books 144; Scala, Florence 31(B), 70(T), 84, 90(L), (Ca'Rezzonico, Venice) 142, (Palazzo delle Regione, Padua) 152, (Palazzo Vecchio, Florence) 150; Courtesy Schwingungsinstitut Hans Jenny, Dornach 68(R)–69; Skoklosters Slott, Balsta, Sweden 209; Gerald S. Hawkins, *Stonehenge Decoded*, Souvenir Press Ltd., London, and Doubleday & Company Inc., New York 128; Armand Barbault, *Gold of a Thousand Mornings*, Neville Spearman Limited, 1975 248(B)–249; Spectrum Colour Library 21(CB); Städelsches Kunstinstitut, Frankfurt am Main 173; Süddeutscher Verlag Bilderdienst 242–243(T); Collection Ajit Mookerjee, Tantra Museum, New Delhi 234; The Tate Gallery, London 73, (Photo John Webb © Aldus Books) 25(B); Times Newspapers Ltd./Robert Harding Associates 165; Ullstein Bilderdienst 21(L), 210; Universitatsbibliothek Heidelberg/Photos Lossen 160(R); A. E. Waite, *Ceremonial Magic*, University Books, Inc., 1961 30(L); Victoria & Albert Museum, London 86, (Enthoven Collection/Photo Eileen Tweedy © Aldus Books) 64, (Photo David Swann © Aldus Books) 25(T), (Photos Eileen Tweedy © Aldus Books) 41, 94–95, 100, 102–103(B), 223, 235; The Warburg Institute/Photo Eileen Tweedy © Aldus Books) 67(T); The Warburg Institute Library/Photo John Freeman © Aldus Books) 221; The Wellcome Historical Medical Museum/Photo David Litchfield © Aldus Books) 21(R); The Wellington Museum/Photos. Eileen Tweedy © Aldus Books 98–99; The Wiener Library, London/Photo Eileen Tweedy © Aldus Books 243(B); Zentralbibliothek, Zürich 164(BL).